Matthias Schmidt

Infrastructural Security for Virtualized Grid Computing

Matthias Schmidt

Infrastructural Security for Virtualized Grid Computing

New Solutions that convey the Security of Grid Computing Infrastructures

Südwestdeutscher Verlag für Hochschulschriften

Impressum/Imprint (nur für Deutschland/only for Germany)
Bibliografische Information der Deutschen Nationalbibliothek: Die Deutsche Nationalbibliothek verzeichnet diese Publikation in der Deutschen Nationalbibliografie; detaillierte bibliografische Daten sind im Internet über http://dnb.d-nb.de abrufbar.
Alle in diesem Buch genannten Marken und Produktnamen unterliegen warenzeichen-, marken- oder patentrechtlichem Schutz bzw. sind Warenzeichen oder eingetragene Warenzeichen der jeweiligen Inhaber. Die Wiedergabe von Marken, Produktnamen, Gebrauchsnamen, Handelsnamen, Warenbezeichnungen u.s.w. in diesem Werk berechtigt auch ohne besondere Kennzeichnung nicht zu der Annahme, dass solche Namen im Sinne der Warenzeichen- und Markenschutzgesetzgebung als frei zu betrachten wären und daher von jedermann benutzt werden dürften.

Coverbild: www.ingimage.com

Verlag: Südwestdeutscher Verlag für Hochschulschriften GmbH & Co. KG
Heinrich-Böcking-Str. 6-8, 66121 Saarbrücken, Deutschland
Telefon +49 681 37 20 271-1, Telefax +49 681 37 20 271-0
Email: info@svh-verlag.de

Approved by: Marburg, Philipps-Universität, Dissertation, 2011

Herstellung in Deutschland:
Schaltungsdienst Lange o.H.G., Berlin
Books on Demand GmbH, Norderstedt
Reha GmbH, Saarbrücken
Amazon Distribution GmbH, Leipzig
ISBN: 978-3-8381-3025-5

Imprint (only for USA, GB)
Bibliographic information published by the Deutsche Nationalbibliothek: The Deutsche Nationalbibliothek lists this publication in the Deutsche Nationalbibliografie; detailed bibliographic data are available in the Internet at http://dnb.d-nb.de.
Any brand names and product names mentioned in this book are subject to trademark, brand or patent protection and are trademarks or registered trademarks of their respective holders. The use of brand names, product names, common names, trade names, product descriptions etc. even without a particular marking in this works is in no way to be construed to mean that such names may be regarded as unrestricted in respect of trademark and brand protection legislation and could thus be used by anyone.

Cover image: www.ingimage.com

Publisher: Südwestdeutscher Verlag für Hochschulschriften GmbH & Co. KG
Heinrich-Böcking-Str. 6-8, 66121 Saarbrücken, Germany
Phone +49 681 37 20 271-1, Fax +49 681 37 20 271-0
Email: info@svh-verlag.de

Printed in the U.S.A.
Printed in the U.K. by (see last page)
ISBN: 978-3-8381-3025-5

Copyright © 2011 by the author and Südwestdeutscher Verlag für Hochschulschriften GmbH & Co. KG and licensors
All rights reserved. Saarbrücken 2011

Abstract

The goal of the grid computing paradigm is to make computer power as easy to access as an electrical power grid. Unlike the power grid, the computer grid uses remote resources located at a service provider. Malicious users can abuse the provided resources, which not only affects their own systems but also those of the provider and others.

Resources are utilized in an environment where sensitive programs and data from competitors are processed on shared resources, creating again the potential for misuse. This is one of the main security issues, since in a business environment competitors distrust each other, and the fear of industrial espionage is always present. Currently, human trust is the strategy used to deal with these threats. The relationship between grid users and resource providers ranges from highly trusted to highly untrusted [125]. This wide trust relationship occurs because grid computing itself changed from a research topic with few users to a widely deployed product that included early commercial adoption. The traditional open research communities have very low security requirements, while in contrast, business customers often operate on sensitive data that represents intellectual property; thus, their security demands are very high. In traditional grid computing, most users share the same resources concurrently. Consequently, information regarding other users and their jobs can usually be acquired quite easily. This includes, for example, that a user can see which processes are running on another users system. For business users, this is unacceptable since even the meta-data of their jobs is classified [124]. As a consequence, most commercial customers are not convinced that their intellectual property in the form of software and data is protected in the grid.

This thesis proposes a novel infrastructural security solution that advances the concept of virtualized grid computing. The work started back in 2007 and led to the development of the XGE, a virtual grid management software. The XGE itself uses operating system virtualization to provide a virtualized landscape. Users jobs are no longer executed in a shared manner; they are executed within special sandboxed environments. To satisfy the requirements of a traditional grid setup, the solution can be coupled with an installed scheduler and grid middleware on the grid head node. To protect the prominent grid head node, a novel dual-laned demilitarized zone is introduced to make attacks more difficult. In a traditional grid setup, the head node and the computing nodes are installed in the same network, so a successful attack could also endanger the user's software and data. While the zone complicates attacks, it is, as all security solutions, not a perfect solution. Therefore, a network intrusion detection system is enhanced with grid specific signatures. A novel software called Fence is introduced that supports end-to-end encryption, which means that all data remains encrypted until it reaches its final destination. It transfers data securely between the user's computer, the head node and the nodes within the shielded, internal network. A lightweight kernel rootkit detection system assures that only trusted kernel modules can be loaded. It is no longer possible to load untrusted modules such as kernel rootkits. Furthermore, a malware scanner for virtualized grids scans for signs of malware in all running virtual machines. Using virtual machine introspection, that scanner remains invisible for most types of malware and has full access to all system calls on the monitored system. To speed up detection, the load is distributed to multiple detection engines simultaneously. To enable multi-site service-oriented grid applications, the novel concept of public virtual nodes is presented. This is a virtualized grid node with a public IP address shielded by a set of dynamic firewalls. It is possible to create a set of connected, public nodes, either present on one or more remote grid sites. A special web service allows users to modify their own rule set in both directions and in a controlled manner.

The main contribution of this thesis is the presentation of solutions that convey the security of grid computing infrastructures. This includes the XGE, a software that transforms a traditional grid into a virtualized grid. Design and implementation details including experimental evaluations are given for all approaches. Nearly all parts of the software are available as open source software. A summary of the contributions and an outlook to future work conclude this thesis.

Zusammenfassung

Ein Grid soll einem Benutzer Ressourcen so einfach zu Verfüng stellen, wie das Stromnetz: Ein Gerät wird an die Steckdose angeschlossen und sofort danach mit Strom versorgt. Im Gegensatz zu einer Steckdose nutzt Grid Computing allerdings entfernte Ressourcen, die bei einem Provider installiert sind. Diese können durch böswillige Nutzer missbraucht werden, die damit nicht nur ihre eigenen Installationen sondern auch die von anderen Benutzern und dem Provider gefährden.

Ressourcen im Grid Computing werden gemeinsam benutzt, d.h. Daten und Programme von konkurrierenden Nutzern oder Unternehmen sind auf der selben physischen Ressource gespeichert. Diese gemeinsame Nutzung stellt eines der Hauptprobleme dar, da Unternehmen sich im Allgemeinen gegenseitig misstrauen und die Gefahr durch Industriespionage omnipräsent ist. Die aktuelle Strategie, um mit diesen Problemen umzugehen, basiert auf dem Vertrauen des Nutzers gegenüber anderen Nutzern und dem Administrator. Diese Entwicklung resultiert aus der Tatsache, dass sich das Grid von einer rein akademischen Spielwiese hin zu einem anerkannten Produkt mit ersten kommerziellen Anwendern entwickelt hat [125]. Im Gegensatz zu kommerziellen Anwendern haben akademische Nutzer meist niedrigere Sicherheitsanforderungen, da Quelldaten und Ergebnisse frei zur Verfügung stehen. Kommerzielle Daten und Anwendungen beinhalten in der Regel geistiges Eigentum, das besonderem Schutz bedarf. In der gemeinsamen Nutzung von Ressourcen im traditionellen Grid Computing liegt also eines der Hauptprobleme, welches die kommerzielle Verbreitung erschwert. Informationen über andere Benutzer und deren Jobs können auf solchen Systemen einfach erlangt werden. In den einfachsten Fällen stellt die bloße Kenntnis, dass ein Konkurrent auf demselben System rechnet, einen Informationsvorsprung dar, der nicht akzeptabel ist, da sogenannte Meta-Daten meist vertraulich sind [124]. Es kann konstatiert werden, dass ein wirksamer Schutz von sensitiven Inhalten im Grid nicht ausreichend vorhanden ist.

Diese Arbeit stellt neue Infrastruktur-Mechanismen vor, die das Konzept von virtuellen Grids weiter voran bringen. Die Arbeiten dafür begannen 2007 und haben zur Entwicklung der XGE geführt. Die XGE ist eine Software zum Erzeugen und Verwalten von virtuellen Grid-Umgebungen. Jobs von Benutzern werden nicht länger nativ, sondern in virtuellen Maschinen ausgeführt. Um die Software einfach in ein bestehendes Grid einzubinden, kann die XGE die Entscheidungen eines bereits installierten Schedulers nutzen und mit der Grid-Middleware auf der Grid-Headnode zusammenarbeiten. Eine neue Grid-fähige, zweigleisige, demilitarisierte Zone schützt die Grid-Headnode vor direkten Angriffen aus dem Internet. Zudem sind die Headnode und die Rechenknoten voneinander isoliert und nicht, wie in einem traditionellen Grid-Umfeld, im selben Netzwerk installiert. Obwohl die demilitarisierte Zone Angriffe erschwert, bietet sie, wie alle Sicherheitslösungen, keinen hundertprozentigen Schutz. Daher ist ein Network Intrusion Detection System um Grid-spezifische Signaturen erweitert worden, damit Angriffe auf Grid-Komponenten verhindert und aufgezeichnet werden können. Um die Daten der Benutzer über die demilitarisierte Zone hinaus zu schützen, ist eine Lösung namens Fence entwickelt worden, die die Daten verschlüsselt vom Rechner des Benutzers in das interne Grid-Netzwerk überträgt. Fence arbeitet dabei mit allen beteiligten Komponenten, inklusive dem Scheduler, zusammen. Ein System verhindert, dass unsichere Kernel-Module und somit auch Kernel-Rootkits zur Laufzeit geladen werden können. Um die Sicherheit der virtuellen Maschinen zu gewährleisten wird ein Malware-Scanner eingesetzt. Dieser nutzt die spezielle Technik der Virtual Machine Introspection um alle laufenden Programme zu überwachen und dabei selber unsichtbar und, für die meiste Malware, unangreifbar zu bleiben. Um die Erkennung zu beschleunigen, können mehrere Erkennungsinstanzen im Grid parallel betrieben werden. Das neue Konzept der öffentlichen, virtuellen Grid-Knoten wird ebenfalls im Kontext dieser Arbeit vorgestellt. Dies ist eine Menge von Grid-Knoten, die aus dem Internet erreichbar und durch dynamische Firewalls geschützt sind. Die Knoten können sich sowohl in einem, als auch in mehreren Rechenzentren befinden. Ein spezieller Web-Service erlaubt es dem Benutzer eigene Firewall-Regeln für seine virtuellen Maschinen zu spezifizieren, ohne damit die Gesamtumgebung zu gefährden.

Das Hauptergebnis der Arbeit sind Lösungen, die dazu beitragen die Sicherheit von Grid-Infrastrukturen auf unterschiedlichen Ebenen zu erhöhen. Alle Ansätze werden detailliert mit Design, Implementierung und Evaluation beschrieben und sind als Open-Source-Software frei verfügbar. Eine Zusammenfassung und ein Ausblick auf kommende Forschung schließen die Arbeit ab.

Contents

Abstract		ii
Contents		ix
1 Introduction		**1**
1.1	Project Framework	2
	1.1.1 Engineering Applications	2
	1.1.2 Financial Business Grid	4
	1.1.3 Plasma Technology Grid	4
	1.1.4 Intelligent System Management for Large Computer Systems	4
1.2	Contributions of this Thesis	5
1.3	Organization of this Thesis	8
2 Fundamentals		**9**
2.1	Introduction	9
2.2	Grid Computing	10
	2.2.1 The Globus Toolkit	11
	2.2.1.1 Globus Toolkit Architecture	11
	2.2.1.2 Grid Resource Allocation and Management	13
	2.2.2 Grid Security Infrastructure	14
2.3	Virtualization	15
	2.3.1 Application and Desktop Virtualization	16
	2.3.2 Network and Storage Virtualization	16
	2.3.3 Server and Machine Virtualization	16
	2.3.4 System-Level or Operating System Virtualization	17
	2.3.5 Xen Virtual Machine Monitor	17
	2.3.6 Live Migration	18
	2.3.7 Libvirt Virtualization API	19
2.4	Cloud Computing	20
	2.4.1 Architecture	20
	2.4.2 Deployment Models	22
	2.4.3 Security Risks	22
2.5	Summary	22

Contents

3 Security for Virtualized Grid Computing Environments   **23**
- 3.1 Introduction 23
- 3.2 Introduction to Job Execution 24
- 3.3 Analysis of the Job Execution Workflow 26
  - 3.3.1 Terminology 26
  - 3.3.2 Analysis of the Head Node Communication and Storage . 27
  - 3.3.3 Analysis of the Host 29
  - 3.3.4 Analysis of the Job Execution 30
  - 3.3.5 Analysis of Multi-Site Computing 32
- 3.4 Methods for Infrastructural Security in Virtualized Grids 34
  - 3.4.1 Virtualized Grid Computing 34
  - 3.4.2 Grid Enabled Demilitarized Zone 36
  - 3.4.3 Lightweight Kernel Rootkit Prevention 37
  - 3.4.4 Malware Detection for Virtualized Grids 37
  - 3.4.5 Dynamic Firewalls 38
- 3.5 Summary 39

4 Host Security   **41**
- 4.1 Introduction 41
- 4.2 Lightweight Kernel Rootkit Prevention 41
  - 4.2.1 Introduction 41
  - 4.2.2 Related Work 42
  - 4.2.3 Design 45
  - 4.2.4 Implementation 53
    - 4.2.4.1 Management System Call 53
    - 4.2.4.2 List Management 56
    - 4.2.4.3 Kernel Module Loading Process 57
  - 4.2.5 Evaluation 58
  - 4.2.6 Summary 60
- 4.3 Malware Detection in Virtualized Grids 60
  - 4.3.1 Introduction 60
  - 4.3.2 Related Work 62
  - 4.3.3 Design 63
    - 4.3.3.1 Architecture 64
    - 4.3.3.2 Operating System Kernel Sensor 66
    - 4.3.3.3 Backend Proxy 66
    - 4.3.3.4 Scan Engine and Executable Analysis 67
  - 4.3.4 Implementation 67
    - 4.3.4.1 Operating System Kernel Modifications 67
    - 4.3.4.2 Kernel-Userland Communication 70
    - 4.3.4.3 Operating System Kernel Sensor 70
    - 4.3.4.4 Backend Proxy and Anti-virus Engine Connection 70
  - 4.3.5 Evaluation 72

4.4	Summary			75

5 Network Security — 77

- 5.1 Introduction . . . 77
- 5.2 Virtualized Grid Computing . . . 78
  - 5.2.1 Introduction . . . 78
  - 5.2.2 Related Work . . . 78
  - 5.2.3 Design . . . 82
    - 5.2.3.1 Image Creation Station . . . 83
    - 5.2.3.2 Architecture . . . 84
    - 5.2.3.3 Hybrid Mode of Operation . . . 86
    - 5.2.3.4 Job Management . . . 88
    - 5.2.3.5 Virtual Machine Management . . . 89
    - 5.2.3.6 Disk Image Distribution . . . 99
  - 5.2.4 Implementation . . . 107
    - 5.2.4.1 Core Components . . . 107
    - 5.2.4.2 LXGEd . . . 110
    - 5.2.4.3 Job Management . . . 111
    - 5.2.4.4 Job Manager . . . 112
    - 5.2.4.5 Virtual Machine Management . . . 113
    - 5.2.4.6 Backend Connection . . . 118
    - 5.2.4.7 Placeholder Virtual Machines . . . 121
    - 5.2.4.8 Remote Interfaces . . . 121
    - 5.2.4.9 Efficient Virtual Disk Image Deployment . . . 122
    - 5.2.4.10 Avoiding Retransmission Overhead . . . 129
    - 5.2.4.11 Storage Synchronization . . . 129
  - 5.2.5 Evaluation . . . 131
    - 5.2.5.1 Execution Time . . . 132
    - 5.2.5.2 XGE Internals . . . 133
    - 5.2.5.3 Scheduler Performance . . . 133
  - 5.2.6 Summary . . . 138
- 5.3 Grid Demilitarized Zone . . . 139
  - 5.3.1 Introduction . . . 139
  - 5.3.2 Related Work . . . 139
  - 5.3.3 Design . . . 144
    - 5.3.3.1 Architecture of the Demilitarized Zone . . . 145
    - 5.3.3.2 End-to-End Encryption . . . 147
    - 5.3.3.3 Optimizing Security Configurations . . . 152
    - 5.3.3.4 Grid-enabled Intrusion Detection . . . 155
  - 5.3.4 Implementation . . . 156
    - 5.3.4.1 Border Network . . . 156
    - 5.3.4.2 Internal Network . . . 157
    - 5.3.4.3 End-to-End Encryption with Fence . . . 157

Contents

		5.3.4.4	Connection to the Globus Toolkit	158
		5.3.4.5	DMZ Head Node Client	160
		5.3.4.6	Cluster Head Node Daemon	161
		5.3.4.7	DMZ Head Node Daemon	161
		5.3.4.8	Grid Enabled Intrusion Detection System	163
	5.3.5	Evaluation		166
	5.3.6	Summary		171
5.4	Dynamic Firewalls for Grid Computing			171
	5.4.1	Introduction		171
	5.4.2	Related Work		172
	5.4.3	Design		174
		5.4.3.1	Secure Infrastructure Communication	175
		5.4.3.2	Dynamic Network Security	178
		5.4.3.3	Inter-Virtual Machine Communication	182
		5.4.3.4	Network Security Web Service	182
	5.4.4	Implementation		183
		5.4.4.1	Rule Set Generation	183
		5.4.4.2	Deployment, Execution and Removal	185
		5.4.4.3	Packet Filtering	185
	5.4.5	Evaluation		186
5.5	Summary			190

6 Experimental Results — 191
- 6.1 Introduction — 191
- 6.2 Efficient Transfer of Virtual Machines — 191
  - 6.2.1 Distribution Methods — 191
  - 6.2.2 Virtual Disk Encryption — 194
  - 6.2.3 Multi-Layered Virtual Machines — 195
- 6.3 Storage Synchronization — 198
- 6.4 Summary — 204

7 Conclusions — 207
- 7.1 Summary — 207
- 7.2 Future Work — 209
  - 7.2.1 Virtual Machine Lifecycle Management — 209
  - 7.2.2 Robustness and Scalability — 209
  - 7.2.3 Energy-efficient Virtual Machine Management — 209
  - 7.2.4 Intrusion Detection — 209
  - 7.2.5 Malware and Rootkit Prevention — 210
  - 7.2.6 Complex Event Processing — 210

List of Figures — 211

List of Tables 215

Bibliography 220

"The only truly secure system is one that is powered off, cast in a block of concrete and sealed in a lead-lined room with armed guards."

Gene Spafford (1956–)

1

Introduction

About a decade ago, Ian Foster presented a three point checklist to define what a grid is [44]. He wrote that grid computing is about coordinating resources that are not subject to centralized control, using standard, open, general-purpose protocols and interfaces and finally, about delivering nontrivial qualities of services. Based on this checklist, grid computing evolved in the following years from research to a mature paradigm that attracted academic as well as industrial users. However, the number of the former was significantly higher than the number of the latter because there is a difference in the trust relationship. Academic users use the grid mostly to compute research task such as calculations or simulations. In general, the input data, the results and possibly the application itself was collected or developed by means of public funding, which means they might have to be made available to the public. Commercial users use the grid for the same tasks, however their data and applications mostly represent intellectual property. While grid computing offers a number of elaborate security technologies, some of them are too weak to protect these assets on the infrastructure layer. One example is the use of shared resources: jobs are executed simultaneously on the same physical resource, allowing that one job is able to gather information about another job. If the job is a malicious one, it could further extend its privileges by exploiting a software's vulnerability. Among others, these stated problems hinder a wider commercial adoption and implementation of grid computing.

Years later, a new computing paradigm appeared and resolved many of the unresolved grid problems: cloud computing. While it took some time to develop a thorough definition of cloud computing, today it is accepted that it is about offering different types of services. This includes applications (called software as a service), computing platforms (called platform as a service) and finally, raw computing resources (called infrastructure as a service). Usually, the last point is realized by using operating system virtualization. Although cloud computing sounds similar to grid computing, it is also a new kind of business model: computing resources are bundled into services and offered on-demand. Customers no longer have to own their own resources, they can rent resources and pay only for their actual usage.

This thesis addresses various aspects of infrastructure security problems present in the grid computing paradigm. Its aim is to introduce a new security infrastructure for grids, which makes grids more attractive to commercial customers while lowering the initial burden of joining a given grid. Some parts of the existing infrastructure were already adopted by cloud computing; thus, several of the approaches protect both worlds: grids and clouds. Securing the computing resources and the network between them represents the main focus of this thesis. In order to strengthen host security, two approaches were designed and implemented to prevent kernel rootkits and malware binaries. Issues dealt with in terms of network security include a novel virtualized grid environment, a grid enabled demilitarized zone, and secure, multi-site computing with dynamic firewalls.

1.1 Project Framework

The following section introduces four projects and corresponding applications which illustrate the need for a secure computing infrastructure. Three of the projects are part of the German D-Grid Initiative [26] and funded by the German Ministry for Education and Research (Bundesministerium für Bildung und Forschung - BMBF) [11]. The remaining project, TIMaCS, deals with the design of system management tools needed for large computing systems. This project is also funded by the BMBF, HPC initiative.

1.1.1 Engineering Applications

By using grid technology, the In-Grid [60] community is able to combine expertise in the areas of modeling, simulation and optimization, which enables all parties to use distributed resources efficiently. Thus, In-Grid provides a grid environment for applications in the field of engineering. The project was part of the first generation of D-Grid community projects (D-Grid I) and was positioned at the interface between industrial and scientific use.

Six typical applications (interactive visualization, foundry technologies, metal forming technologies, groundwater flow and transport, turbine simulation and fluid-structure interaction) are considered showcases in order to cover the three central areas of computationally intensive engineering applications, including coupled multi-scale problems, coupled multi-discipline problems, and distributed simulation-based optimization.

One of the test applications simulates transient turbulence in fluids. Conducting these simulations requires a high amount of computing power, especially processing power. Turbulence studies are well tailored for distributing computing environments such as grids and clouds, since transitional Reynolds numbers can be ideally computed on a single CPU core. Dörnemann et al. [33], who explored the resource characteristics of the application, state that "answering whether turbulence is a persistent phenomenon requires to study the characteristic lifetime of turbulent structures as a function of both flow velocity and domain size. Since the characteristic lifetime even for fixed parameters has to be statistically based on an ensemble of many independent simulations generating the required data, that study requires an enormous amount of CPU time which is contrasted by very low memory and interconnection speed requirements." Figure 1.1 depicts the typical turbulent state on the chaotic saddle. For more information regarding the complexity involved, the reader is referred to the work done by Schneider et al. [119] and Hof et al. [57].

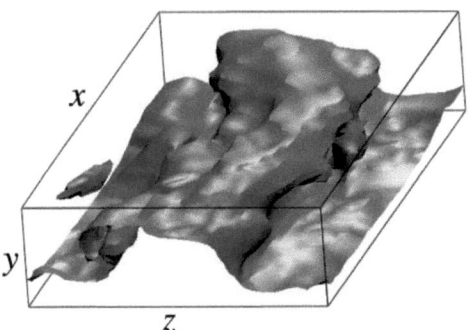

Figure 1.1: Typical turbulent state on the chaotic saddle.

Both the software and the data need protection in this scenario. Simulation software is often developed by small and medium enterprises and might represent years of work. Further, the input data is also highly valuable, a competing company can gain considerable benefits if it is able to steal the data from the grid.

1.1.2 Financial Business Grid

Increasing competition in the German banking sector is leading to increased pressure for restructuring and further automation in IT-related business processes in banks and financial services providers. The Financial Business Grid (FinGrid) project aims to identify suitable services and processes in the financial service sector and to develop grid-based systems that enable financial service providers to reorganize their processes efficiently and to realize applications that have been impossible so far in terms of computational requirements. The project will develop different prototypes that will be used to demonstrate the feasibility of our concepts in terms of security, accounting, monitoring and pricing [41].

Since the financial sector works with sensitive data, e.g. names and account balances of private and business customers, strong security mechanisms are needed. Both the aforementioned prototypes and the customers data must be protected.

1.1.3 Plasma Technology Grid

The plasma technology grid (PT-Grid) aims at offering an online consulting tool for plasma technology applications. The project consists of four main partners that want to bring their modeling tools into the grid. This ranges from academic, open source applications up to commercial tools like ANSYS (Fluent, CFX) and CFD-ACE. The infrastructure is based on established grid technologies, guarantees accounting and billing and should offer an industry-ready security architecture. Thus, the used software, the input data as well as the results represent intellectual property and need special protection [105].

1.1.4 Intelligent System Management for Large Computer Systems

The aim of the TIMaCS project is to build a monitoring framework that is able to deal with the complexity of new, upcoming computer systems, especially ones with several peta-flops. While current monitoring solutions are able to monitor smaller resources, they might not be usable on future-generation systems. TIMaCS tries to overcome this limitation by developing a fast and scalable messaging infrastructure. Attached to the communication bus is a decision engine that is able to start predefined actions in case of an error. Regression test aim at taking preventions actions before an error occurs. Finally, operating system virtualization is used to partition the available cluster into one or more separated virtual clusters [153].

In order to protect the integrity and confidentiality of computations running on backend cluster resources, the TIMaCS project takes advantage of operating system virtualization. Computations take place in sandboxed environments, which provide security to the user as well as to the infrastructure provider.

1.2 Contributions of this Thesis

The research contributions of this thesis are:

- This thesis proposes a novel solution that advances the concept of virtualized grid computing. The work started back in 2007 and led to the development of the XGE, a virtual grid management software that can be used in grid and cloud computing environments. In a grid setup, the XGE provides virtual grid landscapes based on scheduling decisions provided by external schedulers such as Torque [22]. Thus, the traditional shared resource model is replaced with a virtualized model, where all executions happen within a sandboxed container. If used in a cloud environment, the XGE acts as a software platform for the implementation of a private cloud, i.e. it provides infrastructure as a service. The XGE is released under an open source license and available online.[1]

    Currently, the XGE is installed on nodes of the Phillips-University of Marburg, Regionales Rechenzentrum für Niedersachsen (RRZN) at the University of Hannover, CFX Berlin GmbH and Höchleistungsrechenzentrum (HLRS) at the University of Stuttgart.

- A novel dual-laned demilitarized zone is introduced to raise the burden for attacks on the grid head node. Previously, the head node was installed in the same network as the backend computing nodes, so a possible compromise of the head node could also affect the nodes. The demilitarized zone separates the head node from the remaining part of an installation. Furthermore, a cryptographically secured communication channel between the head node and the XGE on the backend network is developed. To detect the attacks that could not be prevented, a network intrusion detection system is modified to recognize grid signatures.

- While the current grid security mechanisms are sufficient to secure job data between the user and the head node, they are not able to secure the data

---
[1] http://mage.uni-marburg.de/trac/xge/

Chapter 1. Introduction

after it was processed by the head node. A novel software called Fence is introduced that supports end-to-end encryption, which means that all data remains encrypted until it reaches its final destination.

- Since it is not possible to protect a system from all possible attacks, this thesis presents two mechanisms to mitigate the outcome of a compromise. An efficient and lightweight solution assures that only trusted kernel modules can be loaded. It is no longer possible to load untrusted modules such as kernel rootkits. Furthermore, a malware scanner for virtualized grids is developed that works with live system call introspection, and thus can detect known as well as yet unknown malware.

- To enable multi-site service-oriented grid applications, the novel concept of public virtual nodes is presented. This is a virtualized grid node with a public IP address shielded by a set of dynamic firewalls. Additionally an encrypted, on-demand virtual private network encapsulates multiple virtual nodes, which, for example, run remote instances of a service-oriented application, in a private network. Furthermore, all virtual machines are also guarded by special firewall rules to prevent internal attacks from malicious users.

The following papers were published during the course of the work on this thesis:

1. Matthias Schmidt, Matthew Smith, Niels Fallenbeck, Hans-Joachim Picht, and Bernd Freisleben. Building a Demilitarized Zone with Data Encryption for Grid Environments. In *Proceedings of First International Conference on Networks for Grid Applications*, pp. 8–16, ACM press, 2007.

2. Matthew Smith, Matthias Schmidt, Niels Fallenbeck, Christian Schridde, and Bernd Freisleben. Optimising Security Configurations with Service Level Agreements. In *Proceedings of the 7th International Conference on Optimization: Techniques and Applications (ICOTA7)*, pp. 367–368. ICOTA, 2007.

3. Matthew Smith, Matthias Schmidt, Niels Fallenbeck, Tim Dörnemann, Christian Schridde, and Bernd Freisleben. Security for On-Demand Grid Computing. In *Journal of Future Generation Computer Systems*, pp. 315–325, Elsevier, 2008.

4. Roland Schwarzkopf, Matthias Schmidt, Niels Fallenbeck, Bernd Freisleben. Multi-Layered Virtual Machines for Security Updates in Grid Environments. In: *Proceedings of 35th Euromicro Conference on Internet Technologies, Quality of Service and Applications (ITQSA)*, pp. 563–570, IEEE press, 2009

5. Matthias Schmidt, Niels Fallenbeck, Matthew Smith, Bernd Freisleben. Secure Service-Oriented Grid Computing with Public Virtual Worker Nodes. In: *Proceedings of 35th Euromicro Conference on Internet Technologies, Quality of Service and Applications (ITQSA)*, pp. 555–562, IEEE press, 2009

6. Matthias Schmidt, Niels Fallenbeck, Kay Dörnemann, Roland Schwarzkopf, Tobias Pontz, Manfred Grauer, Bernd Freisleben. Aufbau einer virtualisierten Cluster-Umgebung. In: *Grid Computing in der Finanzindustrie*, Books on Demand, Norderstedt, pp. 119–131, Oliver Hinz, Roman Beck, Bernd Skiera, Wolfgang König, 2009

7. Matthias Schmidt, Niels Fallenbeck, Roland Schwarzkopf, Bernd Freisleben Virtualized Cluster Computing. In *Research Report High-Performance Computing in Hessen*, pp. 148–149, 2010

8. Matthias Schmidt, Niels Fallenbeck, Matthew Smith, Bernd Freisleben. Efficient Distribution of Virtual Machines for Cloud Computing. In: *Proceedings of the 18th Euromicro Conference on Parallel, Distributed and Network-based Processing (PDP 2010)*, pp. 567–574, IEEE Press, 2010

9. Niels Fallenbeck, Matthias Schmidt, Roland Schwarzkopf, Bernd Freisleben. Inter-Site Virtual Machine Image Transfer in Grids and Clouds. In *Proceedings of the 2nd International ICST Conference on Cloud Computing (CloudComp 2010)*, Springer LNICST, 2010

10. Eugen Volk, Jochen Buchholz, Stefan Wesner, Daniela Koudela, Matthias Schmidt, Niels Fallenbeck, Roland Schwarzkopf, Bernd Freisleben, Götz Isenmann, Jürgen Schwitalla, Marc Lohrer, Erich Focht, Andreas Jeutter. Towards Intelligent Management of Very Large Computing Systems. In *Proceedings of Competence in High Performance Computing CiHPC*, Springer, 2010

11. Matthias Schmidt, Sascha Fahl, Roland Schwarzkopf, Bernd Freisleben. TrustBox: A Security Architecture for Preventing Data Breaches. In: *Proceedings of the 19th Euromicro Conference on Parallel, Distributed and Network-based Processing (PDP)*, pp. 635–639, IEEE press, 2011

12. Katharina Haselhorst, Matthias Schmidt, Roland Schwarzkopf, Niels Fallenbeck, Bernd Freisleben. Efficient Storage Synchronization for Live Migration in Cloud Infrastructures. In *Proceedings of the 19th Euromicro Conference on Parallel, Distributed and Network-based Processing (PDP)*, pp. 511–518, IEEE press, 2011

13. Matthias Schmidt, Lars Baumgärtner, Pablo Graubner, David Böck, Bernd Freisleben. Malware Detection and Kernel Rootkit Prevention in Cloud

Computing Environments. In *Proceedings of the 19th Euromicro Conference on Parallel, Distributed and Network-based Processing (PDP)*, pp. 603–610, IEEE press, 2011

14. Pablo Graubner, <u>Matthias Schmidt</u>, Bernd Freisleben. Energy-efficient Management of Virtual Machines in Eucalyptus. In *Proceedings of the 4th IEEE International Conference on Cloud Computing (IEEE CLOUD)*, IEEE press, 2011

15. Roland Schwarzkopf, <u>Matthias Schmidt</u>, Christian Strack, Bernd Freisleben. Checking Running and Dormant Virtual Machines for the Necessity of Security Updates in Cloud Environments. In *Proceedings of the 3rd IEEE International Conference on Cloud Computing Technology and Science (IEEE CloudCom)*, pp. to appear, IEEE press, 2011

1.3 Organization of this Thesis

The rest of the thesis is organized as follows:

Chapter 2 introduces topics that lay out the fundamentals for this thesis. This includes grid computing, virtualization and cloud computing.

Chapter 3 presents an analysis of the job submission workflow and exposes a number of security issues for both host and network. Based on the analysis the solutions presented in this thesis will be presented.

Chapter 4 presents solutions that solve the host related issues. The design, implementation and evaluation of a lightweight kernel rootkit prevention mechanism and a malware detection engine in virtualized grids is presented.

Approaches that address network security issues are presented in Chapter 5. This includes an approach for virtualized grids including dynamic firewalls and a grid-enabled demilitarized zone. The chapter includes the design, implementation and experimental evaluations.

Chapter 6 presents experimental results not directly related to one specific solution. This includes a survey on efficient distribution of virtual machine disk images including encryption and multi-layer images. Elaborate measurements about efficient storage synchronization conclude the chapter.

Finally, Chapter 7 concludes the thesis and discusses future work.

"You don't live in a world all your own. Your brothers are here, too."
Albert Schweitzer (1875–1965)

2
Fundamentals

2.1 Introduction

This chapter presents an introduction to the topics that lay out the fundamentals for this thesis. It covers grid and cloud computing, virtualization and several components used for development.

The introduction of fundamental concepts starts with an overview of grid computing in Section 2.2. This includes a short introduction to the Globus Toolkit, the de-facto middleware, its architecture and the way how to submit compute jobs. Furthermore, insights of the Grid Security Infrastructure are given.

A technology heavily used in this thesis is virtualization, which is introduced in Section 2.3. After presenting the basic characteristics of the different types of virtualization, a detailed view of the Xen Virtual Machine Monitor is presented. The section concludes with insights on virtual machine live migration and the libvirt API.

Cloud computing is introduced in Section 2.4. Since it consists of three different layers, all three including a detailed description are described.

2.2 Grid Computing

Grid computing aims at providing resources (e.g., compute power, data) as easily as electricity is provided through the power grid. It is quite difficult to find an exact definition for grid computing. Many existing cluster or distributed computing projects call themselves grid computing projects. One of the pioneers of grid computing, Ian Foster, created a three point checklist [44] that further defines the term:

> I suggest that the essence of the definitions above can be captured in a simple checklist, according to which a grid is a system that:
>
> 1) ...coordinates resources that are not subject to centralized control ...(A grid integrates and coordinates resources and users that live within different control domains – for example, the user's desktop vs. central computing; different administrative units of the same company; or different companies; and addresses the issues of security, policy, payment, membership, and so forth that arise in these settings. Otherwise, we are dealing with a local management system.)
>
> 2) ...using standard, open, general-purpose protocols and interfaces ...(A grid is built from multi-purpose protocols and interfaces that address such fundamental issues as authentication, authorization, resource discovery, and resource access. As I discuss further below, it is important that these protocols and interfaces be standard and open. Otherwise, we are dealing with an application- specific system.)
>
> 3) ...to deliver nontrivial qualities of service. (A grid allows its constituent resources to be used in a coordinated fashion to deliver various qualities of service, relating for example to response time, throughput, availability, and security, and/or co-allocation of multiple resource types to meet complex user demands, so that the utility of the combined system is significantly greater than that of the sum of its parts.)

This three points describe the motivational goals of a grid. A grid controls resources used to solve problems in a virtual organization (VO). A virtual organization is either an individual or an organization willing to share their resources with others [43]. A resource could be compute power, software or storage. Service level agreements define how a member of a virtual organization can access the resources. Furthermore, proper accounting and billing is needed to satisfy all attending parties.

Current existing distributed computing paradigms only solve some of the points mentioned above. While it is possible to exchange data and information, there is no integrated solution to manage and control resources. This gap is filled by grid computing. Researchers around the globe invented a number of protocols, tools and services to build virtual organizations during the last years. This ranges from security mechanisms, status and information protocols up to new applications. Due to the dynamic resource allocation, grid computing enhances the previous distributed computing in various ways. Unlike the traditional way, current grid systems expose the local compute resources to a larger number of users via the Internet, using grid middlewares such as Globus [149], gLite [103] or UNICORE [42].

2.2.1 The Globus Toolkit

The Globus Toolkit [149] (often called GT4) consists of a set of components used to build a distributed system. The set contains web services, libraries and tools to build custom extensions. Globus is operated by the *Globus Alliance* consisting of academic institutes, US government agencies and companies like IBM and Microsoft. The toolkit is released as open source, so it is easy to find bugs or to contribute new software.

2.2.1.1 Globus Toolkit Architecture

The Globus architecture is divided in two parts: a server part offering services and the appropriate client part. Various libraries exist to write own services, either in C, Java or Python.

Globus Security is handled by the first component of Globus (as seen in the first column in Figure 2.1). This topic is covered in a separate section, see below.

Data transfer and replication is managed by the second Globus component (column two in Figure 2.1). GridFTP [1] is a protocol similar to the traditional file transfer protocol (FTP) designed to exchange large amounts of data. It was not sufficient to reuse FTP as it lacks supports for concurrent transfers, quality of service parameters and security. GridFTP is coupled to the grid security infrastructure, thus all connections are encrypted and authenticated. Globus offers a built-in server and a client, but it also offers a set of development tools to build own clients. Replicas, distributed copies of data, are managed by the *Replica Location Service* (RLS). It keeps track of all data and enables users to search for distributed data. Users and services can register data after they uploaded it into

Chapter 2. Fundamentals

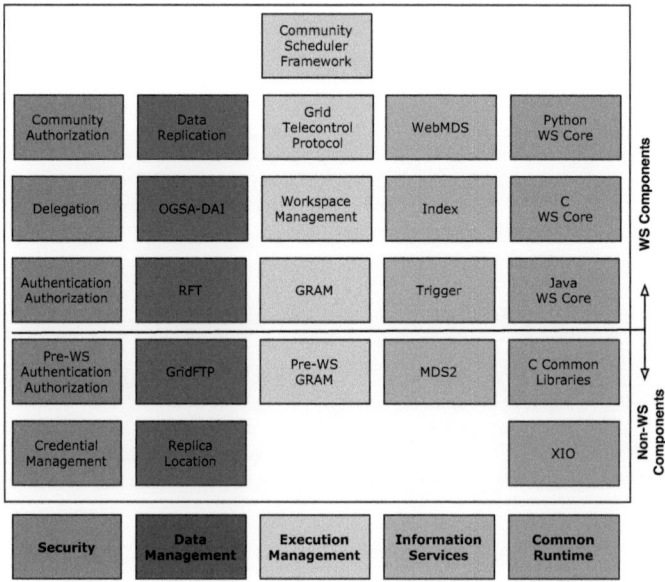

Figure 2.1: Globus Toolkit 4: Components. Source: [149]

the grid. RLS is decentralized, i.e. the registry is distributed between multiple servers. Nevertheless, a centralized solution with only one server is also possible.

Creation, management and deletion of compute jobs is handled by the Execution Management (third column). A distinction is drawn between real web services and pre web services. Pre web services are a set of Unix tools to execute jobs. A further description can be found in Section 2.2.1.2.

The Information Services as seen in the fourth column can be used to control and search resources. Using the *Monitoring and Discovery System (*MDS*)* a user can find out which resources are part of a virtual organization. Part of the MDS are the mphIndex- and the *Trigger* service. Collecting information (e.g., processor load, virtual memory usage, number of jobs) is the job of the index service. All information is available to the user over an interface. Triggering actions upon

2.2. Grid Computing

specific conditions (e.g., limited hard disk space) is done by the trigger service. Finally, WebMDS offers a web site with all collected information.

The *cores*, written in C, Java and Python are the central components of Globus (fifth column). Using this cores it is possible for a grid developer to write his or her own web and WSRF (Web Service Resource Framework) services in the programming language of one of the cores.

2.2.1.2 Grid Resource Allocation and Management

Globus uses the Grid Resource Allocation and Management (GRAM) interface to initialize, execute and monitor jobs. While it is possible to execute jobs directly, GRAM is used when reliable execution, monitoring, credential checking and communication with different batch schedulers are required.

After a user launches a job via GRAM, he or she receives an *Endpoint Reference* (EPR). It is needed to query the job state after launch or to delete the job. GRAM itself is not a scheduler (like e.g. Torque, PBS or SGE), it is only a communication proxy between Globus and the real scheduler.

Users can launch jobs directly on the command line:

```
$ globusrun-ws -submit -c -- /bin/uname -a
Submitting job...Done.
Job ID: uuid:63802811-6fb1-412e-a65a-e3af47e662dd
Termination time: 02/24/2011 10:53 GMT
Current job state: Active
Current job state: CleanUp
Current job state: Done
Destroying job...Done.
```

Listing 2.1: Sample job submission via Globus command line utilities

While this is useful for debugging, it is often desirable to specify additional information like environment variables or resource requirements. This can be achieved using a RSL file, which is a XML file. By sticking to the RSL schema it is possible to describe a job in all details.

```
<job>
    <executable>/bin/uname</executable>
    <directory>/tmp/</directory>

    <argument>-a</argument>

    <environment>
        <name>SHELL</name>
        <value>/bin/sh</value>
```

```
10      </environment>
11
12      <stdin>/dev/null</stdin>
13      <stdout>${GLOBUS_USER_HOME}/uname.stdout</stdout>
14      <stderr>${GLOBUS_USER_HOME}/uname.stderr</stderr>
15
16      <count>1</count>
17 </job>
```

Listing 2.2: RSL description of a sample job

GRAM remains active during the job execution. This enables the user to query the job state or to send a signal. GRAM is tightly coupled to two other components of Globus, the Reliable File Transfer (RFT) service and GridFTP. Both handle the transfer of job input and result data before and after the execution, i.e. if a job is executed on multiple nodes GridFTP can be used to to transfer the job data in advance.

2.2.2 Grid Security Infrastructure

The Grid Security Infrastructure (GSI), formerly known as Globus Security Infrastructure, offers basic security mechanisms. It focuses on three main topics: authentication, authorization and confidentiality. An overview is shown in Figure 2.2. The two diagrams on the left hand side show message-level security (with certificates and classical authentication) and the remaining one on the right hand side shows transport-level security (only using certificates).

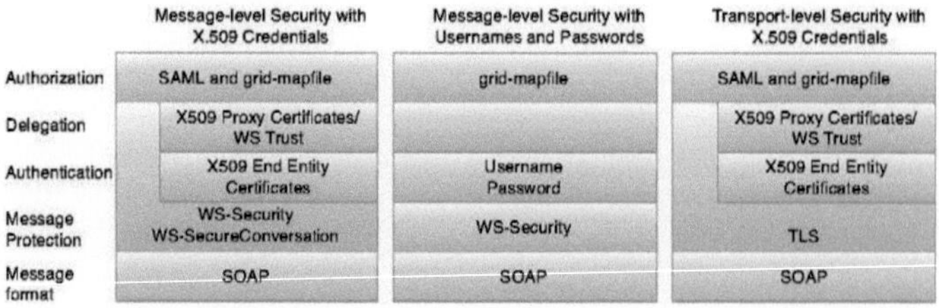

	Message-level Security with X.509 Credentials	Message-level Security with Usernames and Passwords	Transport-level Security with X.509 Credentials
Authorization	SAML and grid-mapfile	grid-mapfile	SAML and grid-mapfile
Delegation	X509 Proxy Certificates/ WS Trust		X509 Proxy Certificates/ WS Trust
Authentication	X509 End Entity Certificates	Username Password	X509 End Entity Certificates
Message Protection	WS-Security WS-SecureConversation	WS-Security	TLS
Message format	SOAP	SOAP	SOAP

Figure 2.2: Grid Security Infrastructure overview. Source: [149]

Authentication is achieved using certificates. Every user owns a certificate signed by a trusted certificate authority (CA). The CA can be either a so-called simpleCA (self-signed CA created by the local Globus administrator) or a real one with a proper registration authority (this is common in academic and industrial grids). Globus can create proxy certificates on demand to enable long running jobs. Without using proxy certificates, a user would have to enter his or her certificate password every time it is forwarded to another Globus component (e.g., from GridFTP to GRAM). As this is not feasible, a proxy certificate is used. A proxy is derived from the user's certificate and consists of a new certificate and a private key. It is signed by the owner, rather than a CA. Proxies have limited lifetimes meaning that the proxy should no longer be accepted by others after the lifetime expired. To support simple grid services, Globus can authenticate a user by his or her user name and a password. While this enables easy debugging and rapid prototyping, one cannot use advanced features such as delegation.

Authorization administers the permissions of a user. The simplest solution is to use a `grid-mapfile`. This plain text file contains a mapping between the users distinguished certificate name (DN) and the local Unix user account. Thus, authorization is delegated to the underlying operating system. Furthermore, GSI can use access control lists for services and the Security Assertion Markup Language (SAML) protocol.

Confidentiality, authentication and integrity checking on the transport layer is done using the Transport Layer Security (TLS) protocol. Since Globus needs certificates to run properly, these certificates are also used to TLS authentication. Additionally, SOAP messages can be secured with the WSSecureConversation specification.

GRAM Security

GRAM also requires a proper certificate (or a proxy certificate) prior to job execution. Furthermore, it relies on the grid-mapfile to map grid users to local Unix accounts.

2.3 Virtualization

Virtualization is the logical separation between services and the underlying physical resources. It is possible to run entire operating systems, applications, or services independent of the underlying system. Virtualization also provides the ability to run the mentioned services on different physical platforms, e.g. it is possible to execute PowerPC binaries on the Intel architecture. For detailed information the reader is referred to the book by von Hagen [166].

2.3.1 Application and Desktop Virtualization

The most prominent example for the *application level virtualization* is the Java programming language. Bytecode produced by the Java compiler runs on the Java virtual machine. Thus, it does not matter if the source and target platform differ, i.e. the bytecode was compiled on a 64-bit machine while it is executed on a 32-bit machine. Consequently, application virtualization describes the process of compiling source code into machine-independent byte code.

The ability to display a desktop from one computer on another computer is called *desktop virtualization*. Prominent examples are Virtual Network Computing (VNC), thin clients such as Microsoft's Remote Desktop and associated Terminal Server products.

2.3.2 Network and Storage Virtualization

Sometimes it is desirable to wrap the underlying, physical network and provide a logical view to the system and/or user. Adding an encrypted layer to the network protects the data from malicious users. Furthermore, an encrypted connection hides the intermediate router as it is presented as a one-to-one connection to the user. Enterprise level concepts such as Virtual Private Networks (VPNs) allow companies to logically connection physically separated sites.

Just like network virtualization, *storage virtualization* is a logical abstraction of physical storage and known since many years. As the name suggests, logical volume managers as used in Linux or BSD are a prominent example. A RAID over one or more disks is also a known example.

2.3.3 Server and Machine Virtualization

The ability to run a whole operating systems inside a container is called *server virtualization* or *machine virtualization*. The container is named virtual machine. Full-virtualization allows the operating system to run unmodified (as in source code changes) because all physical hardware is abstracted. Contrary, a technique called para-virtualization allows faster execution of the virtual machine's instructions, but it also requires modifications to the operating system kernel. Applications benefit from this type of virtualization as they can run unmodified and have a entire software stack (e.g., libraries, dependencies) available. Xen is an example for para-virtualization and Virtualbox for full virtualization.

2.3.4 System-Level or Operating System Virtualization

System-level virtualization allows to run multiple, logically distinct system environments on a single instance of an operating system kernel. It is based on the change root concept available on all Unix systems. Virtualization solutions such as FreeBSD's chroot jails, Solaris Zones, and Virtuozzo are all examples of system-level virtualization.

2.3.5 Xen Virtual Machine Monitor

The Xen hypervisor was first created by Keir Fraser and Ian Pratt as part of the Xenoserver research project at Cambridge University in the late 1990s. In 2003 Barham et al. [8] presented the Xen Virtual Machine Monitor (VMM). Instead of using *full virtualization*, they use a concept called *para-virtualization*. Although full virtualization offers a number of benefits, it also has several drawbacks, especially when used with the Intel x86 architecture. Robin et al. [110] presented a detailed study about the virtualizability of all 250 Intel Pentium processor instructions. Seventeen instructions did not meet the requirements needed by a secure VMM. Several virtualization solutions, like the VMWare GSX Server [162], circumvent these problems in return of higher costs and reduced performance.

Para-virtualization attempts to avoid the drawbacks of full virtualization by presenting a VMM that is similar, but not equal to the underlying hardware. The approach promises higher performance, but it requires modifications to the guest operating system. This prevents that proprietary operating systems (source code is not publicly available) cannot run as Xen guest operating system without special hardware support. In the beginning it was not possible to run Microsoft Windows in a Xen virtual machine, nowadays it is possible, because all new processors have special hardware instructions, like Intel Virtualization Technology (Intel VT) [157] or AMD Virtualization (AMD-V) Technology [3].

Architecture

A Xen system consists of three components: the hypervisor, the kernel and userland applications. Usually, an operating system kernel runs in the processor's Ring 0. Under Xen, instead, a kernel runs in Ring 1 (on 32 bit hardware) as shown in Figure 2.3. Running in Ring 1 means that the kernel still can access memory allocated to applications that run in Ring 3, but it is protected from other kernels or applications. The hypervisor itself runs in Ring 0 and is thus protected from the former mentioned.

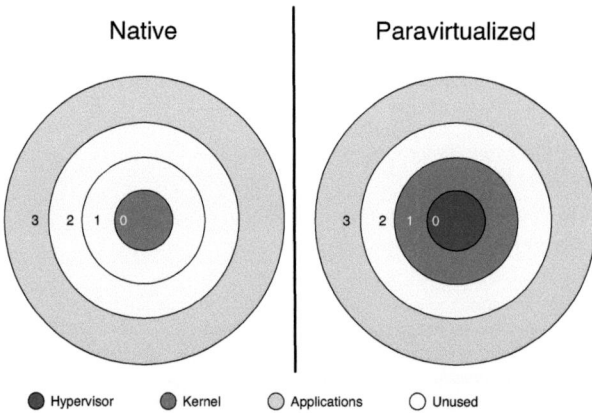

Figure 2.3: Ring usage in native and paravirtualized systems. Source: [18]

Guest virtual machines in Xen are called domain U (domU) and run under the hypervisor's control. The U stands for unprivileged. Upon system boot, Xen starts up a privileged domain, called the domain 0 (dom0). The dom0 is just another domU, but with enhanced privileges. Device drivers are provided by the operating system running in the dom0, as Xen does not include any device drivers by itself. Therefore, the dom0's integrity needs special protection. An unprivileged domain is not allowed to access the hardware directly, all requests are routed through the dom0. Nevertheless, it might be useful to grant access to devices to a domU in certain situations (e.g., direct access to network hardware gives a tremendous speedup).

2.3.6 Live Migration

Live migration is the task of migrating a virtual machine from one physical node to another one while it is running. The process includes the virtual disk image's transfer, CPU registers, content of virtual memory and some other minor things. Usually, the disk image is stored on shared storage, hence no transfer is needed. Since live migration is used by a component developed during the course this thesis, a short introduction follows.

One of the first papers describing live migration was written by Clark et al. [21]. They implemented high-performance migration support for Xen, reducing the downtime of a virtual machine running Quake 3 server to 60 ms. They achieve this using a pre-copy approach in which pages of memory are iteratively copied from the source machine to the destination host, all without ever stopping the execution of the virtual machine being migrated. Their approach finally pauses the virtual machine, copies any remaining pages to the destination, and resumes execution there.

Another approach is taken by Hines et al. [56]. Contrary to Clark, they propose post-copy based live migration for virtual machines. Post-copy migration defers the transfer of a virtual machine's memory contents until after its processor state has been sent to the target host. They facilitate the use of post-copy with adaptive pre-paging techniques to minimize the number of page faults across the network. Furthermore, they propose different pre-paging strategies and quantitatively compare their effectiveness in reducing network-bound page faults.

2.3.7 Libvirt Virtualization API

Several components developed during the course of this thesis use the *libvirt* library. According to the website [29], *libvirt* is the following:

> Libvirt is collection of software that provides a convenient way to manage virtual machines and other virtualization functionality, such as storage and network interface management. These software pieces include an API library, a daemon (libvirtd), and a command line utility (virsh).
>
> An primary goal of libvirt is to provide a single way to manage multiple different virtualization providers/hypervisors. For example, the command 'virsh list –all' can be used to list the existing virtual machines for any supported hypervisor (KVM, Xen, VMWare ESX, etc.) No need to learn the hypervisor specific tools!

libvirt offers language bindings for a variety of languages, among others for the Python programming language, in which most components of this thesis are written in. The example in Listing 2.3 depicts how to use the library to show all running virtual machines on a physical host.

```
import libvirt
import sys

conn = libvirt.openReadOnly(None)
if conn == None:
    print 'Failed to open connection to the hypervisor'
```

Chapter 2. Fundamentals

```
 7      sys.exit(1)
 8
 9 try:
10      dom0 = conn.lookupByName("Domain-0")
11 except:
12      print 'Failed to find the main domain'
13      sys.exit(1)
14
15 print "Domain 0: id %d running %s" % (dom0.ID(),dom0.OSType())
16 print dom0.info()
```

Listing 2.3: Libvirt example: show all running virtual machines

2.4 Cloud Computing

Cloud computing evolved in the last years from a niche product to one the drivers of the IT industry. It is an evolutionary design derived from its ancestors grid [43] and utility computing. Cloud computing offers the same flexibility as utility computing when renting resources such as CPU power or storage and the same flexibility as grid computing when a user submits a job. While cloud computing is a widely used term, there is still no unique definition for it.

2.4.1 Architecture

The most common way to describe cloud computing is to divide it into three different layers as shown in Figure 2.4.

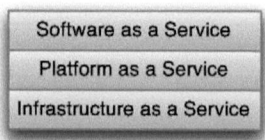

Figure 2.4: Layered cloud computing architecture

Application Layer

The uppermost layer contains the applications running in the cloud. This is also called the *Software as a Service* (SaaS) layer. Contrary to classical applications

2.4. Cloud Computing

installed on the local hard disk, cloud enabled applications or *services* run within the cloud. This means that the user has to connect to an application in order to use its functionality. There are some cloud applications that support an offline mode, but that's more exception than rule. Prominent examples are Google Documents, Microsoft Skydrive Office Web Apps and Exchange Online.

Platform Layer

Also called *Platform as a Service* (PaaS) this layer delivers a computing platform and a solution stack as a service. Computing platform describes some kind of application framework that allows software (here cloud services) to run. A solution framework is a set of libraries and components needed to deliver a fully functional software solution. Prominent examples are Microsoft Azure or Google's App Engine.

Infrastructure Layer

Cloud infrastructure services or often called *Infrastructure as a Service* (IaaS) represents the bottom layer of the cloud stack. In most cases, infrastructure here means virtualized resources, like Xen virtual machines as offered by Amazons Elastic Compute Cloud (Amazon EC2) [2]. The benefits are obvious: usually an IT company has a fix stock of hardware resources to compute their own tasks or tasks from their customers. They need to pay all additional costs like power, cooling and human resources (such as server administrators) on their own. They might even need need to provision additional resources for peak loads such as during Christmas time. These additional resources are often unused, because the overall capacity is to high most of the time. Using remote infrastructure resources in the cloud it is possible for a company to rent additional power on-the-fly, i.e. during peak load times such as mentioned above. Once the high utilization period is over, the resources are returned. Thus, there is no need to have unused computing power on hold until they are actually used.

Furthermore, the pay-as-you-go idea as empowered by the cloud offers great flexibility. If research institutions or companies need to get results quickly, they could easily rent thousands of instances to speed up their computation, given that their software supports it.

2.4.2 Deployment Models

A cloud is a collection of resources in a datacenter, both software and hardware. If the cloud resources are available to customers, e.g. like Amazon EC2, it is called a *public cloud*. Instead, a *private cloud* refers to resources in a private datacenter, e.g. owned by a company and not-accessible to the general public. If a datacenter contains a private and public cloud, interconnected by standardized technologies, it is called a *hybrid cloud* [5].

2.4.3 Security Risks

Contrary to traditional computing paradigms like cluster computing where the client (here the user) had nearly full control over his or her data, cloud computing lead to less control. Services are no longer provided by an in-house computing center, they are provided by an external vendor, i.e. it is by default unknown where the services are executed and where the data is stored. Thus, cloud computing poses a number of security risks, e.g., abuse of cloud computing services, malicious insiders, shared technology vulnerabilities, data loss and leakage, account, service and traffic hijacking and data lock in [161, 84, 13].

2.5 Summary

In this chapter, several topics which lay out the fundamentals for this thesis were presented. This included an overview of the main computing paradigms representing the driver for the upcoming approaches, grid computing. Since virtualization is used by the solutions in this thesis, a detailed introduction was given. Finally, cloud computing as the successor of grid computing is introduced.

"I want to do it because I want to do it."
Amelia Earhart (1897–1937)

3

Security for Virtualized Grid Computing Environments

3.1 Introduction

This chapter outlines the motivation for this thesis. The first section shows the workflow involved in submitting a job to one or more computing sites. The workflow represents the starting point for the writing of this thesis. Then, the workflow is split up into several parts, starting from the initial submission and continuing on through the point of the actual execution. Each part is then analyzed for possible security risks. The final section of this chapter introduces the proposed solution of this thesis.

The focus of this thesis is on securing the infrastructure of grid computing environments. The term *infrastructure* refers to the platforms needed to execute arbitrary services. A service could be either a service that in turn hosts other services (e.g., a service container) or an application. Infrastructure in traditional grid computing refers to the physical machines, equipped with an operating system (Linux in almost all cases), while infrastructure in the context of cloud computing means a operating system virtualized environment. Furthermore, infrastructure also includes the connection between a set of operating systems, either real or virtual.

3.2 Introduction to Job Execution

The motivation for the components designed within this thesis stems from the process of how to submit a job to one or more computing sites. A *job* in the context of this thesis consists of the following parts:

- **Description**: Meta-information describing the job in detail, such as resource requirements (the desired number of CPU cores to run on, the amount of virtual memory that is needed), one or more pointers to the file system where the actual application and dependencies are stored, information about the submitting user and, finally, environmental variables needed to run. Depending on the middleware used, the information could be encoded in XML.

- **Credentials**: It must be impossible to submit a job without proper credentials. In the grid context, the term credentials refer to a unique X.509 certificate per-user, signed by a trusted certificate authority (CA). In the German national D-Grid this could be either the DFN-Verein or the GridKa in Karlsruhe. In terms of cloud computing, the credentials heavily depend on the used IaaS environment. In the case of Amazon EC2 or Eucalyptus, the credentials consist of the account number, an access key and a secret access key.

- **Application**: An application might be a single instance, non-parallel binary or a complex, distributed, service-oriented application.

Figure 3.1 outlines a typical scenario common in traditional grid computing. It presents the path a job follows (shown in green) from the user to a site where it is executed. In this stage, a job consists of a description and the user's credentials. The first step involves the submission of a job to a meta-scheduler. A meta-scheduler, such as Gridway [58], distributes the load and thus all jobs to one or more remote sites. The meta-scheduler receives continuous reports about the current utilization from all participating sites. If one site is heavily loaded, it chooses another site for execution. Thus, after the job arrives, the meta-scheduler chooses between one or more grid sites and forwards the job description accordingly.

The receiver at the site is a software on the so-called head node. In the case of grid computing, this is a middleware like Globus Toolkit [149], UNICORE [42] or gLite [103]. In Figure 3.1 and in the remainder of this thesis, the Globus Toolkit (often called GT4) represents the connection endpoint. Globus processes the request and executes it if the request is valid. This decision depends on

3.2. Introduction to Job Execution

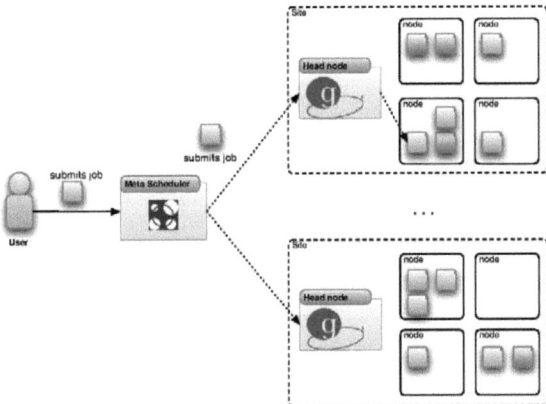

Figure 3.1: Job submission and executions initiated by a user. A meta-scheduler distributes the job to one of the two sites and it is executed on the site's nodes.

several factors. First, the submitting user must be known to the site and his or her certificate must be valid (valid means signed by a trusted CA and not expired). Furthermore, the target application must be either installed on all computing nodes where the actual execution takes places or it must be fetched from a storage location specified in the job description. Execution is declined if one or more of the requirements are not met.

Prior to the actual execution, the job description is forwarded from the middleware to another component, the job scheduler (also known as batch or cluster scheduler). The scheduler has information about all registered computing nodes present on the site. Further, all nodes report continuously to the scheduler. A report includes meta-level information about the system, such as current CPU, RAM and storage utilization and the number of running jobs. Scheduling decisions are based upon this information, i.e., a new job is likely to be executed on a less loaded node than on an overloaded node. The execution of the actual job application is the second-to-last step of the job submission process. Finally, after the execution is terminated, a report and the results are made available to the user.

3.3 Analysis of the Job Execution Workflow

In this section, a security analysis of the workflow presented above is shown. The workflow is split into several parts that are analyzed in detail.

3.3.1 Terminology

Various terms regarding information security are used in a number of different and sometimes conflicting ways in the literature. This thesis uses the following definitions (in conformance with the ISO/IEC 27000 standards on information security [61, 62, 63]):

- **Asset**: Anything that has value to an organization. This includes information, software, hardware and knowledge.

- **Attack**: The attempt to destroy, alter, disable, steal or gain unauthorized access to or make unauthorized use of an asset. An attack might be performed by an individual or a group of individuals. The risk of a successful attack increases or decreases, depending on the attacker's motivation.

- **Authentication**: The act of verifying that an entity is what it claims to be. A prominent real-world analogy is the proof of identity in a bank, where a customer shows his or her photo ID to the bank teller. In the context of grid computing, the user has to present valid credentials to a middleware.

- **Authorization**: After an entity is successfully authenticated, it must be determined what additional information the entity is permitted to access (e.g., read, write, etc).

- **Confidentiality**: The term used to prevent the disclosure of information to unauthorized individuals or systems.

- **Information Security Risk**: The potential that a threat will exploit a vulnerability of an asset or group of assets and thereby cause the organization harm.

- **Integrity**: Data cannot be modified undetectably.

- **Threat**: Potential cause of an unwanted incident, which may result in harm to a system or organization. This could be either a human or an act of nature.

- **Vulnerability**: A weakness which can be exploited by a threat. This could a software bug (e.g., a buffer overflow) or a hardware bug (e.g., a bug in Intel processors leading to Smart Management Bus access [107]).

The following paragraphs describe the steps needed to execute a job on one or more sites providing computational power. These steps, although relatively abstract in their description, unveil a number of security risks.

3.3.2 Analysis of the Head Node Communication and Storage

Figure 3.2 shows the first steps of the job submission process. Only one site is displayed in the figure, nevertheless this analysis also applies to a multi-site scenario.

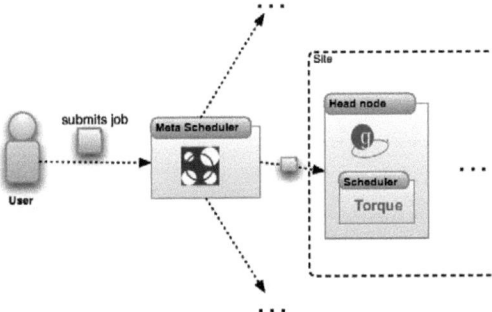

Figure 3.2: Detailed view of a job submission process. An appropriate site is chosen by the meta-scheduler and the middleware acts as the first point of contact.

Although the figure includes a meta-scheduler, the analysis will omit the scheduler as it is only a gateway for communication and decisions between the user and the real head node. Thus, the head node is the primary endpoint of communication for the user. This is also the case if no meta-scheduler at all is used. Communication between the user and the head node is secured with the Grid Security Infrastructure (GSI, see Section 2.2.2 on page 14). GSI includes encryption of the network traffic with the Secure Socket Layer (SSL) protocol and proper authentication. Authentication is done by checking if the user's X509 certificate is signed by a trusted CA. Authorization is done by checking if the user's Distinguished Name (DN) is present in a local, so-called *grid mapfile*. This is a mapping between DNs and local accounts. Depending on the account or the group membership, the user gains permission to access specific resources on the site. Besides the grid users, there might be also local users, i.e., in-house users who access the compute nodes directly and circumvent the head node.

After the authentication and authorization steps are completed successfully, the input data (if not already present) is transferred to the head node. A common way to do this is to specify a GridFTP location in the job description and let the middleware fetch the data automatically. Thus, the job description and the job data are the assets involved in this step. While GSI is sufficient for securing both on the wire, the data still remains unencrypted on the head node's (or any other node's) hard disk.

This poses a major security risk and presents the head node as a primary attack target. Furthermore, the middleware installed even increases this problem. Like most complex IT systems, these middleware solutions exhibit a number security problems [148, 147, 53, 145], which open the entire system to attack. Unfortunately, these security holes not only expose users to attack, but also existing local users who, up until now, have worked in a local and secure environment. This changing nature of grid and cluster computing and the new threats arising thereof is further discussed in articles by Smith et al. [125, 124].

As a result, large computing sites are an attractive target for intruders since they offer standardized access to a large number of machines, which can be misused in various ways. The considerable computing power can be used to break passwords and the large storage capacity is perfect for storing and sharing illegal software and data. The generous bandwidth of the Internet connection is ideal for launching Denial-of-Service (DoS) attacks or for hosting file sharing services, to name just a few attacks. However, more critical than these resource attacks are the attacks on customer data. If a resource provider can not ensure the end-to-end integrity and safety of customer data, widespread industrial adoption of technologies like grid will not be possible.

Summary

While GSI takes care of shielding the user's assets on the wire, it does not prevent the middleware on the head node from storing them without encryption. Furthermore, a middleware's complexity exposes the head node to a number of attacks. To summarize, a more sophisticated solution is needed to raise the barrier for possible attacks and to make the head node itself and the user's assets secure.

3.3.3 Analysis of the Host

The last section illustrates possible vulnerabilities that can occur during the first step of the job execution workflow, especially with the head node. Consequently, this section focuses on possible host vulnerabilities. Host refers to either the head node or any other node. Host security involves countless ways to attack a system. Since it is impossible to incorporate all of these into this work, this thesis presents two possible scenarios of attack.

The head node as a primary target is likely to be compromised if no additional precautions are taken (some will be described in the context of this thesis). Assuming that a node has been compromised, supplementary mechanisms are needed to mitigate the outcome of the intrusion. To persistently retain the control of the attacked system, attackers typically install malware in order to recover full control after rebooting the computing system. This kind of attack is commonly discussed as a *strong intrusion attack*, while temporary attacks between two operating system startups are referred to as *weak intrusion attacks* [15]. The software toolkits that are installed within a strong intrusion attack are commonly called rootkits.

Besides preventing an attacker from maintaining access to the system (even after the security leak is repaired), it is also important to ensure that no malware binaries remain on the host. Malware refers to a wide range of malicious software, such as Trojan horses (used to spy on user's passwords), worms or viruses. Furthermore, they also apply to non-compromised nodes as well. It is desirable for a site administrator to know which applications are currently running on his or her system.

Summary

The head node in particular, as well as all other nodes, represent a target for a possible attacker. Since it is impossible to implement unbreakable security mechanisms, it is important to install mechanisms that mitigate the outcome of a possible compromise. A compromise could result in the installation of a kernel rootkit or malware binaries. In addition to preventing a successful compromise, it is also important to prevent malware from being installed to a given system (either intentionally or unintentionally).

Chapter 3. Security for Virtualized Grid Computing Environments

3.3.4 Analysis of the Job Execution

After the middleware processes the incoming information about a job, it hands over the job to the local scheduler. Based on internal algorithms, the scheduler choses a number of nodes and executes the application. Here, a node means a physical machine with an operating system, such as Linux.

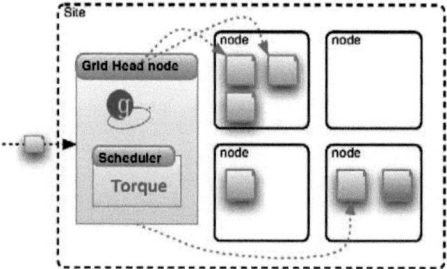

Figure 3.3: Multiple job applications executed on shared resources without any shielding.

Thus, the execution takes place on the actual system together with other running jobs (if any). Running applications are represented by one or more operating system processes. Consequently, all processes have meta-information, e.g. a process ID, used resources and executed application. Since multiple job applications can run on the same node, it is possible for a malicious application to gather information about another running application. This includes the mentioned meta-data. Further, in the case of a misconfiguration, this might include the application data as well.

Figure 3.3 shows an example of how multiple jobs are executed on the same node. A new job (shown in green) is processed on the head node and three instances are executed on two nodes. Three other jobs instances (red and blue) are running at the same time as the green job. A malicious red or blue application could gather information about the green job. In terms of assets, the most important parts of a job are the application itself, the input data and the results. Both crash test model data of a new prototype car or a custom fluid simulation suite represent intellectual property worth substantial amounts of money; thus they need to be protected. A customer will not install his or her own software containing intellectual property on remote resources if the provider cannot guarantee the security. Naturally, most customers are more concerned with the security of their own application and spend less time on the actual operating system.

Job Application Installation

Another issue that arises is the installation and maintenance of the job application itself. This can be done in a number of ways. If the software does not require root access to be installed and the user has a local login, the user can log on to each site and manually install the software in his or her user account. If the user does not have login right (which is quite often the case), the user is forced to copy the application's source code onto the site using GridFTP and then configure and compile the software using batch commands submitted as grid jobs via WS-GRAM [45]. This is a painstaking way to install software since each batch command (i.e. ./configure && make && make install) is submitted as a grid job and scheduled by the cluster scheduler. Outputs from the commands can be returned as the result of the given job or can be fetched with GridFTP. Anyone who has installed moderately complex software on foreign machines can imagine the difficulties involved in installing software in this way, as it can take many iterations to meet all library dependencies.

The state of the art grid fares even worse when software is used that is not available in source code and/or requires root privileges to install (any software supplied as a Debian or RedHat package requires root permissions to install since the package managers require root permissions to run). In these cases, the users cannot install the software on their own, rather the administrators of the local site must be asked to do it for them. This is an administrative hassle, not to mention the security nightmare involved in granting any unknown user software root privileges; thus, this will never happen. The installation process is made even more complicated if the application should offer custom service-oriented interfaces, for these custom services need to be hosted by the grid middleware and as such should require administrative rights to be installed and run with the same rights as the rest of the grid middleware.

Summary

Shared job execution as found in traditional grid computing poses a number of security vulnerabilities. A malicious application could gather the meta-data of other applications running on the same resource. Since job input data as well as the results both represent intellectual assets worth substantial amounts of money, it is important to protect them. Besides the issue with data protection, the use of shared resources also includes the hassles of how to install an application on one or more sites. If the installation is left to the user, this might lead to installation experiments, which could result in an enormous amount of software, possibly containing unknown security vulnerabilities. If an administrator installs software provided by the users, this might lead to possible security risks as the software could be either vulnerable or malicious.

3.3.5 Analysis of Multi-Site Computing

Multi-site computing as already seen in Figure 3.1 is one of the big advantages of grid computing. A meta-scheduler decides about on which site the job is executed. While this might not guarantee the fastest execution, it prevents over-utilization of one site and under-utilization of another.

However, the fact that grid nodes are usually not accessible from the Internet and thus cannot host service-oriented applications hinders the adoption in the business sector, which is greatly interested in the service-oriented computing paradigm. Most grid nodes are kept in private networks, because grid computing evolved from cluster computing, which does not have the need for public nodes. Simply making the nodes of the grid-backend clusters public is not a viable option, since public nodes would clash with the requirements of the traditional batch-job oriented grid and cluster use. Batch-job and service-oriented computing paradigms clash because submitting batch jobs only requires a publicly accessible head node, while the computing nodes can be operated in a private network, reducing the risk of an external attack. Service-oriented grid applications, on the other hand, require a more complex and dynamic setup with accessible compute nodes, which would also endanger all other users on those resources.

If the nodes are accessible to the public via the Internet, new threats arise:

- **Internal attacks against other users**: A malicious user could try to remotely compromise other nodes in order to gain sensitive data or corrupt the work of other users. This can be achieved by exploiting software vulnerabilities. To cope with this threat, users must be carefully shielded from each other.

- **Internal attacks against the infrastructure**: This includes attempts to corrupt parts of the infrastructure or attacks against particular machines (e.g. the head node).

- **External attacks against the computing or infrastructure nodes.** Giving all nodes publicly accessible IP addresses also means that the nodes can be accessed from everywhere in the world. This includes valid connection requests from trusted users and infrastructure services as well as malicious connection requests trying to compromise the node or gain access to sensitive data.

A Sample Multi-Site Application

A sample application that demonstrates the communication requirements of fine-grained service-oriented applications is a multimedia analysis application that runs face and text detection algorithms on confidential video material. The application consists of several grid services that pre-process and analyze large video files. An input video is split into several smaller parts to facilitate parallel execution of the analysis processes. The analysis consists of a face detection algorithm that includes several other algorithms. Every frame of a video snippet is analyzed to find shapes that look like faces. Every face that appears and the length of its appearance are stored, making it is possible, for example, to determine the total time that different characters appear in the material. Depending on the result of a frame's analysis, some deeper analysis might be needed. For instance, if a face was detected, a face recognition service can be called. A video splitter service splits the video into many parts. A face detection service is then run on multiple nodes. Depending on the results of the face detection run, a deeper analysis is performed. Finally, the partial results of all nodes are collected and merged using a result merger service. For more information on the video analysis algorithm, the reader is referred to Ewerth et al. [37].

All connected resources of the presented application are fully accessible if no firewalling technology is used. The classical approach to solving this problem is an all-or-nothing approach that denies or allows all users access to a resource. An Internet connection (if any) is provided by an externally accessible head node. The same applies to node access. In most cases, users are not allowed to log into any of the nodes. This widely used scenario hinders the use of the full service-oriented grid potential. A multi-site, parallel application where all running instances need to share data would not run due to the network restrictions.

Summary

Being able to execute an application on multiple remote sites is one of the big advantages of multi-site grid computing. Nevertheless, this is not possible on most of the sites because the nodes are kept private and not accessible to the outside world. Once this changes, proper mechanisms to shield the nodes as well as the data need to be in place. While this section focuses on grid computing, network security is also an issue for cloud computing.

3.4 Methods for Infrastructural Security in Virtualized Grids

The following sections outline the approaches that will be presented in this thesis. Since this thesis focuses on infrastructure security, a number of security risks related to other areas of grid computing have been omitted. This includes, for example, vulnerabilities of services or service containers. Furthermore, the security analysis is derived from the presented job workflow common in the German D-Grid. While this workflow is very similar to workflows used by other academic or commercial grids, it might contain singularities. Several of the technologies used in this thesis are widely known and mature, e.g. operating system virtualization and firewalls and in combination form the novel concept of virtualized grid computing.

Trusted Computing Base

A system's trusted computing base (TCB) consists of hardware and software components that are critical to its security. Vulnerabilities inside the TCB are an information security risk, which could lead to an attack that itself jeopardizes the security properties of the entire system. The following approaches are based on the standard assumptions made in most other virtualization security architectures [49, 50]. The BIOS, the initial boot loader, and the virtualization hypervisor are all part of the trusted computing base. Since this thesis focuses on infrastructural security, it does not deal with attacks against the TCB.

3.4.1 Virtualized Grid Computing

One of the basic building blocks of a grid environment is a computational cluster consisting of a number of nodes on which job applications are executed. One of the main problems is the shared use of the node's operating system, since it is easy to attack other users within the same operating system once on procures the higher level of privileges needed to install software. An efficient solution for sharing grid computing resources on a single physical machine is to use virtualization.

Xen operating system virtualization provides independent, secure virtual machines in which a modified Linux kernel forms the basis for an essentially unmodified system and application installation on top of it. Several of these so-called domain U instances usually run parallel on a single physical machine, protected from each other and under the control of a domain 0 master operating system instance that can create, suspend and terminate domain U instances on demand.

3.4. Methods for Infrastructural Security in Virtualized Grids

The only instance gaining access to the providing system's hardware like peripheral devices or physical disks is domain 0 (which only the administrator of the system can configure); CPUs, network and disk devices are virtualized for domain U domains and thus controllable by domain 0.

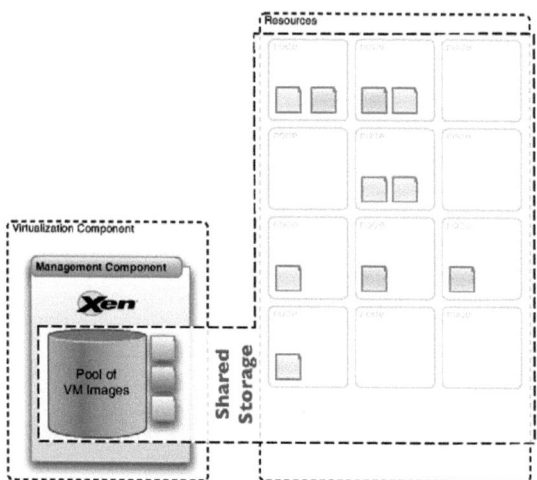

Figure 3.4: XGE connected to backend resources on shared storage

This thesis proposes a novel solution that conveys the concept of virtualized grid computing. Therefore, the XGE, an open source virtual machine manager, was developed. It can run either as a stand-alone application (see Figure 3.4 and 3.5), coupled to an installed resource manager (Torque) or serve as a backend for a web service enabled frontend like Virtual Workspaces. The computing nodes of the XGE run an administrator controlled Xen domain 0 in which user specific Xen domainU images are started when a job is to be executed. The use of virtual computing nodes per user gives the user unprecedented administrative rights. The user can install custom libraries and software autonomously without the cluster administrator's assistance. Since adding a virtualization layer introduces a certain overhead, several mechanisms are presented to overcome this limitation. This includes efficient mechanisms for virtual machine disk image distribution and efficient storage synchronization.

3.4.2 Grid Enabled Demilitarized Zone

When looking at a traditional grid infrastructure, a major drawback of the prominent head node running the middleware became obvious. Being the first point of contact for the legal users, it also is the primary target for attackers. Once the system is successfully compromised, the attacker has access to all nodes, to the user's accounting logs and a variety of other information.

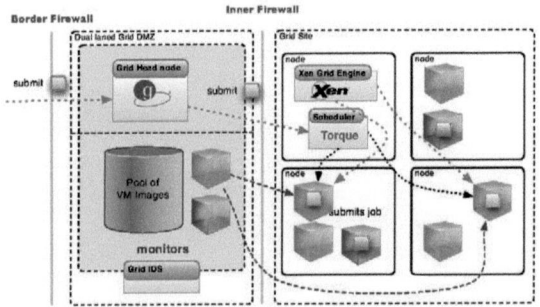

Figure 3.5: Grid DMZ shielding the head node as well as the internal network with all resources

As a solution, this thesis introduces a dual-laned grid enabled demilitarized zone (DMZ) (see Figure 3.5). The head node is now located inside a DMZ and thus completely separate from the backend resources. Communication between the middleware and the virtualization manager (represented by the scheduler and the XGE) on the backend is guarded by cryptographic protocols. Furthermore, only one port remains as communication interface. This greatly reduces the surface open to attack, as designing a small, secure server on the backend is easier than keeping a complex middleware, like the Globus Toolkit, safe.

Grid Enabled Intrusion Detection System

Intrusion Detection Systems (IDS) are a well known technique for detecting intrusions, either via network (NIDS) or directly on the host (HIDS). Most open source or commercial NIDS do not take the recent evolutions of grid computing into account, i.e. they only recognize classic attack patterns such as remote exploitations or flooding attacks on well-known software. Within the context of this thesis, several extensions were developed to detect attacks on different grid computing components.

3.4.3 Lightweight Kernel Rootkit Prevention

A common way for a malicious user to retain control over a compromised system is to install a rootkit. Rootkits are available in multiple variants, ranging from simple ones such as a library-based rootkit, which allows an unprivileged user to gain extended privileges by using a manipulated library, to complex ones like kernel rootkits. Kernel rootkits are usually complex in design and implementation, but due to their nature, they run with the highest access possible, i.e., access to the privileged kernel space. The provided functionality ranges from being able to grant extended privileges to arbitrary processes or to give users remote backdoor access.

In this thesis, an effective and lightweight approach used to prevent kernel rootkits from being installed is presented while allowing an administrator to still be able to load trusted loadable kernel modules.

3.4.4 Malware Detection for Virtualized Grids

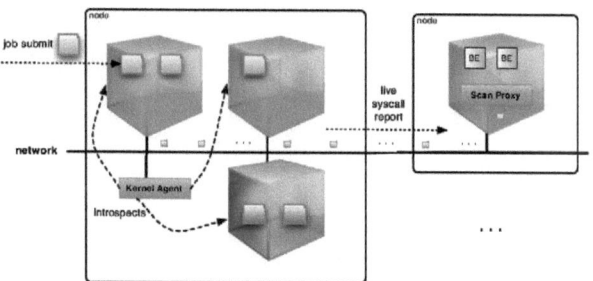

Figure 3.6: Multiple virtual machines introspected by a kernel agent that reports continuously over a middleware to various anti-virus/-maleware backends

Providing virtual machines and thus privileged access within these machines introduces new potential threats that create the need for a new malware detection system. Providers need ways to ensure the security of their infrastructure and the customer's systems. Having a flexible grid infrastructure also opens new pos-

Chapter 3. Security for Virtualized Grid Computing Environments

sibilities to scale up and distribute malware detection software among several systems. Most end-host security solutions negatively and significantly impacts a computer's performance due to huge signature-sets or complex detection algorithms. A large virtual infrastructure can be beneficial here to decrease the slowdown by offloading it to dedicated machines.

This thesis presents an intrusion detection system for virtualized grids to recognize running malware. An overview is shown in Figure 3.6. It is designed to run on virtual machine instances with a backend grid that distributes malware scanning operations between several backends. A flexible framework for a distributed security solution with a minimal overall resource footprint on the end host is presented. To detect well-known as well as yet unknown malware, a traditional signature check is performed and the prerequisites for a live system-call tracer are presented.

3.4.5 Dynamic Firewalls

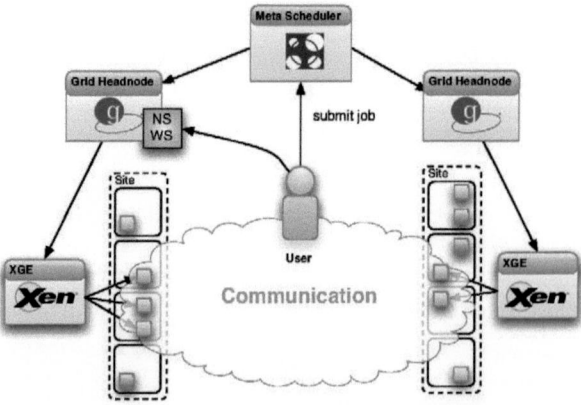

Figure 3.7: Multi-site virtual private network, including the users own computer and the computing nodes of his or her actual job

Data transfer security risks are a serious problem in grid computing environments. Due to exploited vulnerabilities, a malicious user could sniff data in transit between nodes. Encrypted data might prevent the attacker from gaining knowledge about the content, but it still reveals that there is a transfer at all which lasts a certain amount of time and consumes a specific amount of bandwidth. Since this is a leak of meta-data security it should clearly avoided.

Dynamic firewalls that guard virtual machines can mitigate the danger of such breaches in security. The approach presented in this thesis encapsulates virtual machines belonging to the same job or user into a virtual group guarded by firewalls. This is shown in Figure 3.8. A secure by default setting assures that only permitted traffic can leave or enter the virtual group. Communication between machines from different groups is not possible unless explicitly desired. To enforce the filtering and to prevent that the installed firewall is subverted by the users, they are installed outside the virtual machines.

As shown in Figure 3.7, the dynamic firewalls also allow multi-site virtual private networks (VPN) to be built. This VPN encapsulates the user's own computer and all computing nodes that belong to his or her actual job. Encryption ensures that no other party can sniff the traffic.

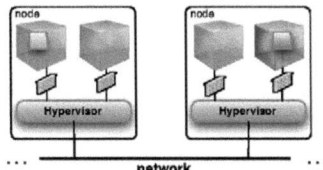

Figure 3.8: Every virtual machine is guarded by a dynamic firewall installed on the administrative domain

3.5 Summary

This chapter presents the workflow involved in submitting a job to a computing site. This workflow is split into several parts that are analyzed for security risks. Based on this analysis, the results of this thesis have been presented.

"The city's central computer told you? R2D2, you know better than to trust a strange computer!"

C3PO

4

Host Security

4.1 Introduction

In the previous chapter, a security analysis of the job submission procedure was conducted. In this chapter, several solutions for host security, including implementation details, experimental results and evaluation, are presented. An effective and lightweight solution prevents kernel rootkits from being loaded while allowing an administrator to still be able to load trusted loadable kernel modules. Furthermore, a prototypical malware detection engine for virtualized grids is presented. Besides being able to use classical anti-virus engines, the solution further monitors the system call stream of all running executables. This enables the detection of yet unknown malware binaries.

4.2 Lightweight Kernel Rootkit Prevention

4.2.1 Introduction

External and internal intrusions are the most serious threats in computer systems that are connected to a network. Attackers can exploit software bugs in core components on a target system to gain superuser privileges, allowing the attacker to take control of the attacked system. The rise of virtualized grid environmental aggravates the stated problem, i.e. customers have access to their own virtual appliances that run on shared physical resources. The former as well as the latter are targets for a possible attacker. Since it is impossible to implement unbreakable security mechanisms, it is important to install mechanisms which mitigate the outcomes of a possible compromise.

There are various types of rootkits available, e.g. application level rootkits that replace the original binaries with a fake binary containing a Trojan horse or library rootkits that replace valid library functions with malicious ones. One of the most sophisticated rootkits is the *kernel rootkit*. It replaces or adds additional functions or device drivers in the kernel space of an operating system. Kernel modules in general enable upgrades to specified parts of a kernel to strengthen the modularity of the operating system. There are two classes of kernel modules: permanent kernel modules, which are loaded when a system is booted and cannot be removed once they are running, and loadable kernel modules, which can be loaded and unloaded when the system is running.

Many kernel rootkits are designed as loadable modules or device drivers, as this is the easiest way to add new functions to the core system. Thus, monitoring the loading process of kernel modules is indispensable to ensure that no malicious modules are loaded. The following section presents a number of approaches that deal with rootkit prevention and executable monitoring in general.

Parts of this section have been published in [113, 114].

4.2.2 Related Work

Kroah-Hartman [76] has proposed signing executables with a fingerprint, which would be stored in an additional section of the commonly used executable linkage format (ELF) [154]. Furthermore, the technique of asymmetric cryptography is used to protect the fingerprint from malware modifications: A private key is used to encrypt the fingerprint stored in the ELF section, while the kernel linker decrypts the signature in order to compare it with the signature of the loaded file. A general problem is the kernel-level implementation of an asymmetric cryptography algorithm. Most current operating systems do not have no such implementation.

A similar way of implementing rootkit prevention is used by Catuogno et al. [15]. They implemented a verification mechanism based on encrypted signatures stored in an additional section of an executable as well. In contrast to Kroah-Hartman, they did not address dynamically loadable kernel modules but executables in general. This is why they assumed that the support of dynamically loadable kernel modules should be disabled. While this solves the problem of loading a

4.2. Lightweight Kernel Rootkit Prevention

kernel rootkit, it significantly reduces the functionality of the system. It is no longer possible to reload devices drivers for example. Furthermore, their approach is not able to handle signed code inside a shared object that is loaded with the dlopen system call. Since this system call is widely used, it represents a major limitation of this approach.

Spinellis [138] describes an unusual form of executable verification. His solution "is based on having the client's software respond to queries about itself" and thus is based on *reflection*. A trusted entity, the server, periodically requests information from the software to be verified, the client. This could be a memory location or predictable processor state. The hashed information is evaluated, and the server can check if the client was tampered. Unfortunately, this approach is a theoretical one and no implementation is provided. Furthermore, it is unlikely to satisfy all assumptions made in the paper in a modern system.

The work by Kruegel et al. [78] focuses on detecting kernel rootkits through static analysis of loadable kernel module binaries. More precisely, the use of behavioral specifications and symbolic execution allows one to determine if the module being loaded includes evidence of malicious intent. The idea for this detection approach is based on the observation that the runtime behavior of normal kernel modules differs remarkably from the behavior of kernel rootkits. For example, a normal module seldom writes directly to kernel memory (except for some device drivers), while a kernel rootkit usually writes directly to kernel memory to alter important system management data structures. Currently, implementation of this approach is only prototypical and the authors state that "our tool is currently available as a user program only. In order to provide automatic protection from rootkits, it would be necessary to integrate our analyzer into the kernel's module loading infrastructure."

An approach that works towards developing a tamper-resistant kernel rootkit detector is presented by Quynh and Takefuji [106]. They put XENKIMONO, which is implemented in a form of a daemon process, into a Xen domain 0 and let it inspect the kernels of other domain Us to detect potential rootkits. XENKIMONO can map the kernel memory of any guest domain and does all the processing, such as reading or writing, on the mapped memory. They perform integrity checking of the kernel memory and monitor critical system processes and network interfaces. If the detector finds any suspicious activity, it can stop the monitored domain U as well as notify the administrator. While Quynh and Takefuji try to detect kernel rootkits, the approach that will be presented in the following prevents kernel rootkits from being loaded.

Van Doorn et al. [160] describe the design and implementation of signed executables for the Linux operating system. Specifically, they sign binaries in the Executable and Linking Format (ELF). A signature is added to an binary by storing it in a new ELF segment. The signature is extracted once the binary is loaded and the ELF format manager in the kernel verifies the signature. This choice implies that every interpreter should be modified in order to verify the signature. In order to avoid verification of the binaries at each execution, a caching exists that is based on a whitelist. While this approach protects the system from executing untrusted executables, it does not prevent an attacker from loading a kernel rootkit.

A Linux kernel module named *DigSig*, which helps system administrators to control ELF binary execution, is presented by Apvrille et al. [4]. If an ELF binary is to be loaded into executable memory regions, *DigSig* searches the file for a signature section. If the section is available and contains a valid signature, loading is permitted, otherwise refused. The main disadvantage of *DigSig* is the assumption that the root account has not been compromised. In case the latter happens, an attacker could either modify the loader process and disable the loading protection or change the key pair (which would require a complete resign run of all executables and libraries, of course). Furthermore, the approach does to take kernel rootkits into account.

Wurster and van Oorschot [173] also propose the use of signatures to protect binaries. While most approaches only allow an administrator to sign binaries once, their approach takes software updates into account, i.e. it is still possible to verify a binary after it has been modified. This is achieved by a set of kernel and binary modifications. Like other approaches, a new ELF segment with a signature is added to every file. When the kernel receives a request to overwrite a file on the system, it first checks the current file on the system. If it is signed, the kernel verifies that the new file can also be verified by a public key contained in the currently installed version of the file. If the signature is verified, then the update is approved; otherwise, it is denied. In line with the previous approaches presented, this approach does not take kernel modules into account.

In the NetBSD operating system, the Veriexec (verified execution) kernel subsystem allows users to monitor files and to prevent their removal, read/write access or execution, if necessary [151]. It implements four levels of strictness: A learning mode for configuration matters, intrusion detection and intrusion prevention mode, as well as a lockdown mode. However, Veriexec does not protect the kernel from modifications by dynamically loaded modules.

Riley et al. [109] present NICKLE, a Virtual Machine Monitor (VMM) based system that transparently prevents unauthorized kernel code execution for unmodified commodity (guest) operating systems. NICKLE is based on memory shadowing, i.e. the trusted VMM maintains a shadow physical memory for a running virtual machine and performs real-time kernel code authentication; thus, only authenticated kernel code will be stored in the shadow memory. Furthermore,

4.2. Lightweight Kernel Rootkit Prevention

NICKLE transparently routes kernel instruction fetches that originate from the guest system to the shadow memory at runtime. This guarantees that only the authenticated kernel code will be executed, initially hindering the kernel rootkit's attempt to strike. NICKLE and the approach presented in this chapter achieve the same goal, kernel rootkit prevention; however, the latter is a lightweight mechanism that is easy to deploy while the former is a quite complex process dealing with shadow memory.

Limbo, a kernel rootkit identification system for Microsoft Windows, was presented by Wilhelm and Chiueh [170]. It checks the legitimacy of kernel modules based on its binary content and run-time behavior before they are loaded into the operating system. The corresponding feature set of a kernel module is obtained using sample execution and the classification uses Naive Bayes. Currently, there no implementation publicly available and the one in the paper, including the training emulator, targets Microsoft Windows.

Petroni et al. [101] present Copilot, a prototype based on a PCI card that detects harmful modifications to Linux kernels. Its aim is to detect cases where an attacker applies a kernel rootkit to an already compromised operating system kernel. Therefore, it retrieves parts of host's virtual memory for examination through Direct Memory Access (DMA) without the knowledge or intervention of the host kernel. An admin station (i.e., a monitoring machine) connects to the card via independent communication. The detection strategy is based on MD5 hashes of the host kernel's text, the text of any loaded kernel modules, and the contents of some of the host kernel's critical data structures. Similar to Copilot is the approach presented by Zhang et al. [176], as they use a separate hardware device: the IBM 4758 PCI Cryptographic Coprocessor. Specifically, the authors describe a method for kernel protection that consists of identifying invariants within kernel data structures and then monitoring for deviations. Although both approaches are a big step towards creating a tamper-proof operating system kernel, they are quite impractical: they require external hardware and they also need special support from the operating system. Thus, these approaches are hard to deploy on a large scale.

4.2.3 Design

Deduced from the related work, a kernel rootkit prevention solution must meet the following requirements:

- The approach should follow the common principle: *keep it simple stupid*. While complicated solutions could provide more features, they also provide more attack surface. Almost all software products contain bugs and security related software is no exception; hence, the solution should be secure, simple and effective.

- It is always possible to prevent kernel rootkits from being loaded by compiling a *fat* operating system kernel, i.e. all required modules are compiled statically into the kernel and loadable modules are denied access entirely. In general, this solution is unacceptable because loadable modules do not only contain devices drives, they could also host the code for network protocols, Quality-of-Service algorithms or symmetric ciphers. Since loading these valid modules does not interrupt the usual work, it should be possible to reload them on demand.

The solution presented in the following section introduces the concept of using authorized kernel modules to prevent rootkit installations via corrupted kernel modules. For this purpose, the operating system kernel is modified to load only previously cryptographically authorized kernel modules.

At first, a short introduction of loadable kernel modules is given. Then, some sample attacks are shown before the design of the solution is presented.

Kernel Modification During Runtime

The BSD Kernel works like a service for user processes. There are three ways to call the kernel: hardware interrupts, hardware traps and software traps. User-level processes usually call kernel service routines through system calls, which are a form of software traps. System calls are implemented by setting a flag, which is checked whenever a process is preparing to exit the kernel. If the flag is set, the kernel will not be exited and the software interrupt code is run. System calls are stored in a system call table. It stores necessary information about each system call, such as the number of arguments and the implementing functions. The kernel is methodically divided into a top half and a bottom half. The latter contains hardware interrupt routines; the former runs in a privileged mode in which kernel data and user process context are accessible. User processes are not permitted to read and write the kernel memory; however, the kernel is allowed to read and write the data of a user process freely.

Kernel modules enable upgrades to specified parts of a kernel in order to strengthen modularity of the operating system. There are two classes of kernel modules: permanent kernel modules, which are loaded when a system is booted and cannot be removed once they are running and loadable kernel modules, which can be loaded and unloaded when the system is running. In BSD, `kldload` respectively `kldunload` utility uses the kernel linker to load or unload a kernel module at run time. In Linux, this can be done by using `modprobe`.

4.2. Lightweight Kernel Rootkit Prevention

In earlier versions of BSD-derived systems, kernel code could not be changed and was completely protected from user changes at run time. The only way to interact with a running kernel was via system calls, which were defined at the time the kernel was built. Today, this is circumvented using kernel modules. However, this raises a security problem: Every user that can acquire root privileges is able to modify the kernel and thus read or write arbitrary memory locations, including the one he or she should not read, such as encryption keys.

How To Attack a Kernel During Runtime

Assuming an attacker gained root privileges on the attacked system (e.g. through a weak intrusion attack), there are two basic ways to infiltrate an operating system kernel.

The first way is to modify the kernel code via direct modifications of the kernel memory, called *runtime memory kernel patching*. The attacker overrides a specific code line in the kernel space either with NOPs (no operation code) to avoid a command being executed (calling a method) or with a jump-argument that leads to a code block created by the attacker (see Figure 4.1). The malloc function is used to allocate memory which is then filled with a malicious function.

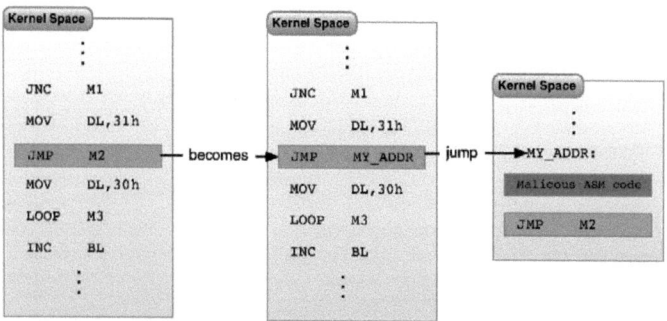

Figure 4.1: Runtime kernel memory patching

The second way is hooking system calls. The attacker has to write a kernel module that acts like a man-in-the-middle between the user and the system call (as shown in Figure 4.2). It catches a specific system call, executes a malicious code and delegates the system call to its correct destination afterwards. Usually, the user will not notice any difference to a normal system call. Nevertheless,

Chapter 4. Host Security

longer execution time or changes in the system call table are indicators for system call hooks [73]. System call hooks can be used for many issues: as a key logger that logs all characters entered into the terminal or to hide malicious processes by removing the according entry in the list of all processes. To summarize, it is possible to alter nearly every aspect of a system by patching the kernel memory or hooking a system call.

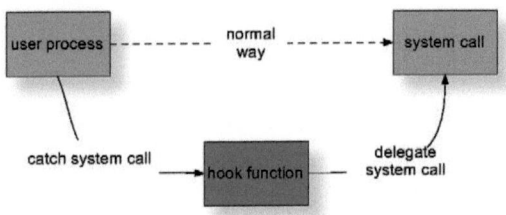

Figure 4.2: Hooking a system call

Listing 4.1 shows a fraction of kernel code that could be used by a kernel rootkit. In order to replace the close system call with a malicious one, the system call table is hooked (line 34) during the module loading process. As soon as the rootkit is unloaded (which is usually not the case), the original table entry is restored (line 36). To obtain root permissions, the attacker has to provide a magic value (which is 31337 in this case [line 1]) as file descriptor, i.e. he or she has to call close(31337) from a userland application. As soon as the kernel detects that magic value, it sets the user and group ID of the calling process to zero, i.e. the process runs with root permissions now (lines 9 through 11). To detect that the rootkit is actually running, the attacker could use the file descriptor 31338. In this case, the kernel returns 42 (line 14 - 15), usually an invalid return code. If any other file descriptor is used (e.g., by all other processes), the original behavior is carried out (lines 17 through 20), consequently the rootkit remains undetected.

```
1  #define ACCESS 31337
2  [...]
3  static int
4  evil_close(struct thread *td, struct close_args *uap)
5  {
6      int ret = 0;
7
8      switch(uap->fd) {
9      case ACCESS:
10         td->td_ucred->cr_uid = 0;
11         td->td_ucred->cr_gid = 0;
```

```
            ret = 0;
            break;
        case ACCESS + 1:
            return (42);
            break;
        default:
            close(td, uap);
            return (td->td_retval[0]);
            break;
        }

        return (ret);
}

[...]

static int
evil_init(struct module *module, int command, void *init_arg) {
    int returncode = 0;

    switch(command) {
        case MOD_LOAD:
            sysent[SYS_close].sy_call = (sy_call_t *)evil_close;
        case MOD_UNLOAD:
            sysent[SYS_close].sy_call = (sy_call_t *)close;
        break;

        default:
            returncode = EOPNOTSUPP;
            break;
    }

    return(returncode);
}
[...]
```

Listing 4.1: Fraction of kernel rootkit code that hooks the system call table and is able to provide root permissions to the calling process

One of the well known kernel rootkits is *adore* [141] and its successor *adore-ng* [140]. It was written for Linux and BSD derived systems and allows an attacker to hide network connections, files and processes. By using the mechanism developed during the course of this thesis, it is no longer possible to load this rootkit.

Secure Levels

Many kernel rootkits are designed as loadable modules or device drivers since this is the easiest way to add new functionality to the core system. Thus, monitoring the loading process of kernel modules is indispensable to ensure that no malicious modules are loaded.

There are various ways to disable dynamic kernel module loading:

- In Linux, it is possible to disable kernel module loading completely. While configuring a kernel, the administrator can set the MODULES option to NO and thus disable the entire kernel loading and processing mechanism. While this completely prevents kernel rootkits from loading, it also affects all legal modules.

- The technique of multiple secure levels is used in various BSD derived Unix operating systems. Any superuser is able to increase the secure level. On the other hand, the only way to lower the secure level is via the init-process, a prototype user process that is only loaded during system startup, so the system has to be restarted. For example, FreeBSD [91], a widely used Unix branch, runs with four different levels of security (compare Table 4.1).

Value	Restrictions
-1	**Permanently insecure mode**, must be compiled into the kernel.
0	**Insecure Mode**, immutable and append-only flags may be turned off. All devices can be read or written.
1	**Secure Mode**, immutable and append-only flags cannot be changed. Disks for mounted file systems and kernel memory (/dev/mem and /dev/kmem) are read-only. Kernel modules may not be loaded or unloaded.
2	**Highly secure mode**: Same as secure mode, plus disks may not be opened for writing.

Table 4.1: Securelevel restrictions

Thus, it is possible to disable dynamic module loading either by disabling modules or via a higher secure level. In this case, one has to take the good with the bad. On the one hand, this avoids critical actions such as arbitrary changes of kernel memory through user programs (which, in fact, is performed by loading a kernel module). On the other hand, the concepts are very restrictive and force users to compile and install the whole kernel instead of merely linking a single file. This step makes a reboot of the modified system necessary and interrupts running applications. Actually, for several applications (e.g. all mission critical applications), this is not a suitable solution.

Enhanced Kernel Module Loading Process

Instead of completely disabling kernel module loading, the BSD secure level concept was enhanced. It allows module loading before raising the secure level.

The following subsection describes the process of kernel rootkit prevention by loading only authorized kernel modules. The state of the secure level is described by two states. If the secure level is lower or equal than 0 (which is the default for single user mode), it is called *insecure mode*; if the secure level is set to 1 or higher, it is called *secure mode*. Furthermore, adding a module to the internal list is called mark/unmark as authorized.

To prevent kernel rootkits, a distinction between safe and unsafe kernel modules must be made. In secure mode, it is only possible to (un-)load authorized kernel modules. It is not possible to load other modules, especially any kind of malware. All authorized modules are kept in a list that resides in read-only kernel memory. The latter is needed to prevent that an attacker could simply modify the list to mask a rootkit as an authorized module. Each entry of the list contains the following information:

- A human-readable description of the kernel module
- A unique cryptographic hash of the kernel module
- Some internal kernel structures to indicate whether the kernel module is currently loaded

The implementation uses a generated SHA-256 hash to provide a unique key for each module. To authorize kernel modules, a userland program has been developed to add or remove kernel modules to the aforementioned list through a system call. This system call refuses execution if it is called without root privileges. Optionally, all dependent modules could be added as well. Any operations on the list can only be made while the system is in insecure mode. A convenient moment would be the initial system setup before it is actually connected to an external network. While the system is running in insecure mode, the userland program is able to mark/unmark modules as authorized. The list, in which the marks are stored, uses transient storage, i.e. the list is initially empty the time when the system is started.

Figure 4.3 shows the possible modifications of a list entry. By default, a kernel module is not loaded and not authorized. In insecure mode, a user can mark a module as authorized and is thus able to load it later when the system is in secure mode. All kernel modules that are loaded during the boot process (e.g. the

Chapter 4. Host Security

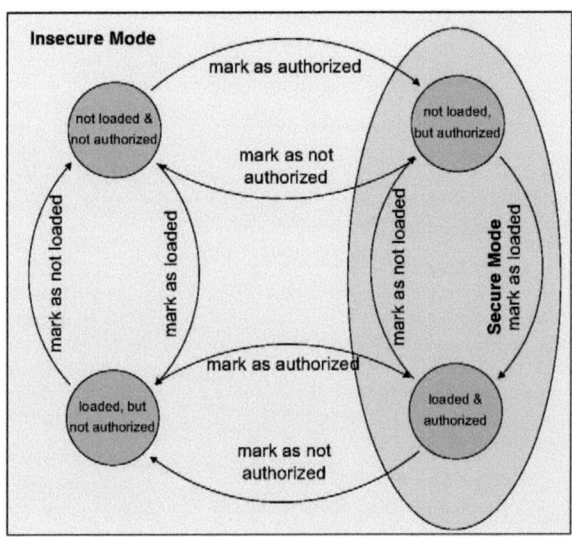

Figure 4.3: Authorized module loading state transition diagram

ACPI subsystem or device drivers) are not authorized. Consequently, they have to be authorized before the system is switched to secure more. Otherwise, they would work as expected, but unloading would not be possible (which might not be necessary, especially if it is a core component). Once the system is in secure mode, only authorized kernel modules can be loaded.

The main features of this process are encapsulated in the dynamic module loading process to check whether a module is marked as authorized or not. To provide this feature, the internal list includes modules and their state. To authorize a module, an authorization function has to open the module file, hash its content and search for matching hashes in the list. If the authorized-flag of the corresponding list entry is set, the module is allowed to be loaded. The unloading process is handled by another function that checks if the module is already loaded. Consequently, there is no need to hash the module again. Every loaded module is equipped with a unique pointer that represents the module. This pointer is used to find the correct module in the list and to decide whether to unload or not. Finally, unloaded modules must be marked as not loaded in the list.

4.2.4 Implementation

This section describes the implementation of the Trusted Kernel Modules concept. Like the operating system kernel (which is the DragonFly BSD Kernel, Version 2.5.0), all parts of kernel rootkit prevention have been written in the C programming language. This section focuses on the functions added to the operating system kernel and omits the userland client. While the client plays an important role, its implementation is straight forward.

4.2.4.1 Management System Call

All main communication between userland tools and the kernel is handled by a newly introduced system call. The fix system call number SYS_vml_manage is created by the global *syscalls.master* template and refers to the new vml_manage function. Parts of this function are shown in Listing 4.2. To ensure that the function cannot be used when module loading is disabled, the appropriate credentials are checked and an error about missing permissions is returned (lines 7 through 8). If the user requests to add a new module entry to the internal list, the identifier and the key are both copied from user space to kernel space into allocated buffers (the actual allocation code is omitted here). Finally, another function is called to mark the modules as trusted ones (lines 11 through 18). The opposing action is to remove a trusted module from the internal list (lines 20 through 25).

```
int
vml_manage(struct thread *td, struct vml_manage_args *uap)
{
    char* identifier, key;
    int len_identifier, len_key;

    if (priv_check(td, PRIV_KLD_LOAD) != 0)
        return (EPERM);

    if (uap->mode == VML_MODE_INSERT) {
        len_identifier =
           imin(strlen(uap->identifier) + 1,MAX_STR_LEN);
        len_key = imin(strlen(uap->key) + 1,MAX_STR_LEN);
        [...]
        copyinstr(uap->identifier, identifier,
            len_identifier, NULL);
        copyinstr(uap->key, key, len_key, NULL);
        return markAsVerified(identifier, key);
    }
```

Chapter 4. Host Security

```
20    else if (uap->mode == VML_MODE_DELETE) {
21        len_key = imin(strlen(uap->key) + 1,MAX_STR_LEN);
22        [...]
23        copyinstr(uap->key, key, len_key, NULL);
24        return markAsNotVerified(key);
25    }
26    [...]
27
28    return EUNKNOWNMODE;
29 }
```

Listing 4.2: Parts of the function that manages the trusted module list

Listing 4.3 shows an important and difficult part of the trusted module loading concept: generating a hash for a module. While generating the hash of a value is rather simple, loading the data of the module into kernel space is not. The first task is to open a virtual node, which is identified by the given filename. A virtual node is an entry in the Virtual File System (VFS), which is an abstract layer on top of the physical file systems. The function has to open the virtual node already in this early stage of the loading process. Later on, it is possible to reuse the provided, convenient functions to read a file from kernel, but, from the security perspective, this would be too late. Thus, the more complex route through the VFS layer has to be taken.

The prerequisites for the loading process are checked in lines 3 through 17. A new *nameidata* structure is initialized. This structure holds pointers to the vnode, the file name and several look-up parameters. Since concurrent access on the *nameidata* structure could lead to an non-deterministic VFS state (and finally to meta-data corruption of the original kernel module), the structure is protected by the global giant lock which ensures exclusive access on single and multi-core systems. Because the user could provide an incorrect path to the system call, the function has to assert that it is working with a regular file and not a directory. Finally, some attributes of the *vnode* that are needed to access the data blocks are obtained (lines 15 through 17).

All data blocks of the kernel module are read in a loop until the end of the file is reached (line 23). The actual read happens through the VFS function from user space to a buffer in kernel space (lines 34 through 37). Since the read bytes can be added to the hash algorithm successively, the memory usage is reduced by reading data piecewise using the same buffer each time. This data can be used to generate the hash key. By using the SHA-256 hash function, the method finally builds a hash value for the complete kernel module (lines 42 and 51). If the internal list contains the generated hash key, the module is marked as to be loaded, otherwise it is not and the appropriate permission denied error is returned.

4.2. Lightweight Kernel Rootkit Prevention

```
[...]

NDINIT(&nd, LOOKUP, FOLLOW | MPSAFE, UIO_SYSSPACE, filename, td);
flags = FREAD;
error = vn_open(&nd, &flags, 0, NULL);
vfslocked = NDHASGIANT(&nd);
NDFREE(&nd, NDF_ONLY_PNBUF);

if (nd.ni_vp->v_type != VREG)
    return NULL;
if (nd.ni_dirp == NULL)
    return NULL;

struct vattr vap;
VOP_GETATTR(nd.ni_vp, &vap, td->td_ucred, td);
if(error)
    return NULL;

[...]

length = vap.va_size;
int steps = 0;
while((steps * BUFFER_SIZE) < length) {
    offset    = BUFFER_SIZE * steps;
    bytesleft = length - offset;
    readbytes = 0;

    if (bytesleft < BUFFER_SIZE)
        readbytes = bytesleft;
    else
        readbytes = BUFFER_SIZE;

    int resid = 0;
    error = vn_rdwr(UIO_READ, nd.ni_vp,
                    (caddr_t) data, readbytes, offset,
                    UIO_SYSSPACE, IO_DIRECT,
                    td->td_ucred, NOCRED, &resid, td);

    if (error)
        goto mem_free;

    SHA256_Update(&ctx, data, readbytes);

    steps++;
}

[...]

MALLOC(buf, char *, SHA256_DIGEST_STRING_LENGTH,
    M_LINKER, M_WAITOK | M_ZERO);
SHA256_End(&ctx,buf);
```

Chapter 4. Host Security

```
52 [...]
```

Listing 4.3: An excerpt of the function that reads the module through the VFS layer from the disk and calculates the hash

4.2.4.2 List Management

The internal list has to hold any information about a module. For example, a module can simply be authorized, not loaded, or it can be loaded but not authorized. Therefore, the list contains one entry per module. The state is indicated by flags or implied by pointers that are not empty. This is shown in Listing 4.4. Every generated list entry holds a unique key, specifically a SHA-256 hash (line 4). The longer the resulting hash value is, the more secure the corresponding algorithm is in reference to brute force attacks. Thus, SHA-256 is a good trade-off in terms of security as well as memory usage and performance.

```
1  struct list_entry {
2      SLIST_ENTRY(list_entry) next;
3      char *identifier;
4      char *key;
5      linker_file_t lf;
6      int flag;
7  };
```

Listing 4.4: Structure of the internal list

The identifier is used to hold the human readable description of that entry (line 3). A `linker_file` pointer points to the corresponding linker file kernel structure (line 5). If the pointer is not NULL, the module, represented by this entry, is currently loaded. By doing this, it is possible to map a loaded module to the generated hash without making changes inside the existing kernel structures. This is needed for module unloading, where the appropriate functions only have the `linker_file` pointer as parameter.

This is a convenient way to map a loaded module to the generated hash without making changes inside the existing kernel structures. To prevent the list from being altered while system is in a secure state, it sis not possible to call the functions responsible for marking-and-authorizing a module. After switching to the secure mode, only authorized modules can be loaded or unloaded; there is no way to authorize kernel modules retroactively.

4.2.4.3 Kernel Module Loading Process

A userland tool is normally used to load modules during runtime. This utility directly uses the system call *kern_kldload*, which basically implements dynamic module loading. Figure 4.4 shows a flowchart of this process. First, the loading function checks the necessary permissions (root-permissions, insecure-mode). If this check fails, loading is aborted and the appropriate error (EPERM) is returned. Next, it calls the module linker, which extracts a usable path name from the given arguments. Then, the main module loading, depending on the binary format, is performed. These formats are compiled into the kernel and cannot be changed dynamically. The common format is the Executable and Linking Format (ELF).

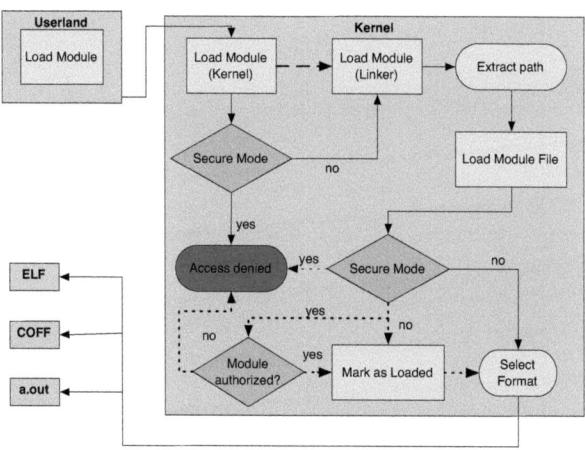

Figure 4.4: Module loading activity

Trusted Module Loading changed this workflow (changes made drawn in dashed lines in Figure 4.4). Loading a kernel module is only permitted with authorization. This requires that the kernel is already in secure mode. If not, the module is just marked as loaded. This is accomplished using the commands in Listing 4.5. Prior to adding a new module to the internal list it has to be checked if the module has already been loaded (lines 2 through 8). If is has not been loaded, memory for a new list entry is allocated and the entry is added after the lists head.

```
1  [...]
2  struct list_entry *cursor;
3  SLIST_FOREACH(cursor, &head, next) {
4      if(strcmp(key, cursor->key) == 0) {
5          cursor->lf = lf;
6          return 0;
7      }
8  }
9
10 [...]
11
12 struct list_entry* entry =
13     malloc(sizeof(struct list_entry), M_TEMP, M_ZERO | M_WAITOK);
14 entry->identifier = NULL;
15 entry->key = key;
16 entry->flag = 0;
17 entry->lf = lf;
18 SLIST_INSERT_HEAD(&head,entry,next);
19
20 [...]
```

Listing 4.5: Marking a kernel module as loaded

Authorizing a module within the unloading process is less complex because the data structures used in the unloading process contain a file pointer that is also registered in the internal list if the module is loaded. If the module is authorized, it is unloaded. Otherwise, unloading is not permitted.

4.2.5 Evaluation

This section focuses on the performance and a qualitative evaluation of the developed lightweight kernel rootkit prevention system. All tests were performed on two 2.53 GHz Intel Core2Duo CPU, 4 GB RAM, connected with Gigabit Ethernet and running DragonFly BSD Kernel, Version 2.5.0.

To measure the module loading overhead, a script was written that cascades module (un-)loading. Since the main overhead is due to hashing the modules, a proper average module size has to be chosen to achieve realistic results. By examining the standard kernel directory, it seems evident that the average size of the kernel modules is 64 KB. In order to be account for some variations in size, 100 KB sized kernel modules were used for testing. Modules were loaded between 250 and 2000 times to be able to measure the correct overhead time.

As shown in Figure 4.5, there is an overhead in every measurement. The module hashing causes the overhead during every module load. Loading modules in either secure or insecure mode (with enabled kernel protection) takes more time than

4.2. Lightweight Kernel Rootkit Prevention

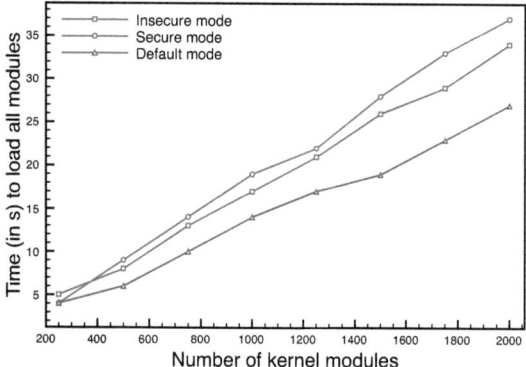

Figure 4.5: Time needed to load up to 2000 kernel modules

loading modules in the default mode (no protection and a stock kernel). This is due to the fact that the kernel rootkit prevention technique has to iterate over the internal list to validate a module. Thus, it involves an additional linear effort. Nevertheless, time is not a critical factor in module loading and the average number of loaded modules should be much lower than in the conducted tests.

In the case of 250 loaded modules in the generic kernel, it takes a module 0.016 seconds on average to load. In a kernel with rootkit prevention, it takes 0.02 seconds on average. This is more than 1.25 times longer, but still not a large delay. If the system is running in secure mode, loading a module will consume more time because there is one additional list iteration involved in the loading process. Generic kernels are not even able to load modules during secure mode. The measured overhead for module unloading is shown in Figure 4.6. Unlike the loading process, the unloading process is not very time consuming. There is no noteworthy time difference regardless which kernel mode is used.

For the sake of completeness, Figure 4.7 shows the time, in seconds, needed to mark up to 2000 kernel modules as authorized including the time needed to execute the *vml_manage* system call, calculate the checksum and store the result in the internal list. Obviously, the time needed to mark modules increases with the number of modules. The previous measurements exposed an overhead both in the loading and the unloading process. Nevertheless, the overhead is insignificant as kernel modules are only loaded once ans do not affect the system's runtime performance.

59

Chapter 4. Host Security

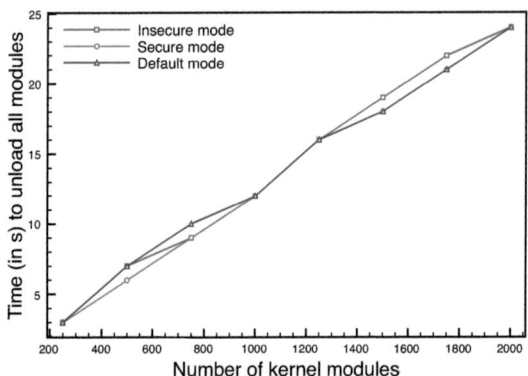

Figure 4.6: Time needed to unload up to 2000 kernel modules

4.2.6 Summary

While the detection rate of malware and anti-virus scanners has steadily improved within the last few years, it is still not a fool-proof solution against recent exploits like zero-day exploits. Many successful attacks lead to the installation of a kernel rootkit to gain permanent control of the target machine and make it possible to get access at later times and misuse the machines as an attack platforms. Consequently, the proposed solution is a lightweight and effective way to prevent loading kernel rootkits all together. Only authorized and thus trusted kernel modules are allowed to load during runtime; loading unauthorized modules is no longer possible.

4.3 Malware Detection in Virtualized Grids

4.3.1 Introduction

Potential threats targeting virtualized grid infrastructures create the need for a new malware detection system, as providers need ways to ensure the security of their infrastructure and the systems of their customers.

While threats apply to a greater extent to infrastructural machines, such as crit-

4.3. Malware Detection in Virtualized Grids

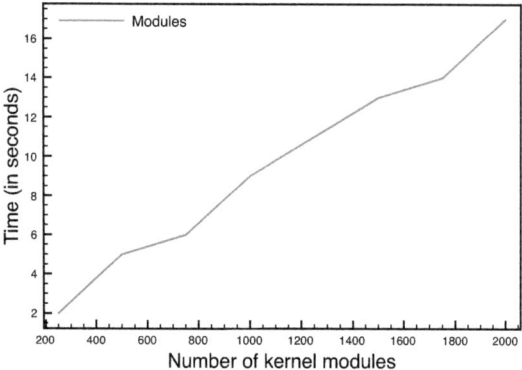

Figure 4.7: Time needed to mark up to 2000 kernel modules as authorized

ical servers (e.g. DNS, DHCP), a grid provider should also be interested in keeping the virtual machines of its customers safe. Most vendors provide virtual machines with full root access, meaning that a user can do basically whatever he or she wants, including destroying the whole machine. Since virtualized grid computing as well as cloud computing is about pay-as-you-go, this should not harm the vendor. Nevertheless, if a user (intentionally or unintentionally) executes malware, this could also affect the provider, e.g. a Spam malware could abuse the outgoing bandwidth and send mass-spam mails. Thus, while granting root permissions to its customers, a provider should still be able to inspect the applications running inside its customers' virtual machines. Furthermore, he or she should be able to take countermeasures if he or she detects a security violation, such as running malware binaries.

Having a flexible virtualized grid infrastructure also opens new possibilities to scale up and distribute malware detection software among several systems. Most end-host security solutions have a major, negative performance impact on the computer caused by huge signature sets or complex detection algorithms. Using virtual grid infrastructures can be beneficial here to decrease the slowdown and offload it to dedicated machines.

Parts of this section have been published in [113, 114].

4.3.2 Related Work

The following section introduces approaches that cover malware detection in virtualized grid and cloud computing environments.

The Automatic Malware Signature Discovery System (AMSDS) [174] has been developed by Yan and Wu. Increasing numbers of zero-day malware take more and more time to analyze and requires signatures to be written; thus it is necessary to provide automatic signature generators. Moreover, the increasing size of signature databases and analysis techniques increase the processor and memory footprint on computers with anti-virus solutions. This can be countered by anti-virus software as a cloud service, which places the workload of analysis and signature maintenance on dedicated machines. AMSDS has a small detection engine with a reduced signature set. This set of signatures can match a great share of malicious software through special treatment and preprocessing of the binary. A file is only sent to the cloud anti-virus service for scanning with traditional anti-virus solutions if the much smaller AMSDS signatures cannot detect a suspicious file. Automatic signature generation is very effective and space-saving compared to classic signature generation. But these signatures can only detect binary executables loaded from either a disk or a network. A binary that is already running on a system, such as a service infected through an exploit, is not covered by this approach.

Laureano et al. [80] have implemented kernel introspection mechanisms into User-Mode-Linux. The authors gather information about the running system by inspecting the flow of the system calls made. Their IDS runs in two different modes: a mode for learning the regular behavior of a system and a so-called monitoring mode where anything unusual generates an alarm and suspicious processes are denied access to specific system calls. The approach simply reports the system calls, there is no fine-grained behavior analysis. Ignoring the system call parameters might lead to a significant increase in false alarms, since it can make a huge difference whether an *open* system call accesses a password file or just a new temporary file.

Oberheide et al. [95] suggest that each node run a lightweight process to acquire executables that enter a system, send them into the network for analysis, and then run or quarantine them based on a threat report returned by a network service. While their evaluations show that they have a fairly high detection rate (using a couple of standard detection engines), they only scan executables as a whole and thus are not able to detect yet unknown malware. The presented behavior should definitely be part of every malware detection system, but it should only accompany other, more sophisticated solutions.

Ether [32], which was developed at the Georgia Institute of Technology in Atlanta, represents a new solution to analyze malware transparently. Ether uses hardware virtualization to stay outside of the target operating system, i.e. there are no detectable components. Actual implementation is based upon the Xen hypervisor and Intel's VT hardware virtualization extensions. Information is gathered in the hypervisor and processed in domain 0. Guest operating systems, such as Windows, run unmodified in the domain U's. Ether seems like a mature product for malware analysis and worth a consideration. Nevertheless, Ether requires hardware virtualization extensions, which are not available on legacy hardware.

Garfinkel and Rosenblum [49] have described a virtual machine introspection based on an architecture that incorperates the isolation, inspection and interposition properties of VMMs. Virtual machine introspection (VMI) describes a family of techniques that enables a virtual machine service to understand and modify states and events within the guest system. Besides this passive monitoring technique, active monitoring of virtual machine-based IDSes has been implemented as well [50]. Although they are facing the gap between the VMM's view of data/events and the guest software's view (which is called semantic gap), their modifications of the guest operating systems are detectable.

Payne et al. [99] present XenAccess, a monitoring library for operating systems running on Xen, incorporating virtual memory introspection and virtual disk monitoring. It enables monitoring applications to safely access the memory state and disk activity. Since the current version of the approach that will be presented in the following is based on the BSD operating system, XenAccess is not useable. Nevertheless, in a future version, based on Xen, it is definitely one of the candidates for virtual machine introspection to chose form.

CloudAV [96] is a software stack developed by Oberheide et al. It is meant to counter the problems that single anti-virus solutions face nowadays with the increase of different malware and new exploitation techniques. Instead of having just one anti-virus solution per host, CloudAV uses multiple, heterogeneous detection engines. This approach is called *N-version protection*. The implementation of the CloudAV system is limited to standard executables, leaving out live code injection and shared libraries. The solution proposed in this thesis also analyzes the behavior of processes during runtime.

4.3.3 Design

Following the related work, requirements for a malware detection engine in virtualized grids can be derived:

Chapter 4. Host Security

- Instead of using a single anti-virus engine, a grid based system should run multiple anti-virus engines simultaneously. This increases the chances of detecting malware significantly, as one engine might not have the signatures for all kinds of malware. Additional detection engines can easily be integrated into the service and multiple engines speed up the process of scanning executables.

- A grid-based system lowers the complexity of host-based monitoring software. Clients no longer need to continually update their local signature database, reducing administrative costs. Simplifying the client software also decreases the chance that it could contain exploitable vulnerabilities [79, 25].

- In general, anti-virus engines scan for traces of known signatures in files (not necessary executables). While this is certainly effective, it does not help to protect against yet unknown zero-day malware. Consequently, a grid-based system should pursue classic anti-virus detection as well as novel ways, such as live system call analysis.

- Traditionally, most malware ran in the user's security context, i.e. it could not influence any installed detection engines. However, recent evolutions in malware [71, 64] have shown that this assumption is no longer true. In order to prevent malware from influencing the detection process, monitoring the system from outside rather than from within is unavoidable. Thus, a grid-based scanner should use techniques like virtual machine introspection [50].

Derived from these requirements a malware detection engine for virtualized grids was developed, which will be presented in the following.

4.3.3.1 Architecture

Contrary to a classic anti-virus setup, a grid-specific design of a malware detection engine should run in a distributed manner and display some special requirements to ensure the security of the service provider's infrastructure as well as the customer's security. The communication paths and different software modules of the proposed design are shown in Figure 4.8. Any program run by the user is executed in a virtual machine. The kernel of this machine then passes all relevant information to a *KernelAgent*. The *KernelAgent* gathers all information by the virtual machines running on the grid resource and then relays them to the *ScanProxy*. The *ScanProxy* provides a front-end to the grid security analyzer services. At this stage, the proxy has to distribute the information to the different services, such as classic anti-virus software or behavior-based analysis solutions.

4.3. Malware Detection in Virtualized Grids

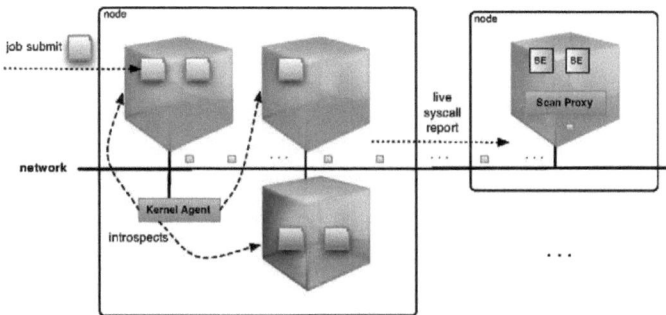

Figure 4.8: Malware scanner architecture

The kernel module is the primary sensor that sits directly in the running virtualized kernel of the guest machine. To avoid any security issues by the way of the kernel module, it has very limited functionality. Its main task is to function as a logging relay and to submit any interesting activities to the *KernelAgent* for further processing.

Process Life Cycle, System Calls

Monitoring a process with respect to its system calls throughout its lifecycle can be a valuable source of information when looking for common patterns in malware behavior. By relaying this information live, not only encrypted executable images and obfuscation, but also in-memory injected malware through an exploit can be analyzed. System calls make it easy to spot specific file accesses or socket operations, such as transmitting data back to an attacker. The relevant information includes the system call, its parameters, return values and the program that made the call.

Obtain Executables

The kernel module should intercept any executable before it is running and submit it to its host agent. This is the way classic anti-virus hooks grab an executable before loading it into their scan engine. They check every executable through static analysis. Applying static binary analysis might not always be the best way to ensure security, especially when confronted with unknown, new malware.

Nevertheless, it still should be part of any malware detection solution. Using this approach, it is easy to take advantage of all the existing anti-virus software. A requirement for any executable analysis is the binary image of the file itself, and for identification purposes, the filename must also be transmitted. Since executables can easily exceed the maximum size of a TCP packet and the integrity must be ensured, transmitting it over TCP is a must.

Contrary to classic anti-virus solutions, no installation within the disk image is necessary, which means the additional security provided by the operating systems is completely transparent to the customer. Moreover, the customer has full control over his or her virtual machine. No matter what the customer does with the image, he or she cannot break or deactivate the malware detection system.

4.3.3.2 Operating System Kernel Sensor

This part collects all the data from the virtual machine kernels running on the host system. This information should then be relayed to the *ScanProxy*. Since there is no other logic involved in this piece of software other than the configuration of what has to be sent to whom, there is almost no need to touch an installed system. To increase performance, methods of caching messages and later on responses are implemented. This is especially interesting for classical executable image analysis. While starting-up several virtual machines, the same executable is run several times. These are often called binaries and include, for example, system services. Submitting and analyzing the executable at every initiation/run costs CPU time and also increases network traffic. This can slow down the start-up time in a feedback-based intrusion prevention system significantly.

Since both groups of information (binary and system call related) have different requirements, splitting up the *KernelAgent* into two separate servers makes sense. One is a TCP-based system call forwarder, the other one should receive binaries and forward them. The binary executable relay must not save any executables to the hard disk. Otherwise, there is a chance of an infection happening on the host system in the event that a malware is installed.

4.3.3.3 Backend Proxy

This component gathers all available information from the hosts and distributes it among the registered scan engines. For each incoming packet containing a system call, one or more receiving scan engines can be used. The proxy then forwards the packet to the registered receivers. It could also act as a global log and caching proxy for the entire virtualized grid. Because every new scan engine is a system call analyzer or a classical anti-virus scanner, it can be enlisted here once or even several times for redundancy purposes. The proxy does not need to have much more logic than the above to keep the system as easy to manage and as immunized as possible. The more complex a code is, the more open a system is to failure through attacks.

4.3.3.4 Scan Engine and Executable Analysis

Considering the previously described framework, several possible scanning backends can be implemented. They can generally be categorized as process-behavior-based or executable-binary-based, such as a classical anti-virus solution, e.g. ClamAV [19]. Every incoming executable has to be placed in a separate container on the hard disk and then analyzed. The received binaries must not be executed, otherwise the security of the scanning computer can be compromised in the event of an infection. By registering several different anti-virus scanners with wrappers, an increased level of security can be achieved. This helps to minimize the vulnerability window that exists between the discovery of a new malware and the release of the signatures by the anti-virus vendors for their products.

To process events such as systems calls, a backend like the software of Wagener et al. [167] can be used with minor modifications. The underlying concept of their approach is that even new malware shares common behavioral similarities to already existing malware. By finding these similarities in behavior graphs, even yet unknown malware can be detected automatically. While Wagener et al. perform system call analysis ahead of time in a secure execution environment, modifications should easily be possible to enable on-the-fly detection.

4.3.4 Implementation

Like the operating system kernel (which is the DragonFly BSD Kernel, Version 2.5.0), the kernel part of the malware detection module has been written in the C programming language. The userland programs are written in Python.

4.3.4.1 Operating System Kernel Modifications

To tap into the relevant parts of the kernel, some static hooks are installed. These hooks redirect or copy valuable information from kernel functions, such as *execve*, to an extra function that passes this information on to the *KernelAgent*.

Obtaining Process Related Information

Getting all process-related information requires the addition of several hooks to the virtual machine kernel. A hook is installed in the function that adds new processes to the kernel's process list and assigns a new PID to them. The list is a linked-list used to keep a global list of all running processes. Another hook that is called at the end of a process lifetime works in a similar fashion. This routine is called by the kernel's *exit1* function to remove a process from the global list of running processes and add it to the list of dead processes. This list is an in-kernel linked-list containing all processes in the ZOMBIE state. This means that they are about to be removed from memory and are finished executing.

The system call hook is called from within the virtual machine's *syscall2* function. It is executed immediately after the real system call has been processed. Getting called after the execution of the system call has the advantage that some parameters that are passed on empty to the kernel and are filled during execution; thus, their contents can be inspected. This is, for example, the case with the *open* system call that has a buffer as its parameter for reading bytes from a file descriptor.

Listing 4.6 shows the kernel function that traces a system call and sends the gathered information to the *KernelAgent*. Basic information such as PID, system call type, name and return code can be extracted from the Lightweight Process (LWP) associated with the real userland process (lines 7 through 12). The challenging part here is determining the parameters (lines 19 through 34). They are passed to the system call function without providing any type-information other than a memory reference. For the kernel, there is no need to know this type-information since the corresponding system call knows what type its parameters should have. As part of the approach, an extra file holds a list of all system calls and their parameter types. Additionally, the error code as returned by the actual system call is provided for analysis purposes. This has the advantage that the data flow can be recorded, such as the returned file descriptor from an open call and later on any *read* system calls to this file descriptor. Finally, the structure is sent to the *KernelAgent* (line 38).

```
1  [...]
2  void
3  vsyscalltracer(struct lwp *lp, int code, int narg,
4      register_t args[], int retcode)
5  {
6      struct vsyscalldata vsd;
7      vsd.type = VSD_SYSCALL;
8      vsd.code = code;
9      vsd.retcode = retcode;
10     vsd.pid = lp->lwp_proc->p_pid;
```

4.3. Malware Detection in Virtualized Grids

```
11      memset(vsd.name, 0, 1024);
12      snprintf(vsd.name,1024, "%s", lp->lwp_proc->p_comm);
13
14      int i = 0, len=0;
15      char buf[VSD_MAXPARAMLEN];
16      char tbuf[VSD_MAXPARAMLEN];
17
18      memset(vsd.params, 0, VSD_MAXPARAMLEN);
19      while(i < 10 && syscalltypes[code][i] != 0) {
20          memset(buf, 0, VSD_MAXPARAMLEN);
21
22          if (syscalltypes[code][i] == STR) {
23              copyinstr(args[i], tbuf, 1024, &len);
24              snprintf(buf,VSD_MAXPARAMLEN,"|p%i:%s",i,tbuf);
25          } else if (typesizes[syscalltypes[code][i]] == 4) {
26              int t = (int) args[i];
27              snprintf(buf, VSD_MAXPARAMLEN,"|p%i:%i", i, t);
28          } else {
29              snprintf(buf, VSD_MAXPARAMLEN,"|p%i:%i", i,
30                  syscalltypes[code][i]);
31          }
32          i++;
33          snprintf(vsd.params, VSD_MAXPARAMLEN,"%s%s",vsd.params, buf)
                ;
34      }
35      if (i==0)
36          snprintf(vsd.params, VSD_MAXPARAMLEN, "||");
37
38      send_vsd(vsd);
39  }
```

Listing 4.6: Kernel function that traces system calls

Obtaining Executables

The binary loader hook is placed in the virtual machine's *kern_execve* function, which is the actual place of execution and not the system calls' first entry point, *sys_execve*. To avoid unnecessary calls to the logging hook, it is only called after *exec_check_permissions* has been successfully returned. After this call, it is certain that the executable is valid and has the appropriate permissions. Logging takes place before the first page of the executable gets mapped into the memory and is executed. In a feedback-based intrusion detection system, it would still be possible to stop the execution at this stage, should the binary be infected with malware. The whole binary is then submitted to the *KernelAgent* using TCP.

4.3.4.2 Kernel-Userland Communication

To keep the protocol overhead as small as possible and be as responsive as necessary, a simple protocol is implemented by using UDP in the kernel. Approaches based on TCP would have brought up some additional delays, which is a problem when monitoring real-time events such as system calls.

Listing 4.7 shows the static structure that will be passed to the sending function (send_vsd()). This structure holds name and parameters of the system call as well as information about the process.

```
struct vsyscalldata {
    char name[1024];
    char params[VSD_MAXPARAMLEN+1];
    int type;
    int pid;
    int code;
    int retcode;
};
```

Listing 4.7: vsyscall data structure

4.3.4.3 Operating System Kernel Sensor

The *KernelAgent*'s main task is to collect the data from all virtual kernels running on the machine and forward it to its *ScanProxy*. This part is implemented using the Python programming language. Whenever a new packet is received, a background thread is started to process the received packet. This implies that it is parsed and then the whole packet is sent forward to the configured *ScanProxy*.

4.3.4.4 Backend Proxy and Anti-virus Engine Connection

This software module is similar to the *KernelAgent* on the receiving part. Instead of one configured receiver for relaying, like in the *KernelAgent*, there is a list of receivers. This list can be configured for each entry to relay only specific types of traffic (e.g. only NEWPROC, ENDPROC and SYSCALL) or any traffic for a catchall or logging daemon. Due to this fine-grained configurability, the incoming packets must be inspected and checked against the list of receivers to ensure that every receiver obtains only events for which is has subscribed.

A TCP variant of the *ScanProxy* has also been written for scanning executable files with an anti-virus software such as ClamAV. Just as within the UDP *ScanProxy*, a list of receivers/backends can be configured. All incoming binaries are relayed to

4.3. Malware Detection in Virtualized Grids

them. The *ScanProxy* only keeps the executable's data in memory; nothing gets written to the hard disk. This backend checks incoming binary files with ClamAV for known viruses. Incoming files are received over TCP connections to ensure that the received binaries are in order and complete. As in the *KernelAgent* and the *ScanProxy*, the name of the executable is also submitted. Every received binary is saved in a temporary quarantine folder, where it is scanned. After scanning is complete, the file is deleted to ensure security of the backend system.

Example System Call Stream

The following section presents a sample output of *ktrace*[1] showing a malware binary. Like *strace* under Linux, *ktrace* shows all system calls of a BSD binary during execution. Listing 4.8 shows a shortened system call dump of malware that steals the Unix password file (/etc/passwd), sends it over a UDP channel through the network and creates a copy of the command shell with *setuid* permissions.

A UDP network *socket* is opened in line 2. An open system call is performed to get a file handle for reading the password file (line 4). Then, the file is read block by block and transferred using the socket (lines 7 though 13). Finally, the file handle is closed. In order to retain control, a copy of the command shell is placed into the temporary directory (lines 15 through 30). Most system calls are generated by the copy process, but the call in line 27 sets the *setuid* bit of the copy, i.e. the shell will be executed on behalf of the owner, which is the superuser.

```
 1 [...]
 2 CALL    socket(PF_INET,SOCK_DGRAM,0)
 3 RET     socket 3
 4 CALL    open(0x804888f,O_RDONLY,<unused>0)
 5 NAMI    "/etc/passwd"
 6 RET     open 4
 7 CALL    read(0x4,0xbfbff554,0x100)
 8 CALL    sendto(0x3,0xbfbff554,0x58,0,0xbfbff544,0x10)
 9 RET     4
10 [...]
11 CALL    read(0x4,0xbfbff554,0x100)
12 GIO     fd 4 read 0 bytes
13 RET     read 0
14 CALL    close(0x4)
15 RET     close 0
16 CALL    sigaction(SIGINT,0xbfbfed10,0xbfbfecf8)
17 RET     sigaction 0
18 CALL    sigaction(SIGQUIT,0xbfbfed10,0xbfbfece0)
19 RET     sigaction 0
20 CALL    sigprocmask(SIG_BLOCK,0xbfbfecd0,0xbfbfecc0)
21 RET     sigprocmask 0
```

---

[1] http://leaf.dragonflybsd.org/cgi/web-man?command=ktrace

Chapter 4. Host Security

```
22 CALL   fork
23 RET    fork 49122/0xbfe2
24 CALL   wait4(0xbfe2,0xbfbfed28,<invalid>0,0)
25 RET    wait4 49122/0xbfe2
26 [...]
27 CALL   chmod(0x80488b5,S_ISUID|S_IRUSR|S_IWUSR|S_IXUSR|S_IRGRP|
28        S_IXGRP|S_IROTH|S_IXOTH)
29 NAMI   "/tmp/suidshellcopy"
30 [...]
31 CALL   exit(0)
32 [...]
```

Listing 4.8: ktrace dump of a malware binary stealing the password file

4.3.5 Evaluation

The performance and a qualitative evaluation of the developed malware detection system is presented in this section. All tests were performed on two 2.53 GHz Intel Core2Duo CPU, 4 GB RAM running DragonFly BSD, Kernel Version 2.5.0, connected with switched Gigabit Ethernet network.

Since the main modifications to the virtual machine kernel occurred in the process and system call handling code, measuring performance impact is best done by spawning several processes and by performing rapid system calls; thus, data or process intensive tasks are not relevant for the benchmark.

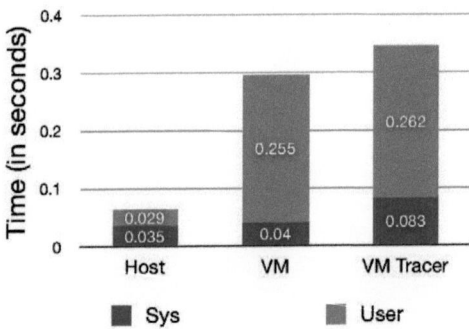

Figure 4.9: Comparing host, virtual machine and modified virtual machine speed

A test case that queries the kernel for network, user and other arbitrary informa-

4.3. Malware Detection in Virtualized Grids

tion is executed 50 times, and the average run time is calculated. The results of the benchmark are presented in Figure 4.9. The lower bars, named *sys*, indicate the time spent executing system calls on behalf of the executed program. The upper bars, named *user*, represent the time spent doing calculations, iterations or general actions in userland. The diagram clearly shows that the host operating system easily outperforms the virtualized kernels. Even though the time spent executing system calls is nearly identical between host and the virtual machine kernel, the time spent in userland is much more compared to the time when running on the host directly. Enabling the tracer functionality of the virtual machine kernel doubles the time spent in the kernel, but the userland portion stays constant. Since the in-kernel time for system calls is so low compared to the total execution time (0.06 seconds), this impact on the performance can be ignored.

Another experiment measured the time needed to intercept a 8 KB binary in a running virtual machine with the *KernelAgent*, transfer it over the network and scan it with the ClamAV engine. Over 350 trials were conducted to get a robust mean, which is 0.5 seconds. The measured overhead of 0.5 seconds before the actual execution starts is negligible in the described grid environment, as most jobs will be long-running computational jobs. Furthermore, the use of caching techniques will even reduce the overhead, as every (unchanged) binary is only scanned once.

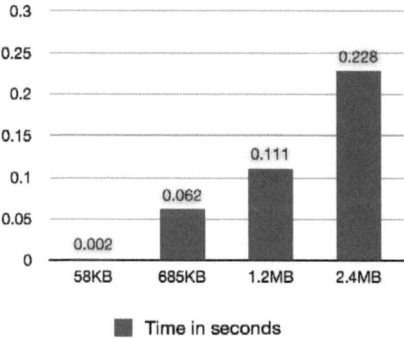

Figure 4.10: Transfer times for various binaries from the KernelAgent to the antivirus backend

Figure 4.10 shows the times needed to transfer various binaries of different sizes over the developed middleware between *KernelAgent* and the *ScanProxy*. Multiple measurements were conducted with different binary sizes representing different types of malware (the average file size of the standard system binaries is about 1.2 MB). For Binary 1 (58 KB), the average time is 0.001 seconds, for Binary 2 (685 KB), the average time is 0.06 seconds, for Binary 3 (1.2 MB), the average time is 0.1 seconds, and for the biggest binary (2.4 MB), the average time is 0.2 seconds. Thus, the transfer time increases with the size of the binary.

Figure 4.11 shows the time needed to send an executable from the kernel to the *KernelAgent*. In the first measurement (leftmost bar), there was no *KernelAgent* running and thus the kernel waits until the connection times out, which takes 0.34 seconds on average. The second process (bar in the middle) sends the binary prior to execution and blocks until transmission is completed, which takes 3.8 seconds on average. In the third process (rightmost bar), a worker thread is created that sends the binary file in the background. This way, execution can proceed without waiting for the file to be sent, which is time consuming. In average, this takes 0.88 seconds. An interesting fact is that sending a binary with an extra thread takes about twice as long as waiting for the timeout because the *KernelAgent* is not running. The increased speed of multi-threading can be seen when comparing its time with a version where execution starts only after transmission of the binary file is completed. The non-multithreading version takes about four times as long.

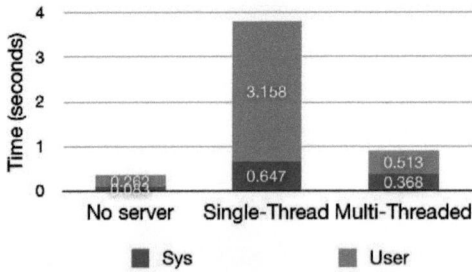

Figure 4.11: Benchmark comparing speed of a modified kernel without running TCP receiver for binaries, single-threaded and multi-threaded transmission

Currently, copying data inside the operating system kernel is done by using static memory instead of dynamic memory allocated with *kmalloc*. While static memory is less flexible, allocation is faster and the chances of undetected memory leaks are low, compared to dynamic memory. Figure 4.12 shows the time needed to pass around data with static and dynamic allocated memory. While the former action takes 0.282 seconds on average, the latter takes 0.307 seconds on average. As a consequence, all operations that need are called frequently and whose performance is critical should avoid dynamic memory allocation, if possible.

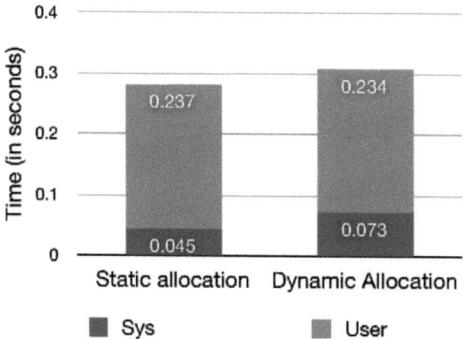

Figure 4.12: Time needed to pass data in the kernel using static and dynamically allocated memory

The presented experiments evaluated several aspects of the grid-based malware detection system. While it introduces some performance penalties, it increases the security of the monitored systems.

4.4 Summary

In this chapter, an approach for combined malware detection and rootkit prevention in virtualized grid computing environments was presented. All running binaries are intercepted by a small, in-kernel agent and submitted to one or more backend units where the actual classification process occurs. Furthermore, live-scanning of all binary system calls is performed to detect yet unknown exploits or malware. Due to the in-kernel nature of the agent, it is completely transparent to the user as well as to malicious binaries trying to detect any countermeasures. The distributed architecture utilizes existing grid resources and the connection of different analysis engines. Furthermore, lightweight modifications to the module loading process of the operating system kernel prevent that attacker from loading kernel rootkits. While the presented approaches are developed in the context of virtualized grids, they can also be used in cloud computing environments.

"If, ten years from now, when you are doing something quick and dirty, you suddenly visualize that I am looking over your shoulders and say to yourself, "Dijkstra would not have liked this", that would be enough immortality for me."

Edsger W. Dijkstra (1930–2002)

5
Network Security

5.1 Introduction

In this chapter, network security solutions for grids are presented, including implementation details, experimental results and evaluation. At first, a novel architecture for virtualized grids is introduced. While jobs in traditional grid computing use shared resources, the presented solution encapsulates jobs in virtual execution environments. Since adding a virtualization layer poses new challenges, several mechanisms are presented to address them. This includes efficient mechanisms for virtual machine disk image distribution and effective storage synchronization. Since is is impossible to protect a prominent node, like the grid head node, from all possible attacks, mechanisms are needed that make it more difficult for a possible attacker to access the system. Therefore, a novel grid demilitarized zone that guards the grid head node is presented. The introduction of a demilitarized zone also created the need for a software that allows job resources to be transported to the backend computing resources securely. This is done by a novel set of components that tightly fits into a grid environment. Furthermore, the security of the demilitarized zone is extended through a Network Intrusion Detection System to detect several grid-specific attacks, especially Denial-of-Service attacks against the Globus Toolkit 4, i.e. the grid middleware used. Finally, this chapter presents the concept of public nodes. While it is common in clouds that virtual machines within nodes can be reached from the Internet, it is unknown in grids. Dynamic firewalls guard the virtual machines belonging to a job from internal and external attacks. In order to provide a certain degree of freedom to the user, a web service is available that allows secure, fine-grained configuration of the firewall settings.

5.2 Virtualized Grid Computing

5.2.1 Introduction

As stated in Section 3.3.4, shared use of computing resources is one of the major problems of traditional grid computing. Jobs running on the same node could interfere with each other: A legal job could use too many resources or fill up a temporary file system (e.g., /tmp), which might also affect other jobs. Furthermore, a malicious job could try to gather information about another job. In order to mitigate such situations, there is a need for a clear separation between different user's jobs.

The following section presents a number of projects that attempt to achieve this goal. Based on the related work, the requirements for the proposed solution are defined. Then, the design for the proposed solution is presented and evaluated via a number of experiments.

Parts of this section have been published in [118, 127, 126, 116, 121, 115, 39, 117, 163].

5.2.2 Related Work

Grid Computing and Virtual Machines

This sections presents related work that addresses the use of virtual machines as execution environments within the context of grid computing.

Figueiredo et al. [40] presented a case study about grid computing on virtual machines. They outlined the benefits to grid computing by using operating system virtualization, especially in terms of security, usability and legacy support. While this paper outlined the road towards virtualized grid computing, their solution does not work with a scheduler that has already been installed on a system. Because this is a requirement of the German D-Grid, the solution is not acceptable.

VMPlant [77] is a grid service for automated configuration and creation of virtual

5.2. Virtualized Grid Computing

machines based on VMware, which can be cloned and dynamically instantiated to provide homogeneous execution environments within distributed grid resources. This work focuses on defining a framework for virtual machine management and the representing software requirements through a directed acyclic graph. In line with the previous approach, VMPlant does not work with a scheduler that has already been installed on a system.

VSched [85], which is included into *Virtuoso*, is a system for distributed computing using virtual machines to mix batch and interactive virtual machines on the same hardware. Implemented as a user-level program, it schedules virtual machines created by VMware GSX Server [162]. VSched is designed to execute processes within virtual machines during idle times. Processes are executed while users are not producing a high CPU load, e.g. while only using a word processor or surfing the web. VSched focused on implementing a user-level scheduler and thus is not prepared for the use in high-performance computing environments, such as the German D-Grid.

The Globus team presented *VirtualWorkspaces*, an approach to distributed virtual machines in grids [177, 68, 66, 48]. The project uses Xen virtualization technology to dynamically create and deploy virtual machines. Unfortunately, this project was in an early stage and allowed the creation of just one virtual machine per job. Furthermore, a user has to trigger the Virtual Workspace service manually to get a virtualized execution environment. The project has been abandoned today and merged with the Nimbus project, which is presented in the following.

Keahey et al. [67] presented the idea of using virtual environments in grid computing. Their work resulted in the development of the *Nimbus* project [94]. It allows the dynamic creation of virtual machines in which grid jobs are executed, and therefore uses Xen virtualization technology. In contrast to the solution that was developed during the course of this thesis, Nimbus offers an on-demand set-up mechanism that provides virtual clusters, but it cannot be used in traditional cluster scenarios, in which a scheduler decides where jobs will be executed.

Kiyanclar et al. [72] presented Maestro-VC, a paravirtualized execution environment for secure on-demand cluster computing. Maestro is similar to the *VirtualWorkspaces* project presented above. A gateway receives an XML request from a number of clients describing a number of virtual machines. A global scheduler is in charge of building the virtual cluster. While Maestro demonstrates a good number of features needed for virtualized grid computing, it still lacks some details. There is neither support for multi-site grid computing nor for personalized VPN connections to the submitting user. Furthermore, it does not deal with live migrations of virtual machines.

The challenges of system-level virtualization for High Performance Computing are presented by Valle et al. [159]. They speak about different topics, such as an ideal hypervisor, possible virtual system environments, fault tolerance, I/O, storage, resource management and administration. Their work raises interesting questions about the use of virtualization in grid and cloud environments and outlines a number of requirements that have to be fulfilled.

Engelmann et al. [34] conducted a study on how to use virtualization to provide management and utilization of high performance computing systems. Their approach uses a platform virtualization to execute virtual machines. Furthermore, they state that techniques are used "in order to provide a powerful abstraction for portability, isolation, and customization of the entire software suite of a HPC system." In line with the approaches presented above, no implementation was provided that is able to work in an existing grid computing environment using an already installed scheduler.

Könning et al. [74] described the development efforts in providing a virtualized environment concept and prototype for scientific application development and deployment. Virtualized Environments can be specified in XML and consist of a number of system files in a chroot environment unique to each individual user. chroot was chosen by the authors since it has a negligible overhead. Nevertheless, chroot is not an optimal solution for a secure environment since it is possible to escape from a chroot jail if no additional protection (such as kernel hardening patches) are present.

OpenNebula, was developed by Sotomayor et al. [132, 136] to enable efficient scheduling in virtualized environments. It uses leasing, and not jobs, as the fundamental resource provisioning abstraction. *OpenNebula* is able to build a private, a public or a hybrid cloud computing environment. In cluster or grid computing environments, job resources (in terms of compute nodes or virtual machines) are provided by the batch scheduler. It is not possible for a user to choose his or her own resources. Therefore, it is not easily possible to integrate *OpenNebula* in a classic grid computing setup using an existing scheduler.

The authors of OpenNebula also present Haizea [135, 133, 134], a resource lease manager that can act as a scheduling backend for OpenNebula, providing leasing capabilities not found in other cloud systems, such as advance reservations and resource preemption, which are particularly relevant for private clouds. Haizea seems like a promising solution that bridges the gap between grids and clouds and is similar to the combination of solutions that will be presented in this thesis.

Smith [123] presented an approach towards service-oriented on-demand grid computing. He used operating system virtualization to shield users' jobs from each other. The Business Process Execution Language (BPEL) is used to integrate the system into existing business workflows. Furthermore, a server rotation mechanism protects the grid head node from unknown stealth attacks by refreshing the head node transparently using virtual machine disk images. An intrusion detection system using a streaming database system is presented to detect attacks, which could not be prevented.

Virtual Disk Image Distribution

Related work and discussion on the topic of efficient distribution of virtual machine disk images is presented in the following.

Sapuntzakis et al. [112] show how to move the state of a running computer across a network quickly, including the state in its disks, memory, CPU registers and I/O devices. The authors use several techniques to migrate a VMWare virtual machine from one node to another. The paper focuses on distribution over slow links (the primary example is a 384 kps DSL link). To achieve this goal, a self-made COW layer is used that is connected to the VMWare GSX Server. This layer attaches a bitmap to every COW disk. If a block is written/freed on one of the disks, the associated bitmap entry changes. Thus, instead of transmitting the entire COW disk, only the bitmap file is transferred and compared against an older, already existing version, and only the blocks that have changed since the last update are transmitted. To speed up the transfer over low-bandwidth links, only a hash instead of the data itself is transferred. If the receiver has the data matching the hash on local storage, it uses this data. If not, it requests the data from the server. As the authors state in the paper, the presented approach is not intended for high-bandwidth environments. Nevertheless, their approach presents a number of good inspirations related to disk image distribution.

Nelson et al. [93] describe the design and implementation of a system that uses virtual machine technology to provide fast, transparent application migration. The system is called *VMMotion* and is part of the VMWare VirtualCenter product. The actual migration involves severals steps: the selected virtual machines's memory is pre-copied to the destination, while the original machine continues running. Then, the virtual machine is suspended and transferred to the destination. The destination takes over control and resumes the suspended machine. Finally, the remaining memory state is copied. The actual transfer process happens over SCSI storage. All virtual machines are attached to a Storage Area Network (SAN); thus, the SCSI disk can be reconnected to the destination machine. Due to the fact that VMWare is not usable on most academic grid sites, this approach is not feasible.

Kozuch et al. [75] present an approach called Internet Suspend/Resume (ISR). ISR is a hypothetical capability of suspending a machine on one Internet site, traveling to another and resuming it there. To achieve this, the authors use VMWare and distributed file systems (NFS). All virtual machines are stored on a shared folder, which itself is shared with all participating machines. Upon suspension, the machine is shut down and saved on the disk. This disk can now be used to resume the machine on a remote destination. While this scenario is feasible for closed environments, it is not feasible for grid computing. Due to the fact that the disk image could be accessed by others, this could lead to a potential information leak. The authors also present some thoughts on further improvement, especially in the area of image deployment. Their thoughts served as an inspiration for the work done in this thesis.

Wolinsky et al. [171] describe a system of virtual machine-based sandboxes deployed in wide-area overlays of virtual workstations (WOWs). They feature a DHCP-based virtual IP address allocation, a self-configured virtual network supporting peer-to-peer NAT traversal, stacked file systems, IPSec-based host authentication, and end-to-end encryption of communication channels. The authors assume that almost all of the work done in the area of disk image distribution has been performed in conjunction with virtual machine migration. This means that an application or the operating system as a whole is migrated over a network. All important operating system aspects (i.e., saving the state of the CPU, network, memory, etc.) are covered by migration. Thus, distributing the disk image over the network is only part of a complex procedure and not covered in detail.

5.2.3 Design

Based on the related work presented in the last section, the following requirements for a virtualized grid management software can be derived:

- It is important to chose a mature virtualization hypervisor. Since operating system virtualization technology is used to achieve isolation between jobs on the same node, it has to be known as fool proof. Furthermore, as performance is important for grid computing, it is not an option to use non-accelerated solutions. Non-accelerated means that there is operating system kernel support for, e.g., fast memory and I/O access.

- Since the setting for nearly all software developed during the course of this thesis is the German national D-Grid, a number of requirements have to be fulfilled. Among others, this includes effortless interaction with the installed grid middleware, such as the Globus toolkit. Implementing one's own client to submit (grid) jobs is not acceptable, as it could lead to confusion on part of the user.

- While implementing a fully-featured scheduler capable of virtualization is advantageous because there is no hassle in dealing with foreign code and concentrating on the work of virtualization, it has the disadvantage that implementing a scheduling logic that supports advanced features like node reservation or backfilling is a very demanding task and could shift the focus away from the virtualization and security work. Thus, a grid virtualization solution should utilize the decisions of a scheduler that has already been installed.

- In order to boot, every non-diskless virtual machine needs a disk image (aka *virtual machine disk image*) that contains the root file system. Thus, the approach has to make sure that the disk image is distributed to a node prior to the actual boot process. Apart from the time of raw disk image distribution, the network load caused by the distribution process itself is a critical factor. A simple and incomplete distribution method could lead to significant traffic on the core network components, possibly leading to long-lasting transfers, congestion or, in the worst case, packet loss.

5.2.3.1 Image Creation Station

Using a virtualized grid creates the need for a software that provides virtual machine images on demand. While the software that will be presented in the following can use virtual machine images from most image creation software, it is mostly used together with the Image Creation Station (ICS). It is a software developed at the Distributed Systems Group at the University of Marburg, mainly by Niels Fallenbeck. For further information the reader is referred to the following papers: [126, 39].

Motivation

One of the biggest changes for on-demand grid computing compared to traditional grid computing is the requirement that users must be able to install custom software with root privileges autonomously (and preferably without the hassle of a job-based installation procedure). To satisfy this requirement, a software installation process based on virtualization technology is introduced. A user receives a private virtual environment which looks and behaves exactly like a node of the grid to be used. The user has root access and can install software in the same way as software is installed on a local machine. This functionality is provided by an Image Creation Station (ICS) developed for this purpose.

Virtual Machine Creation

The ICS consists of two parts: a front end and a back end. The front end is a website that allows the user to define some basic parameters for the virtual machine. The website is accessed in a protected manner using a X.509 user certificate. The identity of the X.509 certificate is also used to imprint the created virtual machine to the user. The configuration options a user has include: which architecture the image should use (32 or 64bit) and how big the virtual machine's disk image should be and what name should be used to identify the image (a user can have several images at the same time).

Once the user has selected the required options, an image can be created and then booted. Once the image is finished, it is booted using a dynamic IP address. Since this takes a couple of minutes, a notification email is sent containing the dynamically chosen location of the image and the login information. The ICS accepts a GPG public key with which the email can be protected. If a Globus installation is added to the nodes, the same X.509 certificate used for the website can be used to log onto the image. Alternatively, a SSH public key can be passed to the ICS during the image creation process, and the ICS will configure the image to accept SSH login authentication for the corresponding private key.

Once the user is logged in, software can be installed with root privileges in the traditional way, which greatly eases the installation process compared to the traditional grid installation techniques. A user can make any modifications to the operating system configuration and installation, any required shared libraries and third-party software. This also paves the way for more fine grained service-oriented applications, since a service hosting environment can be installed on the worker nodes without endangering other users. Figure 5.1 shows the ICS front end.

A user can create several (different) images giving each image a separate name. The ICS deploys the images to the cluster and provides the image-to-user-mapping which is later used by the XGE to select the correct virtual machine.

5.2.3.2 Architecture

A new software for managing virtual machines in grids was designed derived from the requirements: the XGE Version 2. The aim of the first version, also developed at the University of Marburg back in 2006 [38], was to interrupt long-running serial compute jobs in favor to massively parallel jobs. The version described below shares, besides the name, no components with the old version.

The XGE is divided into several parts, which are all independent threads ensuring

5.2. Virtualized Grid Computing

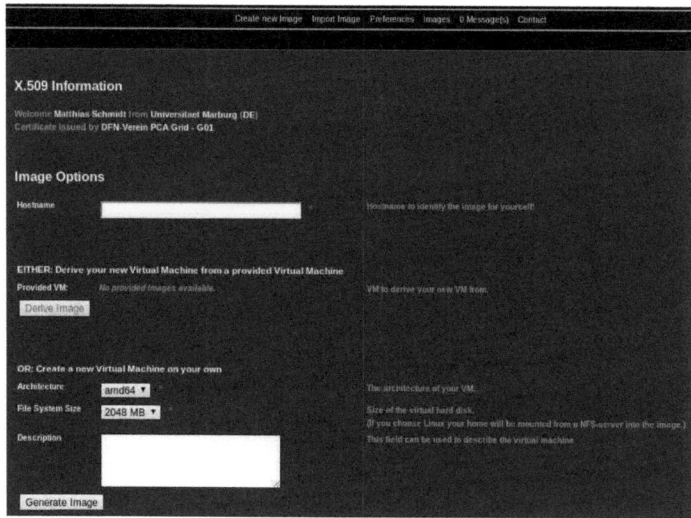

Figure 5.1: Image Creation Station

maximum concurrent operation. This partitioning was an early decision in the design process as deployment and execution speeds are important. If the initial time for the stated two processes take too long, an impatient user could abort the operation entirely. This, in turn, leads to increased load on all resources, as all of the users' virtual machines would need to be stopped and the nodes would need to be brought back into a consistent state. Nevertheless, the highly multi-threaded architecture needs proper synchronization to avoid leaving the system in an inconsistent state.

The architecture is shown in Figure 5.2. A new request is submitted by either a local scheduler or directly by a user. Depending on the submitter, another XGE module is in charge: either the *Watchdog* or the *ConnectionHandler* (see Section 5.2.3.3). A number of different modules manage the jobs: *Job*, *JobManager* and *JobServer* (see Section 5.2.3.4). All operations related to virtualization are handled by the *JobVMManager*, the *VNodesManager* and the *Backend* (see Section 5.2.3.5). The *DBManager* is connected to a database and is queried by nearly all modules (see Section 5.2.3.5). Disk image distribution is operated by the *Distribution* module, the *ImageManager* and two remote components installed on each node, *LXGEd* and the *Image Daemon* (see Section 5.2.3.6).

Chapter 5. Network Security

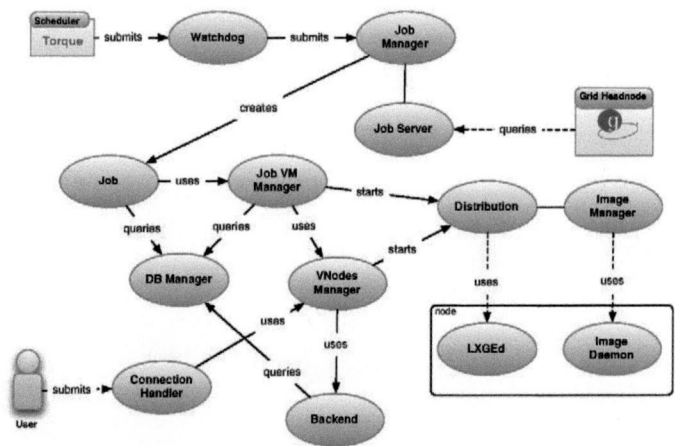

Figure 5.2: The architecture of the XGE. The figure shows all modules and their relationship to each other.

5.2.3.3 Hybrid Mode of Operation

The XGE supports a hybrid model of operation that is driven by the user or the scheduler. While the former is especially useful for creating virtual clusters on-demand, the latter is compatible with an existing scheduler (e.g., Torque or the Sun Grid Engine).

Placeholder Virtual Machines

To make the XGE transparent to a scheduler, the scheduler should not realize that it is operating on virtual machines, as it would then see nodes appearing and disappearing. This would break the scheduler's ability to properly schedule jobs because the nodes allocated to the job queues are constantly changing (when nodes disappear for a while, the scheduler believes the nodes have crashed and cannot be used for further jobs; thus, it reschedules everything). To prevent this from happening, the XGE uses placeholder virtual machines that are registered with the job queues. Every placeholder virtual machine contains a scheduler daemon (e.g., Torque's pbs_mom or SGE's sgeexecd) which lets the scheduler know about a number of nodes and makes scheduling decisions. When a job is scheduled, the placeholder virtual machine exchanged with the user virtual machine transparently, so that the scheduler does not notice any change.

Scheduler Interface

The following execution flow is performed when a job is submitted to the scheduling system: (1) A job is submitted to the scheduler. (2) Based on its scheduling configuration and the given constraints (required number of CPUs, RAM, etc.), the scheduler decides on which nodes the job will be executed. (3) Before the scheduler notifies the execution daemons on the chosen nodes, it is interrupted and hands control over to the XGE. (4) The XGE shuts down all placeholder virtual machines on the chosen hosts and starts the users' own virtual machines. (5) When all virtual machines are up and running, the XGE runs the user specific firewall configuration scripts and then hands back the control to the scheduler. (6) The scheduler continues as normal and executes the job. (7) After execution, a pre-defined epilogue script is called, which activates the cleanup procedure of the XGE. (8) All virtual machines belonging to the job are shut down, and the XGE boots up the placeholder virtual machines. When all placeholder virtual machines are back, the control is passed back to the epilogue script, which terminates itself.

To fulfill the steps described above, the XGE needs requires some additional information:

- The most important information is a list of virtual machines chosen for job execution.

- For proper identification and for account and billing purposes, the user name is also needed. If an ID is provided, the XGE uses that ID for outside communication. In general, most schedulers use their own unique naming scheme for jobs, as does the XGE. Since a mapping between the scheduler's ID and the XGE's own ID is useful for communication with third-party software (e.g., the installed grid middleware), an internal mapping between both is generated and maintained.

- If the submitter specified some kind of resource requirements (number of virtual CPUs, amount of virtual memory, number of network interfaces, etc.), this information is given to the XGE.

- By default, the XGE is bound to one of the scheduler's dedicated queues. This ensures that only jobs that are ready for virtualization are processed by the XGE. Furthermore, it allows the administrator of a grid site to run virtualized and non-virtualized jobs simultaneously.

- The XGE also saves any names that the scheduler provides for jobs, which may or may not be the same as their IDs.

The scheduler writes all of the information to a plain text once it is finished with its scheduling decision. This text file is stored in a subdirectory, known to both the scheduler and the XGE. Listing 5.1 shows a job description file generated by Torque.

```
1 [job]
2 name = 162.int12909
3 id = 162.int12909
4 queue = vqueue
5 script = testjob.sh
6 user = matthias
7 memory = 1024
8 hosts = node001c0 node002c3 node002c4
```

Listing 5.1: Job description file as provided by a scheduler

This file is read by the *Watchdog* daemon, which continuously monitors the shared job directory. Once it finds a new entry, it checks if the job is already known. This might be the case if the XGE was restarted (either deliberately or because it crashed). If the job is already known, the *Watchdog* ignores it. Otherwise a new *Job* object is created and registered with the *JobManager*, and further processing takes place. It also extracts the aforementioned information and saves it into the job's attributes.

User Interface

While the Watchdog communicates with the scheduler, the *ConnectionHandler* communicates with the user's client. It is a separate thread within the XGE and hosts a XML-RPC server. Hence, all clients have to speak XML-RPC and implement the interface. As direct requests do not belong to a job, there is no need to register a job object in the *JobManager*. The *ConnectionHandler* directly uses the functions provided by the *VNodesManager*, which will be explained later.

5.2.3.4 Job Management

As already mentioned, the *Watchdog* registers new jobs with the *JobManager*. A job is precisely described by a set of attributes with the values originating from the scheduler. Besides the provided values, there are attributes specific to the XGE:

5.2. Virtualized Grid Computing

- Every job is identified by a Universally Unique Identifier (UUID) [81]. This guarantees unique identification during runtime. Even after the runtime, the ID stays unique, as a timestamp is used during the generation process.
- A creation and a completion timestamp, which can be used for account and billing.

While the *JobManager* handles jobs, the *JobServer* module handles possible machine-to-machine communication. Thus, it runs as a separate thread and is also able to spawn new worker threads on-demand. Furthermore, it is equipped with a network interface which listens on a predefined TCP port. The decision to enhance the *JobManager* with the *JobServer* was due to the fact that it knows everything another machine would like to know and it is independent from the remaining system. Even if malicious network packets crash the *JobServer*, the core system that deals with job handling could still work and could finish all operations until the *JobServer* is restored.

To provide a unique interface to either clients and machines, all network communication is handled in XML. A client sends a request to the interface and the XGE sends the correct answer or an error. The possible queries from the client to the job manager range from simple status calls about a certain job to complex status reports, which include detailed information about, e.g., the number of virtual CPUs, several timestamps needed for accounting and billing, the disk space used and network traffic statistics of all virtual machines, and the CPU time consumed. To handle multi-site applications across network boundaries, a permanent communication channel between all running XGEs is needed, which is established between the respective *JobServer* modules. The purpose of the channel is to exchange information that needs to be present on all of the XGEs involved. Strong cryptography and authentication ensures that this information stays confidential and cannot be intercepted by malicious entities.

5.2.3.5 Virtual Machine Management

The virtual machine management part of the XGE is completely separate from the job management part. It does not know anything about jobs or how to create, manage or delete them. It operates with the *Backend* on a lower level and provides a public interface. This interface is used by the job management and the *ConnectionHandler*.

Every single virtual machine is described by an object called VM. It has a number of attributes that save information about the name of the virtual machine, the path to the disk image, the amount of virtual memory, the number of virtual CPUs, the MAC address and multiple fields for consumed resources (e.g., CPU time

Chapter 5. Network Security

used and transferred network packets). If a virtual machine belongs to a job, its VM object is created by the *JobVMManager*; otherwise the *ConnectionHandler* creates it.

Core Components

The *VNodesManager* is the core component responsible for virtual machine management. By using the *Backend* module interface, it is able to convey hypervisor operations such as boot, shutdown, destroy and migrate virtual machines.

On the initial start-up, the *VNodesManager* has to connect to the aforementioned *Backend*, which itself is connected to all nodes, to gather information about virtual machines that are already running on the system. If there were machines that the XGE was not aware of, they could be destroyed. This would be especially fatal if these were regular machines and not placeholders. The state of all running machines is saved into the internal database.

Figure 5.3 shows a simplified view of the stacked architecture that is involved in virtual machine operations. The virtual machine, represented by a VM object, is processed by the *VNodesManager*, which itself uses an interface provided by the *Backend* module. Interaction with the hypervisor occurs through the *libvirt* library. Remote communication between nodes occurs through the libvirt daemon, which runs on all nodes. This daemon uses the local hypervisor's operations to start, stop, etc. virtual machines.

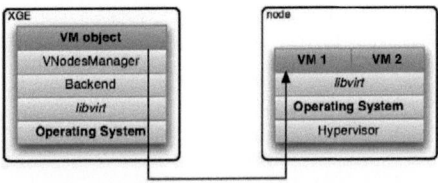

Figure 5.3: Stacked architecture for virtual machine handling

Start Virtual Machines

The last step prior to job execution is to boot all virtual machines that belong to the users job. As this process consumes a certain amount of time (between 5-30 seconds depending on the node's performance), it is executed for all nodes simultaneously. Synchronization ensures that neither the scheduler nor the user

5.2. Virtualized Grid Computing

is triggered until all virtual machines are properly booted. An early notification could let the originator execute an application on a non-existent virtual machine. Synchronization happens by polling the state of the virtual machine: if the machine is either running or blocked, it is alive. At first, checking for a blocked state seems cumbersome; however, that is how Xen, for example, denotes that a virtual machine is running.

If the XGE operates in scheduler mode, it has to shutdown a running placeholder machine first. Since the scheduler is interrupted during the XGE's operations, it will not notice that the placeholder is exchanged with the user's real machine. Shutting down a great number of placeholder machines could take some time and hence slow down the job workflow. Even worse, if the shutdown process (and the following start-up process) takes too long, the scheduler assumes that the job submission failed and cancels the job. That works even though the scheduler is interrupted because the monitoring logic runs in a separate thread. Therefore, the placeholder images are designed for minimalistic virtual machines, consisting only of a kernel, an initial ramdisk, and the scheduler's execution daemon (more details in Section 5.2.4.7 on page 121). Using such an embedded combination has the advantage that the whole operating system is stored on a memory disk and not on the hard disk. Accordingly, the XGE can destroy (i.e., pull the plug) the placeholder, which takes only a fraction of a second.

Once the placeholder is gone, the user's virtual machine begins the boot process. Low level operations are carried out by the *Backend* via the *libvirt*. If the boot process fails, the XGE aborts the process and reports an error back to the requester. Now, it is important to bring the system back to a consistent state. Since the placeholder is down, the scheduler's execution daemon is also down. After a timeout, the scheduler believes that the node has crashed and thus reschedules everything. In order to avoid this situation, the XGE has to restore the placeholder.

Once a virtual machine is booted, it automatically retrieves an IP address from a DHCP server. Due to a static mapping between IP and MAC addresses, it is easily possible for an administrator to identify a running virtual machine. This could come in handy if an unexpected error occurs or if there are suspicious packets on the network. The IP address contains the number of worker nodes as well as the CPU core on which the machine is running. The same information is encoded into the MAC address. A sample address for a virtual machine could be 172.16.8.110 with the MAC 1A:00:00:00:08:6E. The range of the network here is 172.16.0.0/16 where the third byte encodes the CPU core and the fourth byte, the number of the worker node. Since the local nodes have four CPU cores, the network consists of four subnets (172.16.8.0/24 through 172.16.11.0/24). The example would be decoded to a machine running on the first CPU core on node 110.

Stop Virtual Machines

Shutting down a virtual machine is similar to the process of starting it up, only in reversed order. Once a shutdown request is requested either by the user or the scheduler, the XGE has to check if there really is a machine running. In general, this check is always positive, but due to administrators actions or system failures, it could be negative. If there is no machine running, the XGE reports a warning and skips further actions. In order to restore a consistent state, the XGE has to restart a placeholder. However, this only occurs when there is a scheduler involved, as starting a placeholder in a non-scheduler driven environment could lead to occupied nodes.

Prior to the actual shutdown, all information gathered during the virtual machine's lifetime is written into the database. Among others, this includes CPU time consumed, maximum amount of virtual memory used and network traffic statistics. All of this information is held by the hypervisor during runtime and disappears after shutdown; hence, they have to be copied to persistent storage for accounting and billing purposes.

Virtual Machine Migration

In virtualized grid computing environments where many virtual machines run dynamically (i.e. they are created and destroyed over time) on clusters of physical hosts, the possibility of migrating virtual machines between differed hosts is an essential feature. It enables dynamic load balancing, energy efficient machine utilization, and eases maintenance. An important property of the employed migration mechanism is transparency for the virtual machines: a user should not notice that his or her virtual machine is being migrated, and the virtual machine's operation should continue seamlessly during the migration process.

Most current live migration implementations (e.g., the Xen migration facility) do not take disk storage (including swap space on a disk) into account. Disk storage is assumed to be located on a shared medium that can be accessed by both the source and the destination host involved in a live migration.

This leads to several problems:

- Disk access over a network always introduces a decrease in performance compared to local disk access.

- The virtual machine depends on a shared storage facility and a functioning network connection to work properly.

5.2. Virtualized Grid Computing

- Each virtual machine instance needs its own working copy of a disk image due to local modifications, although in a virtualized grid environment many virtual machines might share the same basic image.

A solution that is better suited to the requirements of a virtualized grid environment should allow a virtual machine to access its disk storage locally during normal operation. This implies that a live storage migration that only affects the virtual machine performance negatively during a migration process is needed in addition to the migration of main memory and CPU state. Furthermore, it is desirable to share basic disk images between virtual machines to reduce the number of copies.

The following subsection describes the approach built into the XGE to satisfy the the requirements stated above.

Usually, each computing node needs persistent storage to operate, containing user data, a custom software stack, etc. All of the data written during a virtual machine's lifetime in a virtualized grid environment is temporary because it is disregarded after shutdown. Thus, the virtual machine's disk space is divided into two parts: a basic part containing the base operating system and a writable part containing all new data written during virtual machine operation. Live migration is simplified if the base part is never altered, i.e. it can be copied to the destination host without losing any updates issued by the virtual machine during migration; only the writable part has to be considered.

However, a write operation not only writes new data to a disk but might also modify or delete existing data from the basic part. For example, the file /etc/mtab will be altered upon each mount call. Hence, the two parts need to be merged in some way. These requirements are met perfectly by a union file system, as implemented, for example, by *aufs* or *unionfs* (which has been deprecated). Previous work [121] showed that a union file system can be used as a root file system.

There are several possible ways to create a layered root file system:

- The simplest way is to use a temporary in-memory file system (tmpfs) as a writable layer (see Figure 5.4(a)). The main advantage of this approach is that the setup is transparent to live migration: since all data resides in main memory, it is transferred to the destination host during the normal memory copy process without taking any special measures. A positive side effect from the virtual machine's point of view is the increased I/O performance for disk accesses. For this setup to work properly, a sufficiently large amount of RAM needs to be allocated to the virtual machine. However, there are two kinds of workloads that are not suited for this approach: memory intensive workloads requiring a very large amount of RAM and workloads that write a great deal of data to a disk (and possibly never - or at least only rarely occasions - access it again).

- Another possibility is to use a real disk image as a writable layer (see Figure 5.4(b)). It is better suited for workloads that produce a great deal of disk output. Whatever is written to the disk does not clutter up the main memory.

- A hybrid approach is a further possibility: instead of using a disk image as a writable layer, a large tmpfs is provided in conjunction with a large swap partition (that resides on disk). Figure 5.4(c) illustrates the resulting setup. This has the advantage of supporting workloads that use a great deal of memory and disk-intensive capabilities. All data written to the writable layer and not accessed again for some time will be swapped out to a disk; thus, the main memory does not fill up with unused file system content.

The challenge with the last two approaches is that they are not transparent to live migration. Current virtual machine hypervisor implementations like Xen do not support live migration of virtual machines with local persistent storage but assume shared storage (including any swap space) that is accessible from both the source and the destination host. However, for performance reasons, it is desirable that a virtual machine has local access to its disk images. Hence, a mechanism is needed to transfer the disk images seamlessly to a new host, as presented below.

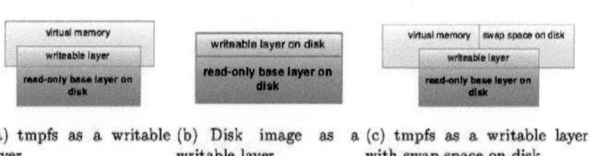

(a) tmpfs as a writable layer (b) Disk image as a writable layer (c) tmpfs as a writable layer with swap space on disk

Figure 5.4: Multilayer Disk Images

Disk Image Synchronization

Using local persistent storage poses some challenges when performing live migration of virtual machines. The main problem involves transferring a consistent disk state to the destination host while the virtual machine keeps running and thus is altering the disk state. Hence, the task is divided into two parts: copying the data and tracking changes (and somehow sending them to the destination host).

5.2. Virtualized Grid Computing

The proposed synchronization mechanism works as follows: at the beginning of the migration process, the source host starts to copy the disk image to the destination. At the same time, all subsequent disk writes from the virtual machine to be migrated are trapped and issued synchronously to the local and the remote disk image. Synchronously means that the acknowledgment of the disk write is delayed until the remote host has confirmed it. Once the background copy operation is finished, the normal live migration process begins; during the entire live migration process, the two disk images operate in the synchronized mode. After the virtual machine is resumed on the destination host, the disk images are decoupled, which means they are no longer dependent on the source host.

To perform the actual synchronization, the DRBD [86] kernel module is used; it is integrated into the mainline Linux kernel since release 2.6.33. DRBD is designed for high availability clusters that mirror a disk from the primary host to a secondary backup host and thus act as a network-based RAID-1. Figure 5.5 shows the design of the module. It presents itself to the kernel as a disk driver and hence allows a maximum of flexibility: it does not pose restrictions on the file system used above or on the underlying disk driver managing the actual disk accesses. And it is transparent to the kernel block device facilities, which means that buffering and disk scheduling are left to the kernel as usual. The module can operate in two modes: standalone and synchronized. In standalone mode, all disk accesses are simply passed to the underlying disk driver. In synchronized mode, disk writes are both passed to the underlying disk driver and sent to the backup machine via a TCP connection. Disk reads are served locally.

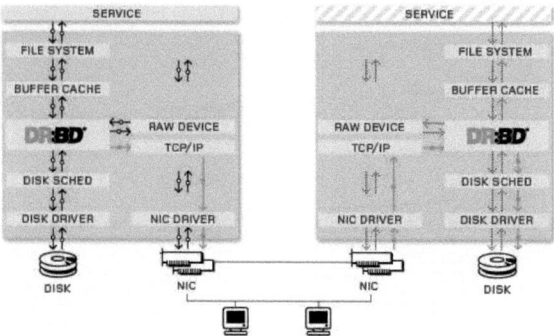

Figure 5.5: DRBD module overview. Source: [86]

Although designed for a high availability setup where disks are mirrored across the network during normal operation, the DRBD module can be integrated into the live migration process for migrating local persistent storage. The source host plays the role of the primary server, and the destination host plays the role of the secondary server. During normal operation, the source host runs in standalone mode; hence writes are performed only on its local disk, and there is no dependence on other hosts. During live migration, the DRBD driver is put into synchronized mode, which causes all disk writes to be performed synchronously on both hosts while the entire disk is synchronized in the background. Once the migration is finished and the virtual machine is resumed on the destination host, the DRBD driver on the destination host is put into standalone mode and the source host is disconnected, removing all dependencies between the two physical hosts.

The properties of this approach are as follows:

- There is nearly no performance overhead during normal operation of a virtual machine because all disk writes are performed locally.

- The solution is reliable. If a migration fails, the virtual machine can keep running on the source host. Due to the synchronous writes on both hosts, the virtual machine has a consistent disk state on the destination host after a successful migration.

- There are no residual dependencies. Once the virtual machine is resumed on the destination host, no dependency on the source hosts remains. In particular, no disk writes are ever issued on an inconsistent disk (such as, for example, in the approach of Luo et al. [87]).

- The total migration time is increased compared to a memory-only migration. The additional time grows linearly with disk size. The total migration time can be reduced as follows:
  - If a layered files system is used (as described above), the size of the writable layer can be kept small, reducing the amount of data to synchronize. The read-only layer can be fetched from a separate image pool simultaneously or might even already be cached at the destination host so that no extra copy process is needed.
  - DRBD allows for checksum-based synchronization, which means that only blocks that differ on source and destination are transferred. If sparse image files are used on both sides, all unused blocks are implicitly zero-filled and are hence identical on both sides, reducing the total amount of data to copy.

- Background disk synchronization and the transfer of the main memory are performed sequentially, so that they do not affect each other in a counterproductive way. Since both tasks generate network traffic, the memory

5.2. Virtualized Grid Computing

dirtying rate would exceed the transfer rate (due to the parallel disk synchronization) much faster, resulting in the abort of the iterative copy phase and thus a longer downtime of the virtual machine. Furthermore, disk synchronization usually takes much longer than copying the memory; hence, an exact timing would be difficult.

- No additional virtual machine downtime is introduced because the virtual machine can be resumed without any further delay once the live migration process of the virtualization system in use has finished. In contrast, the approach of Bradford et al. [12] delays all disk I/O of the virtual machine until the remaining writes are applied to the disk on the destination host. This can cause an additional delay for write-intensive workloads.

- Write-intensive workloads are implicitly throttled by the synchronous nature of the disk writes, such that the disk write rate never exceeds the network transfer rate, which would render any disk synchronization mechanism useless. Bradford et al. [12] employ explicit write throttling whenever the write rate exceeds a predefined threshold. Luo et al. [87] actively stop their pre-copy phase if the disk dirty rate is higher than the transfer rate, resulting in a much longer post-copy phase where the destination host still depends on the source host and the virtual machine runs with decreased performance.

- The amount of bandwidth consumed by background synchronization can be dynamically configured in the DRBD driver. This enables the administrator to find an appropriate trade-off between total migration time and performance degradation of the virtual machine due to high network consumption.

- Synchronization is completely transparent to the running virtual machine.

- The approach is independent of a special virtualization environment; thus, it can be used with any hypervisor that supports live migration.

Backend

All low level virtual machine operations in the XGE are done using an interface provided by the *Backend* module, which itself is connected to the *libvirt* library.

On initial startup, connections to the *libvirt* daemons running on all nodes are opened. These connections are simple TCP connections, either encrypted, using SSH [30] or TLS [31], or unencrypted. By default, the XGE uses SSH. In order to send commands to remote machines, the XGE instructs *libvirt* to forward them to the daemons. There is only one connection per node, which will be closed upon shutdown to avoid zombie processes and connections.

The interface provided by the *Backend* offers functions to e.g. start, stop and migrate virtual machines. In order to avoid errors, there is always a requirements check prior to the actual *libvirt* call. Due to its simple design, this module can easily be extended with more functionality.

Database

Persistent storage within the XGE is realized using a database. In order to be independent of a specific Database Management System (DBMS) such as MySQL [98] or PostgreSQL [102], SQLite [139] is used. SQLite is a small, lightweight database that stores all databases in a binary-encoded text file.

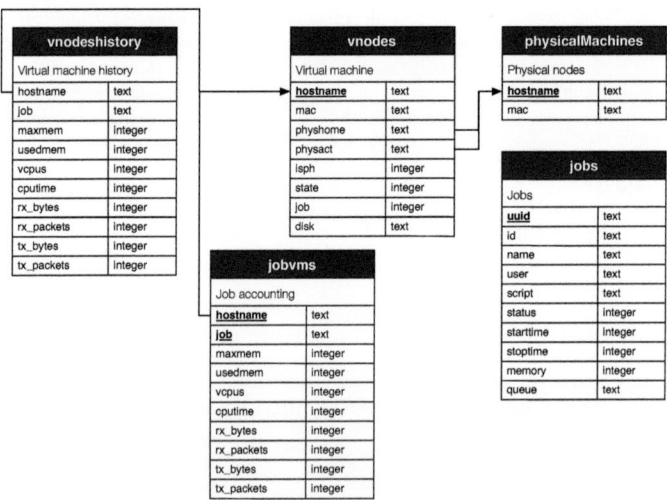

Figure 5.6: Database tables

Figure 5.6 shows all database tables and connections. The primary table is the *vnodes* table that contains information about each virtual machine present in the system including the unique host name (the primary key). Among other entries, it also contains the home's host name and the actual node. Here, home node

5.2. Virtualized Grid Computing

means the node where the virtual machine was started for the first time. Keeping this host name is important as the machine could be migrated to another node. In order to start a placeholder machine after shutdown, the XGE has to know the original host name. The actual host name is changed every time a machine is migrated. Both fields refer to the *physicalMachines* table that contains the unique host name; hence, it is the primary key for all nodes, including their MAC address.

Jobs are saved into the *jobs* table, which contains identification and various statistical fields. Since every job has to be unique within the system, the *uuid* field is used as primary key. In order to save accounting information, a *jobvms* table exists. As soon as a job is finished this table is filled with the consolidated values from a virtual machine that belongs to it. Thus, the host and the job name are the primary keys. The *vnodeshistory* table is temporary and contains account information about a particular virtual machine. It is filled every time a machine is migrated or shut down. The contents of this table are used to assemble the final accounting report.

All database operations are handled by the *DBManager* module. It creates the whole database, including the table layout on the first startup, and offers an interface to other modules to query, update or delete database values.

5.2.3.6 Disk Image Distribution

Prior to being able to boot the virtual machines, the (virtual machine) disk images need to be present on the machines. This section presents several methods for distributing virtual machine images from one node with the source of a set of selected nodes as the destination.

Network File System

The traditional way to distribute a number of disk images in a virtualized grid site would be to use the Network File System (NFS) [14]. NFS is well-established and provides a simple way, for both the administrator as well as the user, to make files available remotely. The central NFS server stores the disk images and the nodes retrieve copies on-demand. This leads to multiple point-to-point transfers. Furthermore, when multi-gigabyte files are accessed by a large number of nodes simultaneously, NFS shows erratic behavior. This leads to a number of crashes during tests. To avoid this behavior, the nodes would need to synchronize their transfers, so as not to interfere with each other. Further common problems with NFS such as stale NFS file handles (which can, for instance, be caused by a re-exportation of the NFS exports), can lead to stalling virtual machines or even nodes. Finally, NFS is not well suited for use in a multi-site computing scenario. Exporting NFS outside a local network is complicated and is difficult to secure. For these reasons, a simple unicast deployment algorithm was developed to serve as a benchmark instead of NFS.

Unicast Distribution

A straightforward method for distributing virtual machine images is sequentially copying them to the destination nodes. The benefits of this method are that it is fairly simple to understand and implement and it works in multi-site scenarios; however, its drawbacks include long transfer times and network congestion.

Binary Tree Distribution

To avoid network congestion and to allow parallel transfers, a binary tree-based distribution method can used. In this method, all computing nodes are arranged in a balanced binary tree with the source node as its root (see Figure 5.7). The balanced tree property guarantees that the depth of the leaves differs by at most by one. Since a balanced tree has a height of $log_2(n)$ with n being the number of nodes, the transmission time is $O(t \cdot log_2 n)$, where t is the time needed to transfer a virtual machine image from source to destination.

All transfers are synchronized to avoid that a transfer on a child node starts before the data from the parent is available. Correct synchronization can be achieved by either synchronizing every level of the tree or by synchronizing every node. Whereas the first method is easier to implement, the second method guarantees a higher throughput and thus lower transmission times.

This method reduces the time needed to transfer a virtual disk image to all nodes as compared to the unicast distribution method. The method can be used for multi-site computing if either all nodes are located inside the same subnet (e.g., if two remote sites are connected with a Virtual Private Network (VPN) or if the nodes have public IP addresses ([2]).

The binary tree is in fact a Fibonacci tree. A special feature of the Fibonacci tree is that it is rebalanced using rotations after insertions or deletions. Thus, if the distribution of a virtual machine image is interrupted due to a node failure, the tree needs to be rebalanced to guarantee a seamless transfer. Besides rebalancing, there are some further actions involved to resume the transfer to all nodes that are now rebalanced. It is possible for a node to have a different parent after re-balancing, so the transmission for that node must be restarted. The child

5.2. Virtualized Grid Computing

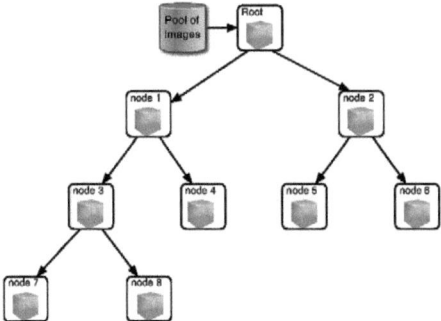

Figure 5.7: Binary tree distribution

nodes of that node stall automatically until they have sufficient data to continue the transmission.

Peer-to-Peer Distribution

Another method is to use peer-to-peer (P2P) technologies for disk image transfer. The BitTorrent protocol [10] was chosen. Bram Cohen designed the protocol in April 2001 and released a first implementation on 2 July 2001. The protocol allows users to distribute large amounts of data between multiple, network-connected machines without congesting the network compared to standard file distribution.

BitTorrent was designed as a protocol for fast, efficient and decentralized distribution of files over a network. Every recipient downloading a file supplies this file (or at least parts of it) to newer recipients also downloading the file. This reduces the overall costs in terms of network traffic, hardware costs and overall time needed to download the whole file.

The node hosting the source file starts a *tracker* that coordinates the file's distribution. Furthermore, a file (a so-called *torrent file*) containing meta-data about the source file tracker's (URL) is generated and must be distributed to all clients (either active with a push mechanism or passive with all clients downloading the torrent file from a web server). Clients, also called *peers*, connect to the tracker that tells them from which other peers pieces of the file are available for download. A peer that shares parts or the entire file is called a *seeder*. Using this technique, sharing files between multiple peers benefits from high speed downloads and reduced transmission times compared to other techniques. An overview of all described components is shown in Figure 5.8.

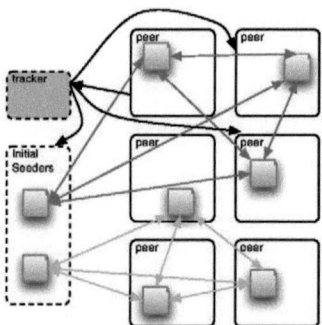

Figure 5.8: Distributed file sharing between multiple peers including a tracker

To distributed data over BitTorrent the seeder has to generate a *torrent file* containing meta-data information about the files to be shared and about one or more *trackers*. The file contains, among other entries, the following information [23]:

- The URL of the tracker
- The *suggested name* for the file
- The *piece length*. All files are split into fixed-size pieces which are all the same length, except for the last on which might be truncated. Most commonly its 256 KB.
- The *length* of the file.

The tracker coordinates the file's distribution. New peers connect to the tracker which informs them about all other peers which store parts of the requested file. Thus a client requesting a file acts simultaneously as a consumer and as a seeder (peer-to-peer). This reduces the load on a single server as its equally distributed after a certain time and it reduces the overall download time.

Due to its distributed nature, BitTorrent perfectly fulfills the needs of multi-site computing. It can be used to distribute disk images between two dedicated virtual machine image pool nodes on remote sites if the networks where the actual compute nodes reside are private or not connected in a VPN. The distribution from the pool node to the compute nodes can also be accomplished by BitTorrent or another suitable protocol. If the network setup permits it, a direct virtual machine image transfer to the compute nodes is desired to save additional local distribution time on each site.

To distribute a virtual machine image to the compute nodes, a torrent file containing the URL of the tracker needs to be generated. The tracker in this case is the source node hosting the disk images. Furthermore, a seeder for the disk image needs to be started on the source node. To begin with the actual distribution process, BitTorrent clients are started remotely on all compute nodes. They connect to the tracker, load and seed the virtual machine image immediately. After the process is finished, all nodes carry the complete and correct virtual machine image. The distribution of two virtual machine images is illustrated in Figure 5.9.

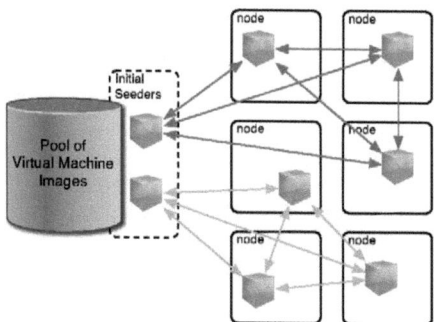

Figure 5.9: Distribution of two disk images via BitTorrent

Multicast

The distribution of virtual machine images via multicast is the most efficient method in the local area network environment. The design of the multicast module can be kept simple if no ordering guarantees are given by the master node. Ensuring reliability in this case is delegated to both the sender and the receivers. The former can handle data reliability by tuning either the number of redundant packets (increasing the CPU load) or by tuning the stripe size, i.e., the number of packets sent in a block (this could decrease the CPU load but increase the loss of data). IP-based multicast can also be used to transfer the data. It is supported by most networking hardware out of the box. Modern hardware can handle multicast transfers even better, i.e. it is possible to distribute the multicast packets only over selected links according to their multicast group membership. This is accomplished if the switches support IGMP *Snooping* or the *Cisco Group Management Protocol* (CGMP). The switches can inspect the Internet Group Management Protocol (IGMP) packets and adjust their switching tables accordingly. This transfer method is likely to be scalable to large-scale installations, e.g. the ones used by modern infrastructure providers, since the hardware used is capable of scaling to thousands of hosts and multicast groups.

Multi-Site Transfer

Although multicast is an ideal method for transferring data within a local area network, it is not the preferred method for transferring data over network boundaries since routing multicast packets between networks might require special protocol support at the network core, such as the Distance Vector Multicast Routing Protocol (DVMRP). Furthermore, it could be possible that data is shared between two private, physically separated desktop grids or clouds within the same organization, but the network policy forbids that data is transferred via multicast over the network backbone connecting the two.

It is also possible to use a combination of two methods when performing multi-site computing. If the nodes in a private site are not directly accessible because they do not have public IP addresses, it is not possible to use e.g. BitTorrent directly. Here, it is possible to transfer the disk images or only selected layers to publicly accessible pool nodes to cache the data there and transfer it locally via multicast afterwards.

Encrypted vs. Unencrypted Transfer

If private data (whether it is sensitive data or not) is transferred over an insecure link or over network boundaries, it should be encrypted. However, encryption involves additional costs: the cryptographic computations produce CPU load on both the sender and receiver, and the average transfer rate is reduced. Unencrypted transfers are favorable if the data itself is public and nobody cares if it is stolen. Furthermore, if the network is isolated from the outside world (which is common in high performance computing setups today), the increased transfer rate is a benefit compared to an encrypted transfer.

5.2. Virtualized Grid Computing

Avoiding Retransmission Overhead

To avoid the retransmission of a virtual machine image that is already present and to avoid the need for huge amounts of disk space at the destination nodes, an approach based on copy-on-write (COW) layers is proposed. A layered file system is a virtual file system built from more than one individual file system (layer) using a COW solution like UnionFS [158]. A virtual machine image is realized by a COW virtual disk consisting of three or more layers. At first, only a *base layer* is present. This layer contains a complete installation of a Linux operating system. On top of the base layer, a *site layer* is placed. It contains all modifications needed to run this virtual machine image on a particular site, such as a local or a remote site like Amazon's EC2 service. Special configuration information depending on the infrastructure, as in LDAP settings, name servers, and NFS server, are stored in the site layer. The third layer is the *user layer* that contains all modifications made by the user. The size of this layer ranges from small (only a basic software stack with special libraries and e.g. MPI programs is installed) to very large (a complex, proprietary application with a license server is installed).

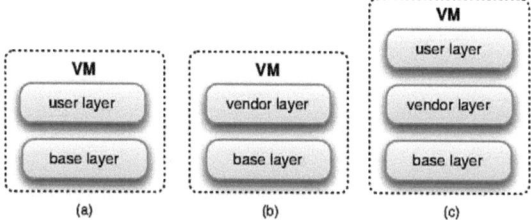

Figure 5.10: Usage scenarios for a layered virtual machine

There are different usage scenarios for layered virtual machine images, as shown in Figure 5.10. The user may set up the user layer of a virtual machine completely on his or her own, leading to a two-layered image (a). Alternatively, a software vendor (or one of its sales partners) may provide a layer containing one of its products (b). Even in this case, the user may set up a custom layer on top of the vendor layer, containing extensions or other required tools (c). Moreover, other usage scenarios might be possible and should be supported.

Usually, a large number of similar jobs are submitted to a site, where each job represents a part of the problem to be solved. A simulation process is typically divided into numerous independent tasks that will be executed concurrently on

Chapter 5. Network Security

many compute nodes. These jobs are executed in multiple instances of the virtual machine, and they are most likely executed consecutively. Retransmitting the user layer again every time is contradicting to the whole idea of image distribution compared to the use of NFS. Thus, the user layer (as well as the base and possible vendor layers) should be cached locally on the individual nodes. To ensure that a cached layer is in a working state when it is used to form a root file system, it is best to make sure that it is not changed with respect to its original state. This can only be achieved by prohibiting write access to the layer during runtime.

Using COW virtual disks has several advantages. The base layer remains nearly the same over a long period of time. An update, for example, is only necessary if security or errata patches have to be installed. This allows us to store the base layer on the compute nodes and avoid expensive retransmissions. It also removes the need for a large amount of disk space because the large base layer is cached. Updates to the site layer are also quite rare; thus, it can also be stored on the compute nodes. Only the user layer changes often, as users tend to install new software, re-install existing software or change settings. Thus, most of the time, the user layer is the only part of a virtual machine image that needs to be retransmitted, leading to significant savings in the overhead for retransmission.

Integration

All of the mechanisms presented are integrated into the XGE. Multicast and binary tree are not enabled by default; rather the disk image distribution is done with BitTorrent. Unicast or sequential distribution is available as a fallback if there is no BitTorrent compatible infrastructure.

The BitTorrent distribution is explained here in greater detail. A daemon, the *image daemon*, runs in the background on all nodes and waits for commands from the XGE, specifically the *ImageManager*. It runs as separate thread and triggers the distribution process. Therefore, it sends a fetch request to all imaged's. A submodule of the imaged, the *TorrentClient*, downloads the disk image. Nodes that already have the disk image serve as seeders and help to expedite the process. Once the distribution is finished, the sending nodes stop seeding.

Since a user's virtual machine can run multiple times on one node, the disk image also has to be present multiple times. As it is a waste of bandwidth to repeatedly download an disk image to a node, the XGE implements a caching strategy. Therefore, a disk image is only downloaded once and then duplicated with local copy operations. By using read-only disk images (with a writable copy-on-write layer on top), the need for local copies vanishes. Here, it is sufficient to create a symbolic link. As there is absolutely no write access on the disk image, the hypervisor boots it.

5.2.4 Implementation

The XGE is completely written in the Python programming language [47] and currently has more than 8000 lines of code. By using the *libvirt* library [29], the XGE can work with multiple operating system virtualization backends without having to extend or change the code. Currently the XGE is well tested with the Xen Virtual Machine Monitor and the Kernel Virtual Machine (KVM).

5.2.4.1 Core Components

The XGE consists of a number of core components that handle all the low-level work and build the connection between all other non-core modules.

Depending on the initial connection, different parts are responsible. If the XGE is used with a job scheduler, the *Watchdog* takes over. Otherwise, if the XGE is directly controlled by a user via the client interface, the *ConnectionHandler* takes over.

Initial XGE start-up is managed by the *main* class that makes sure that all requirements needed to operate are met. To identify problems during the initial start-up, the logging component is initialized at first. Now the LXGED is started on every registered node. This daemon (explained in detail in Section 5.2.4.2 on page 110) opens up a permanent connection to the XGE to e.g. retrieve remote commands. If the administrator wants to distribute the virtual machine hard disk image with BitTorrent, an instance of the *imaged* (see Section 5.2.4.9 on page 125) is also launched on all nodes. It handles all BitTorrent-related communication between the XGE, the corresponding node and the tracker. Finally, the *VNodesManager* (see Section 5.2.4.5 on page 113) and the Watchdog are started. This step concludes the start-up phase.

Watchdog

Communication between the XGE and a job scheduler occurs through a shared directory on a common file system. After the scheduler successfully processes a job (and decides on which nodes the job will be executed), it creates a new sub-directory within this shared directory. This is by default /opt/xge/jobs. Within this directory, the scheduler creates a file named job.conf containing the job configuration details.

The Watchdog continuously monitors this directory for new job directories dropped by the scheduler. Once it detects a new one, it tries to registers a job within the

Chapter 5. Network Security

XGE. If the XGE is restarted (either deliberately or because it crashes), the Watchdog can detect known job directories. These jobs are ignored and not processed again. Unknown jobs are then registered, i.e. a new job object is created. This process is explained in detail below.

ConnectionHandler

Given that the XGE is not controlled by a scheduler, the ConnectionHandler processes requests issued by a client. To be independent from the given infrastructure, local as well as remote communication with the ConnectionHandler is possible. Therefore, it runs as a separate thread implementing a XML-RPC server. The server itself is also able to start child threads to handle multiple connections at once. IP address and port of the server are defined by the local administrator.

The ConnectionHandler exposes a number of functions to the client, such as starting and stoping virtual machines as well as placeholder machines, or migrating a virtual machine from one node to another. Furthermore, it is possible to request a variety of status information from all known virtual machines. While this is interesting for the user, it is also important for other services, such as accounting and billing services.

Any error triggered by the ConnectionHandler (and thus, initially by the user) is caught, handled and delegated back to the client. This enables the client to catch the exceptions and notify the user appropriately. This is shown in Listing 5.2. The call to start-up a virtual machine is shown in lines 10 and 11. If any exceptions occur, they are caught and sent back to the client.

```
[...]

@staticmethod
def startVM(name, diskImagePath, mem, cpus):
    if mem <= 0:
        mem = config.memory
    if cpus <= 0:
        cpus = 1
    try:
        VNodesManager().startVM(VM(name, image=diskImagePath,
            disk=diskImagePath, memory=mem, mac=None, vcpus=cpus))
    except (VMException, XgeException), e:
        raise xmlrpclib.Fault(1,'%s:%s' % (e.__class__.__name__,e))

[...]
```

Listing 5.2: Part of the ConnectionHandler that starts a virtual machine, catches and forwards possible exceptions back to the requester

5.2. Virtualized Grid Computing

To retain knowledge about all internal processes and to provide information to users and other services, the XGE saves a number of data in a database, here SQLite [139]. While SQLite is very flexible, it also has a reduced instruction set and lacks the performance of mature databases. Since the XGE is not a high-performance component, these two drawbacks are negligible. The *DBManager* handles all database operations within the XGE.

```python
class DBWorker(threading.Thread):
    def __init__(self, dbname, queue):
        self.requests   = queue
        self.dbname     = dbname
        threading.Thread.__init__(self)

    def run(self):
        self.conn = sqlite3.connect(self.dbname)
        self.cur  = self.conn.cursor()
        while True:
            (what, tuple, event, result) = self.requests.get()
            self.cur.execute(what,tuple)
            self.conn.commit()
            result.extend(self.cur.fetchall())
            event.set()

[...]

def executeWrapper(self, what, tuple=()):
    result = []
    event  = threading.Event()
    self._requests.put((what,tuple,event,result))
    event.wait()
    return result

[...]
```

Listing 5.3: Database worker class, which handles concurrent access to the SQLite database

Due to the fact that the Python SQLite connection is unable to handle concurrent requests and because database queries need to be issued from many threads in different contexts during regular XGE operation, it is necessary to open and close the database connection for each request. Therefore, a worker had to be implemented to wrap the actual database interface (see Listing 5.3). Initially the DBWorker receives a queue object from the DBManager that holds SQL requests, results and events. The queue module is already thread safe, which ensures that the XGE code does not have to deal with concurrency issues here.

Every thread that wants to connect to the database has to use a number of functions provided by the DBManager. These functions access the database through a wrapper method (line 19 - 24). Query requests are transferred to the DBWorker using a producer-consumer setup.

5.2.4.2 LXGEd

LXGED consists of two components: a daemon running on each registered node and a client integrated into the XGE. Communication between the two components occurs using XML-RPC. Exceptions are forward between the daemon and the client, ensuring that possible failures can be processed.

One of the important functions of the LXGED is to copy hard disk images when sequential deployment is used. The responsible code on the daemon is shown in Listing 5.4. The disk image sPath on the source node will be copied to dPath on the destination node (line 4). If read only disk images are used and the disk image is already present on the destination node, creating a symbolic link is sufficient since this saves time and bandwidth. Writeable disk images cannot be linked; this, a real remote copy is necessary. This is done using the rsync [155] program because it is able to copy sparse files efficiently. A sparse file occupies only the actual disk space consumed on disk. It is limited by its maximum size recorded in its inode. For example, a 10 GB sparse file occupies only 500 MB on the system if this is the number of actual used blocks. Most programs used to transfer files between remote machines (this also applies to most programs for local copies) are not able to cope with sparse files. Thus, using such a program would result in a 10 GB file on the remote disk. The opposite is true for rsync, which detects sparse files and transfers only the effectively used blocks.

```
[...]

@staticmethod
def copyLocalFile(sPath, dPath, doLink=False):
    ret = 0
    if doLink:
        try:
            os.symlink(sPath, dPath)
        except OSError, e:
            raise xmlrpclib.Fault(1, '%s:%s' % (e.__class__.__name__
                , e) )
    else:
        cmd = ['rsync', '-aPqS', sPath, '-e', 'ssh', 'root@localhost
            :'+dPath ]
        try:
            ret = subprocess.call(cmd)
        except (OSError, ValueError), e:
            raise xmlrpclib.Fault(1, '%s:%s' % (e.__class__.__name__
                , e) )
```

```
18 [...]
```

Listing 5.4: Method in the LxGEd used to copy virtual machine hard disk images between client and daemon node

5.2.4.3 Job Management

After the Watchdog daemon recognizes a new job given by the scheduler, a *Job* object is created. This object contains all information about a job and can be used to communicate to the attached methods. To describe all aspects of a job, the object inherits from the *JobInformation* class. This class holds a variety of information that is important to both the user and the XGE.

Listing 5.5 shows some attributes of the JobInformation class. A `uuid` generated by the XGE is used to identify a job uniquely. Furthermore, a job could contain an `id`. This is is either the same as the uuid or the ID provided by the scheduler. In the latter case, a XGE job could be identified with a scheduler ID. This might be handy for accounting and billing services. A job has a specific state, encoded by an integer:

Waiting (0) : The job is queued in the XGEs internal structures and waits until all of its virtual machines are started.

Running (1) : All of the job's virtual machines are booted and the scheduler has started the execution of the application.

Finished (2) : Execution is complete and all virtual machines are down.

Error (3) : An error has occurred. The exact failure is reported to the user and the XGE tries to correct a possible unsafe system state (e.g., one half of the users virtual machines run, the other half refused to boot).

To be able to identify the submitting user's home directory, the XGE also records the user name. This is necessary because the XGE saves a status and error log file in every users' home directory.

```
1 class JobInformation(object):
2     def __init__(self, uuid, tid):
3         """ UUID of the job """
4         self.uuid = uuid
5         """ ID related to traffic shaping """
6         self.tid = tid
7         """ ID of the Job (set to UUID if not overwritten) """
8         self.id = uuid
```

Chapter 5. Network Security

```
 9          """ Network UUID (set by the calling instance) """
10          self.nuuid = ''
11          """ List of associated hosts """
12          self.hosts = []
13          """ List of associated VMs """
14          self.vms = []
15          """ Job status (0=waiting, 1=running,
16              2=finished, 3=error) """
17          self.status = 0
18          """ Creation timestamp """
19          self.timestamp = 0
20          """ Stop timestamp """
21          self.stoptime = 0
22          """ Name of the job """
23          self.name = ""
24          """ Owner of the job """
25          self.user = ""
26          """ Maximum of memory allowed for VMs """
27          self.memory = 0
28          """ Queue of the job """
29          self.queue = ""
30          """ Script """
31          self.script = ""
32 [...]
```

Listing 5.5: Abstract of the JobInformation class describing vital details about a XGE job

5.2.4.4 Job Manager

A central component of the XGE that manages jobs is the *JobManager*. It can create new jobs, delete old ones or manage a variety of aspects associated with jobs. Therefore, a global list containing all jobs is used.

Listing 5.6 shows a method used to register new jobs. Since concurrent access from multiple threads is possible, entries within this method must be synchronized (line 3). Given that the job is already in the internal list, it is not added again and the method returns (lines 4 through 7). To gain information about the job, the job configuration file created by the scheduler is parsed. In the event of an error, the job state is set to *Error*, a notification is sent to the scheduler and an error is returned to the caller (lines 9 through 16). If no parsing error occurs, the job is appended to the internal list, a message handler is created and finally, the job is started (lines 18 through 22).

```
1 [...]
2 def registerJob(self, job):
3     self.__jobLock.acquire()
```

5.2. Virtualized Grid Computing

```
 4      for i in self.__jobList:
 5          if str(job.name) == str(i.name):
 6              self.__jobLock.release()
 7              return False
 8
 9      if job.parseConfig() < 0:
10          job.status = 3
11          try:
12              notifyResourceManager(self, "running")
13          except XgeException:
14              pass
15          self.__jobLock.release()
16          return False
17
18      job.addMessageHandler()
19      self.__jobList.append(job)
20      job.startJob()
21      self.__jobLock.release()
22      return True
23
24  [...]
```

Listing 5.6: Method to register a job in the XGE

5.2.4.5 Virtual Machine Management

A virtual machine is described by a VM object. This object contains attributes for the number of virtual CPUs, the maximum amount of virtual memory and the path to the hard disk image. Virtual machines can be bound to a job or created on-demand upon a user's request. In the former case, the virtual machines are bound to a JOB object, in the latter case the VM objects are created directly by the *VNodesManager*.

The VNodesManager is the core component for virtual machine management. Through its backend bindings, it is able to execute virtual machine operations, e.g. start, stop or migrate. Initially, the VNodesManager connects to the operating system virtualization backend chosen by the administrator. This happens using the *libvirt* library. Only one backend can used at a time. Listing 5.7 shows how a connection to either KVM (line 4) or Xen (line 7) is set up.

```
1  [...]
2
3  # initialize the backend with xen as default
4  if self.c.backend == "kvm":
5      self._backend =
6          Backend(self.physicalMachines, self.virtualMachines,
7              "qemu+ssh://")
8  else:
```

113

```
 9      self._backend = 
10          Backend(self.physicalMachines, self.virtualMachines,
11              "xen+ssh://")
12
13  [...]
```

Listing 5.7: Initialization of the backend connection in the VNodesManager

If no backend connection is possible (e.g., because the wrong operating system kernel is in use), the XGE stops immediately.

Start Virtual Machines

One or more virtual machines can be started either through a job or directly via a client. The former case involves the *JobVMManager*. Nevertheless, the communication with the backend is handled by the VNodesManager in both cases. The JobVMManager's primary task is to check if all required dependencies for starting the virtual machine are met and to distribute the hard disk images to the nodes.

Listing 5.8 shows how a virtual machine named vm is started with the VNodes-Manager. Start-up is only possible if the virtual machine is registered and the if the calling thread can obtain a lock (lines 4 through 5). If not, the caller is blocked and has to wait until the current operating thread finishes its work. Locking is necessary here because multiple XGE threads could try to access the vm object.

The control flow is now divided into two parts (lines 8 and 24). If the administrator enabled placeholder images, the method has to check if the virtual machine is indeed a running placeholder image. If it is, the placeholder is destroyed. If not, another virtual machine is already running and no new machine should be started. Finally, starting is delegated to the backend (lines 14 through 18) and the machine's description is written to the database.

```
 1  [...]
 2  def startVM(self, vm, event=None, uuid=None):
 3      vnode = vm.name
 4      self._checkName(vnode)
 5      self._locks[vnode].acquire()
 6      _node = self._dbm.getNode(vnode)
 7
 8      if self.c.ignorepl == 0:
 9          if _node["state"] == 2 and _node["isph"] != 1:
10              self._locks[vnode].release()
11              raise VMException("VM is occupied")
12
```

5.2. Virtualized Grid Computing

```
13          try:
14              if _node["state"] == 2:
15                  self.destroyVM(vnode)
16              vm.mac = _node["mac"]
17              self._backend.startVM(vm,
18                  _node["physicalmachineact"],ph=False,event=event)
19              self._dbm.updateNode(vnode,
20                  {"state":1,"isph":0,"job":uuid,"disk":vm.image})
21          except XgeException:
22              self._locks[vnode].release()
23              raise
24      else:
25          if _node["state"] == 2:
26              self._locks[vnode].release()
27              raise VMException("VM is occupied")
28          try:
29              vm.mac = _node["mac"]
30              self._backend.startVM(vm,
31                  _node["physicalmachineact"],ph=False,event=event)
32              self._dbm.updateNode(vnode,
33                  {"state":1,"isph":0,"job":uuid,"disk":vm.image})
34          except XgeException:
35              self._locks[vnode].release()
36              raise
37
38 [...]
```

Listing 5.8: Method used to start a virtual machine in the VNodesManager

Shut down Virtual Machines

One or more virtual machines are shut down once the execution is finished and the scheduler has informed the XGE about that step, or if the user requests, the termination. Listing 5.9 shows the code responsible for the shutdown. If the virtual machine vm is not marked as running, no action needs to be taken (lines 9 through 11).

If the virtual machine belongs to a job and is not a placeholder, a set of status information is saved in the database (lines 13 through 20). The actual shut down command is sent to the backend and, if placeholder images are activated, such a placeholder virtual machine is started (line 26 - 28).

```
1 [...]
2
3 def shutdownVM(self, vm, event=None, restore=True):
4     vnode = vm.name
5     self._checkName(vnode)
6     self._locks[vnode].acquire()
```

```
     _node = self._dbm.getNode(vnode)

     if _node["state"] != 2:
         self._locks[vnode].release()
         return
     try:
         if self.c.ignorepl == 0:
             if not _node["job"] is None and _node["isph"] == 0:
                 self._dbm.insertNodeHistory(
                     self.generateHistoryEntry(vnode, _node["job"]))
         else:
             if not _node["job"] is None:
                 self._dbm.insertNodeHistory(
                     self.generateHistoryEntry(vnode, _node["job"]))

         physicalMachine = _node["physicalmachineact"]
         self._backend.shutdownVM(vnode, physicalMachine, event)
         self._dbm.updateState(vnode, 3)

         if self.c.ignorepl == 0:
             if restore:
                 thread.start_new_thread(self.startPH, (vnode,))
     except XgeException:
         self._locks[vnode].release()
         raise

[...]
```

Listing 5.9: Method used to stop a virtual machine in the VNodesManager

Virtual Machine Migration

Migrating a virtual machine is shown in Listing 5.10. A virtual machine called vnode is migrated from its current physical location to a new node called destination. As with the process used to start a virtual machine, the method checks a number of requirements and the calling thread has to obtain a lock (lines 3 through 11). Due to migrations, the node of a virtual machine changes often; thus, the method has to retrieve the current node name from the database (line 12). All operations on virtual machines save the current node in the database. If the virtual machine is already running on the destination node, the migration is aborted (lines 14 through 16).

Prior to the actual migration process, the hard disk image has to be transferred to the destination node. Otherwise the hypervisor refuses to migrate. A disk image transfer is not needed only if the disk image is stored on shared storage (line 26). Otherwise, the disk image is transferred either with BitTorrent (lines 27 and 28) or with the sequential copy method (line 30). Once the transfer is finished, a call to start the migration is given to the backend code and the new node is saved in the database.

Finally, a variety of status information (for further details, see Section 5.2.4.3 on page 111) is saved in the database (lines 38 and 39). This is necessary as the hypervisor and thus the backend change during a migration. The old backend invalidates all status information after the migration and the new backend starts counting from zero. To enable proper accounting, the XGE needs to keep track of all status information even during migrations.

```
[...]
def migrateVM(self, vnode, destination):
    self._checkName(vnode)
    self._checkDom0(destination)
    self._locks[vnode].acquire()
    _node = self._dbm.getNode(vnode)
    _state = _node["state"]

    if _state != 2:
        self._locks[vnode].release()
        raise VMException()
    _act = _node["physicalmachineact"]

    if _act == destination:
        self._locks[vnode].release()
        raise VMException()
    try:

        disk = _node["disk"]
        history = None

        if _node["isph"] == 0:
            if disk is None:
                raise XgeException()

            if self.c.useshared == 0:
                if self.c.depmode == "bittorrent":
                    ImageManager().deployTorrent(disk, [destination
                        ])
                else:
                    DeploySequential(disk, {destination:[vnode]})

            if not _node["job"] is None:
                history =
                    self.generateHistoryEntry(vnode, _node["job"])

        self._backend.migrateVM(vnode, _act, destination)
        self._dbm.updatePhysicalMachine(vnode, destination)
        if not history is None:
            self._dbm.insertNodeHistory(history)
```

```
41        self._locks[vnode].release()
42    except XgeException:
43        self._locks[vnode].release()
44        raise
45
46 [...]
```

Listing 5.10: Method used to migrate a virtual machine in the VNodesManager

5.2.4.6 Backend Connection

The *Backend* class is responsible for all communication with the underlying hypervisor. While the first version of the XGE implemented its own functions to communicate with the hypervisor, the recent version uses the *libvirt* library developed by RedHat. Consult Section 2.3.7 on page 19 for further details about *libvirt*.

One instance of the libvirt daemon runs on every node. This daemon sends commands to the local hypervisor (such as start or shutdown) and receives responses. All libvirt daemons are permanently connected to the XGE backend with a TCP based connection protocol. These connections remain open until the XGE is stopped. It is important to explicitly close them at the end. Otherwise the underlying network connections remain open, leaving the system in an inconsistent state.

Listing 5.11 shows the code that opens a connection to the libvirt daemon. An URI is created by looping over the available nodes (lines 4 through 7). Depending on virtualization software used the URI is different, i.e. to connect to a Xen node, the URI is xen://hostname, whereas a connection to KVM requires the following URI: qemu://hostname/system. Line 9 links to the method shown in lines 23 through 28 that opens the actual connection. After the connection is set up, the method tries to retrieve the virtual machines that are already running on each node (lines 11 through 19). This is important if the XGE is used either in a mixed environment, i.e. there are virtual machines managed by the XGE and manually by users, or if the XGE crashed and the internal recovery process is in progress. If there is already a virtual machine running on a node, the XGE will not touch it (i.e., replace the machine with a placeholder or another machine).

```
1 [...]
2
3    for physicalMachine in physicalMachines:
4        if self._c.backend == "kvm":
5            beUri = uri+str(physicalMachine)+"/system"
6        else:
7            beUri = uri+str(physicalMachine)
```

5.2. Virtualized Grid Computing

```
 8
 9          _conn = self.openConnection(beUri)
10          self.connections[physicalMachine] = _conn
11          _domains = self.getDomains(_conn)
12          for d in _domains:
13              _name = d.name()
14              if _name in _tmp:
15                  self.domains[_name] = d
16                  self._initialDomains[_name] = physicalMachine
17                  _tmp.remove(_name)
18      for t in _tmp:
19          self.domains[t] = None
20
21 [...]
22
23 def openConnection(self, uri):
24     try:
25         conn = libvirt.open(uri)
26         return conn
27     except libvirt.libvirtError:
28         raise XgeException("Failed to open backend connection")
29
30 [...]
```

Listing 5.11: One TCP connection is opened to the libvirt daemon running on every node

Once the *Backend* class has an open connection to the libvirt daemons, it is able to execute commands on behalf of the VNodesManager. Listing 5.8 showed the code in the VNodesManager used to start a virtual machine; Listing 5.13 shows the actual backend code.

The code tries to start a virtual machine a second and a third time if the previous attempt fails (line 3). The actual start-up occurs in lines 5 through 10. The virtual machine is started and the calling thread waits in the WaitBoot method for the event that the machines is booted. Even though the thread is busy waiting and locks the caller, it is necessary to avoid races with an involved scheduler. If the method would return immediately after the libvirt daemon is instructed to start the machine, the XGE would notify the scheduler. Assuming this information is correct, the scheduler would try to launch the executable within the machine. If the machine is still booting (which takes between 10 and 30 seconds, depending on the hardware), the execution would fail and lead to the abortion of the entire job.

A similar procedure is needed after a shutdown command. Here, it is also important to avoid races; thus, the XGE waits until a machine is really down. Since every virtualization software (e.g., Xen or KVM) reports different codes for, running or finishing to libvirt, the XGE can not rely on this information. This means that although libvirt reports that a machine is down, it is possible that the machine is still running or in the process of being shut down. Therefore, the CPU time is checked for a zero value, as this can only occur if the machine is indeed not running.

If an error occurs (lines 12 through 16), the XGE checks the error codes and raises an exception. If the libvirt daemon reports a critical system error during the first attempt, the XGE tries to re-establish the connection.

```xml
<?xml version="1.0" encoding="UTF-8"?>
<domain type='xen'>
    <name>node005c0</name>
    <uuid>550e8400-e29b-11d4-a716-446655440000</uuid>
    <os>
        <type>linux</type>
        <kernel>/boot/vmlinuz-2.6.32-5-xen-amd64</kernel>
        <initrd>/boot/initrd-2.6.32-5-xen-amd64</initrd>
        <cmdline>root=/dev/xvda1 ro selinux=0 3</cmdline>
    </os>
    <on_poweroff>destroy</on_poweroff>
    <on_reboot>restart</on_reboot>
    <on_crash>restart</on_crash>
    <memory>1048576</memory>
    <vcpu>4</vcpu>
    <device>
        <disk type = 'file'>
            <source file='/images/node005.img' />
            <target dev='xvda1' />
        </disk>
        <interface type='bridge'>
            <source bridge='xenbr0' />
            <mac address='1A:00:00:00:56:05' />
            <script path='/etc/xen/scripts/vif-bridge' />
        </interface>
    </devices>
</domain>
```

Listing 5.12: XML document describing a virtual machine

In order to start a virtual machine, the XGE has to create a descriptive XML document. A sample document describing a Xen virtual machine is shown in Listing 5.12. Like the XGE, libvirt also uses a name and a UUID to identify each virtual machine (lines 3 through 4). Lines 5 through 10 define the operating system kernel, which is a Linux kernel with an initial ramdisk in this example. Depending on the virtualization software, a number of hardware devices can be configured. In this example, the machine has one hard disk image that is a plain file on the local system (lines 17 through 20). Furthermore, one network interface is set up. This interface is bound to the local network bridge xenbr0.

5.2. Virtualized Grid Computing

```python
def startVM(self, vm, physicalMachine, ph=False, event=None):
    xml = createXML(vm, ph)
    for i in range(2):
        try:
            _dom = \
              self.connections[physicalMachine].createXML(xml,0)
            if not self.domains[vm.name] is None:
                self.domains[vm.name].__del__()
            self.domains[vm.name] = _dom
            WaitBoot(_dom,event).start()
            return
        except libvirt.libvirtError, err:
            if err.get_error_code() == libvirt.VIR_ERR_SYSTEM_ERROR \
              and i == 0:
                self.recover(physicalMachine,vm.name)
            else:
                raise VMException("Could not start VM")
```

Listing 5.13: Backend method used to start a virtual machine

5.2.4.7 Placeholder Virtual Machines

To keep the placeholder virtual machines as small and flexible as possible, they consist of merely a Linux kernel and a ramdisk, i.e. they are not dependent on persistent storage. As a consequence, it is possible to destroy a placeholder, which consumes less time than a regular shutdown. In order to communicate with the scheduler, an execution daemon (e.g., Torque's pbs_mom or SGE's sgeexecd) is installed.

5.2.4.8 Remote Interfaces

Two remote interfaces are offered by the XGE to communicate with services as well as users. The first interface, called the *JobServer*, is only for machine to machine communication; the *ConnectionHandler* can be used by client software.

An example of how to use the JobServer would be the connection between a grid middleware and the XGE. While developing this thesis, such an connection was implemented using the Globus toolkit as middleware. Furthermore, Globus hosted a service for accounting and billing that collected the following information from all of a job's virtual machines:

- Amount of virtual memory used
- Number of virtual CPUs

- CPU times consumed
- Bytes and packets transferred
- Bytes and packets received

Based on this record, a report and a bill is created for a potential customer.

The JobServer requires that all messages (the one it receives and the one it sends) are valid XML. This eases machine-to-machine communication and provides messages that humans can read in the event that debugging is necessary.

5.2.4.9 Efficient Virtual Disk Image Deployment

In this section, the implementation of different methods for virtual machine disk image transfer is described. By default, the XGE transfers all disk images with *BitTorrent*, a peer-to-peer software designed for large data transfers. As a fallback, *unicast* or sequential deployment is available. This means that all disk images are transferred one by one to the nodes. A distribution algorithm based on a *binary tree* is also available, but no longer enabled in the default distribution. Finally, experimental support for *multicast* is implemented.

Unicast Distribution

Unicast or sequential deployment is the simplest method available in the XGE. While it is naturally the slowest method, it works in almost all network environments without any additional dependencies (e.g., BitTorrent requires a configured tracker and multicast might require special network configuration).

Initially, the deployment process is started by the JobVMManager that has a list of target nodes, which is needed to distribute the disk image to its exact destinations. Then, a new thread running an instance of the *DeploySequential* class is launched. Listing 5.14 shows the code responsible for the distribution.

Prior to the actual distribution, the size and the file system modification timestamp of the source disk image is determined. If there is already a disk image on the remote node and if both values match, distribution is skipped to save time and bandwidth (lines 22 and 36). While this is not as reliable as computing a checksum (e.g., a MD5 or SHA-1 hash), it does indeed save time. Computing a MD5 checksum of a small 1 GB disk image takes about 35 seconds and creates increased CPU load.

```
1 [...]
```

5.2. Virtualized Grid Computing

```python
for physicalMachine in self.hosts:
    if len(self.hosts[physicalMachine]) == 0:
        continue

    li = 0
    rc = {}
    lock = thread.allocate_lock()
    threads = []
    for virtualMachine in self.hosts[physicalMachine]:
        _xged = LXGEdClient(physicalMachine)
        if li == 0:
            li += 1
            retries = 0
            while retries < 3:
                retries += 1
                initialImg = virtualMachine
                oPath    = os.path.join(self.c.rd, virtualMachine)
                rMTime   = _xged.getMTime(oPath)
                rSize    = _xged.getSize(oPath)
                if rMTime == _imgMTime and rSize == _imgSize:
                    break

                rCopy = CopySequentialRemote(virtualMachine,
                    self.image, oPath, physicalMachine, rc, lock)
                rCopy.start()
                rCopy.join()

                rSize = _xged.getSize(oPath)
                if rSize == _imgSize:
                    break
        else:
            dPath    = os.path.join(self.c.rd, virtualMachine)
            rMTime   = _xged.getMTime(dPath)
            if rMTime == _imgMTime:
                continue

            lCopy = CopySequentialLocal(virtualMachine,
                oPath, dPath, physicalMachine, rc, lock, self.c.
                    doLink)
            lCopy.start()
            threads.append(lCopy)

            rSize = _xged.getSize(dPath)
            if rSize == _imgSize:
                break

    for t in threads:
        t.join()

[...]
```

Listing 5.14: Fragment of the sequential virtual machine hard disk image distribution code

The XGE attempts to transfer a disk image three times (line 16) to circumvent possible network problems (e.g., network is congested and thus the transfer times out). Lines 25 through 28 show how the remote copy process is started as a separate thread. The `join` statement ensures that the thread is not returned until the transfer is finished. Finally, the remote size has to be checked against the known size. If they match, the transfer is successful (lines 30 through 32).

If one virtual machine is scheduled to run multiple times on a node (e.g., 4 instances of one virtual machine run on a node with 4 CPU cores), multiple remote copies of the disk image would be a waste of time and bandwidth. Therefore, only one remote copy is created; all other disk images are copied on the local disk. For read only images, a file system link is sufficient; thus, they do not have to be copied at all. Lines 33 through 46 show the code which starts a local copy thread. Since the local copy processes can run simultaneously, the `join` occurs later (line 48 through 49).

Binary Tree Distribution

Binary tree distribution is more complex than the unicast distribution method. A binary tree is generated once the scheduler knows all of the destination nodes. The root of the tree is always the node carrying the disk image. A multi-threaded implementation ensures that the copy operations are performed simultaneously, i.e. the disk image is copied from the first node to its two children in the tree. Once a reasonable amount of data (a variable threshold; in the implementation, it is set to 50 MB) has arrived at the children, a new copy-thread for every child is spawned. Thus, a continuous flow of data is maintained through the entire tree.

To ensure that a new copy-thread is started without having any data to transfer, all copy actions are synchronized. A node must not send data until it has sufficient data to start a transfer. For example, if the network transfer between two nodes in the tree is interrupted, all children are blocked until the interruption is resolved. To avoid endless waiting, the copy process is aborted after a certain interval of time. Depending on the local administrator's preferences, it is possible to repeat a transmission or completely cancel the copy process.

Every method runs as separate thread, of course. Furthermore, the methods have the same caching strategy as mentioned in the theories above. If a disk image

5.2. Virtualized Grid Computing

with the same name already exists on the destination node and if the size and the modification timestamp match, the actual copy is skipped. Local copies are also created on the hard disk, without it being necessary to start an additional network transfer.

Peer-to-Peer Distribution

As already mentioned above, the peer-to-peer distribution method is based on BitTorrent. Is is implemented as a distributed application with a client-server architecture. A daemon, called the *imaged*, runs on every registered node and acts as a server. The client component is the *ImageManager* that runs as separate thread within the XGE. It sends fetch or seed requests to the image daemons on the other hosts. XML messages are used as the communication protocol.

The components will be explained in detail in the following sections. Since the BitTorrent distribution method is the default in the XGE, it will be explained in greater detail compared to the other methods.

ImageManager

The most important of the ImageManager's process is the one that starts the distribution. Part of this process is shown in Listing 5.15. A disk image and a list of nodes are passed to the deployment function, which tries to deploy this disk image to all of these nodes. First, a number of variables need to be set, including the seeding nodes, the disk image name, and the destination directory (lines 2 through 6). Next, the ImageManager fetches the torrent file from the node carrying the file (line 12). Even if the head node already has the file on its local file system, it is necessary to fetch a fresh copy since the torrent file might have changed (e.g. because the disk image was modified in the mean time). After the file is retrieved, the hash sum (which uniquely defines the torrent) is extracted for later use (line 18).

```
def deployTorrent(self, image, hosts):
    seeders = list(set(self.physicalMachines) - set(hosts.keys()))
    destDir = os.path.join(self.baseDir,os.path.dirname(image))
    imageName = os.path.basename(image)
    torrentPath = os.path.join(self.torrentRoot, image + ".torrent")
    torrentUri = self.torrentHost + ":" + torrentPath

    [...]

    localTorrent = os.path.join(destDir, imageName + ".torrent")
    try:
        fetchFile(torrentUri, localTorrent)
```

Chapter 5. Network Security

```
13          e = lt.bdecode(open(localTorrent, "rb").read())
14          if e is None:
15              raise XgeException.XgeException("deployment error ")
16
17          info = lt.torrent_info(e)
18          hash = str(info.info_hash())
19      except XgeException:
20          raise XgeException("deployment error")
21
22  [...]
```

Listing 5.15: First part of the method used to distribute a disk image via BitTorrent

Listing 5.16 shows the core of the disk image distribution on side of the client. The code is completely multi-threaded since a single-threaded implementation is opposite to the design goals of BitTorrent. BitTorrent relies on many hosts that seed and download data simultaneously. A FetchController thread is started for each host in lines 8 through 11. To satisfy BitTorrent's aforementioned design goals, a number of SeedController threads are started in lines 14 through 16. These threads send seed requests to all registered nodes. If a node already owns a complete copy of the disk image, it will continue until the other nodes have finished downloading. An event-based mechanism is used to stop the seeders (line 6 and 20).

```
1  [...]
2
3  fetchThreads = []
4  fetchLock = thread.allocate_lock()
5  fetchResult = [0]
6  stopEvent = threading.Event()
7  id = os.path.join(destDir, imageName)
8  for (host,vnodes) in hosts.items():
9      t = FetchController(host, self.port, vnodes, torrentUri,
10                 id, self.imageDir, fetchLock, fetchResult, hash,
                   self.doLink)
11     t.start()
12     fetchThreads.append(t)
13
14 for host in seeders:
15     t = SeedController(host, self.port, torrentUri, id, stopEvent,
           hash)
16     t.start()
17
18 for t in fetchThreads:
19     t.join()
20 stopEvent.set()
21
22 if fetchResult[0] != 0:
```

5.2. Virtualized Grid Computing

```
23    raise XgeException("deployment error")
```

Listing 5.16: Second part of the method used to distribute a disk image via BitTorrent

BitTorrent Client

The *TorrentClient* uses the library *libtorrent-rasterbar* [130] to implement the client part. Listing 5.17 shows the client's main loop. First, it checks if new torrents were submitted and starts them (line 3). Once new torrents are submitted, the loop starts again from the beginning (line 7). Finally, it handles stop requests (if any) and checks the status of all running torrents (lines 9 - 10).

```
1  def run(self):
2      while not self.stopped:
3          self.startNewTorrents()
4          if len(self.runningTorrents) == 0:
5              self.waitForNewTorrents()
6              if self.stopped: break
7              continue
8
9          self.handleStopRequests()
10         self.checkStatus()
11         time.sleep(self.interval)
12     self.stopAllTorrents(True)
13     self.saveResumeData()
```

Listing 5.17: BitTorrent client within the imaged

The TorrentClient checks the status of all running torrents regularly. Torrents progress through different states, as seen in Figure 5.11. First, a torrent is in the state *new*. Once the torrent is recognized by the TorrentClient, the state it set to *downloading*, or in the event of an error, to *error*. A torrent keeps seeding the image after it finished downloading (encoded by the transition to *seeding*). Finally, the torrent's state is set to *finished* and the torrent is removed from the session. The sink state *stopped* occurs only if deliberate termination is requested.

Multicast

The multicast distribution method is based on UDPcast.[1] It provides an easy and seamless way to transfer data via multicast. Every node has a receiving client installed and the sender is installed on the machine that hosts the disk images. Once a transmission is started, the sender starts the multicast distribution and all

---
[1] http://udpcast.linux.lu/

Chapter 5. Network Security

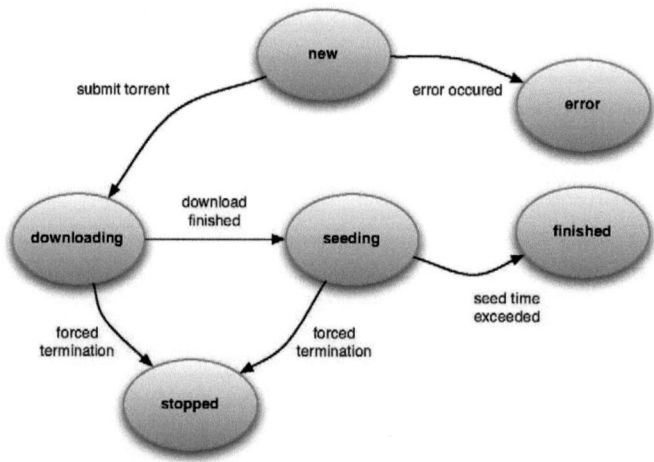

Figure 5.11: Possible torrent states in the TorrentClient

receivers store the disk image at a predefined location. All distributing threads are synchronized and shut down once the transfer is complete.

Cross-Site Transfer

Depending on the network structure, the XGEs are either aware of the public IP addresses of all nodes in multi-site computing environments, or they know at least the IP addresses of a publicly accessible virtual machine disk image pool node. By default, the XGEs assume that the compute nodes are accessible to the public. Otherwise, it is up to the local administrator of the site to configure it appropriately. BitTorrent is used when disk images are transferred between two remote sites and the local distribution.

Encrypted vs. Unencrypted Transfer

Depending on the distribution method, the transfer can be either encrypted or unencrypted. For example, BitTorrent and Multicast traffic is commonly unencrypted; thus, additional security mechanisms like IPsec [70] must be put into place. The binary tree method can be used with unencrypted (to save bandwidth and CPU overhead in protected network environments) or encrypted (for use in non-confidential networks) transfer. Authentication is achieved by using public key cryptography. The source node has a secret key and all destination nodes have the source node's registered public key. Traffic encryption is performed using OpenSSL [97], which itself uses an asymmetric key for the handshake and a symmetric key for the actual encryption procedure.

5.2.4.10 Avoiding Retransmission Overhead

To avoid the retransmission of a disk image that is already present and to avoid the need for huge amounts of disk space on the destination nodes, the implementation is based on copy-on-write (COW) layers.

The presented three-layer COW disk image architecture is based on Advanced UnionFS [158]. The base layer hosts a Debian GNU/Linux stable-based Linux distribution with a Xen-capable kernel. All tools needed to ensure seamless out-of-the-box operation are included, such as the complete Debian package management, standard compilers and interpreters, and a basic set of libraries including development headers. The base layer can to run on every infrastructure supporting the Xen virtual machine monitor. The site layer contains several additions needed to run the generic base image on different sites. The changes to the base layer include special settings, such as name resolution (DNS), IP configuration (DHCP-based, static addresses or peer-to-peer auto configuration), or user management (LDAP or NIS interfaces). Typically, the site layer is rather small in size, often between 10 KB or 1 MB.

The user layer contains all the modifications made by the owner. To ensure that the modifications made by the user will not prevent the virtual machine image from running (if, say, the user deleted some crucial system files), the base layer as well as the site layer are mounted read-only during execution time. Furthermore, the site layer overwrites any of the user's changes to configuration files that are also touched by the site layer. Of course, this limits the user's freedom of image customization, but having limited freedom is better than having no running virtual machine at all (or ever worse, a virtual machine that is stuck in the boot process and blocks resources).

5.2.4.11 Storage Synchronization

The synchronization mechanism the uses DRBD devices has been implemented as part of the XGE. The controller that handles the synchronization mechanism has been written in Python. The current implementation works with Xen as the backend hypervisor, although most of the code does not depend on Xen.

DRBD Device Configuration

A two-node setup consists of a pair of DRBD devices that are identified by their path in the file system. Since the DRBD endpoints communicate via two separate TCP connections, they have to agree on port numbers on both sides. Hence, a DRBD endpoint is identified by host name, port number and path. To reduce the global configuration overhead, the nodes manage their resources locally (see next section). The actual device names are abstracted from symbolic links.

DRBD devices work in different modes throughout their lifetime. Usually, a DRBD device runs in standalone mode as a pure bypass to the backing block device. In this mode, disk I/O performs with nearly native speed. In the pre-migration phase, the DRBD device on the source node is connected to the endpoint on the destination node, and the two of devices run in primary/secondary mode (only the source node is allowed to write to the device) during the initial synchronization. Just before the actual migration starts, the devices are put into primary/primary mode. This is necessary because Xen checks for write access on all associated block devices before initiating a live migration. From the devices' point of view, this mode allows both ends to issue write requests simultaneously. However, this will never happen in the local setup due to the nature of a live migration: a virtual machine is always running on a single node and thus will always access the device through only one endpoint at a time.

Node Setup

Apart from kernel and RAM disk, a virtual machine has one or more associated disk images: a read-only base layer (the user image), a writable disk layer (if it does not reside in the memory), and, possibly a separate disk image used as swap partition. Disk images may be physical devices, logical volume manager (LVM) partitions, or disk images, and the choice is left to the XGE configuration.

The virtual machine never alters the base layer; hence, all instances on one physical host that use the same base image can share a single copy. When initially necessary, the image is downloaded once (e.g., via BitTorrent) and cached into a local image pool. All writable disk images are attached to DRBD devices so that all I/O are intercepted by the DRBD driver. Each virtual machine has a directory that contains (symbolic links to) all of its disk images. Due to the symbolic links, the disk image names can easily be kept consistent within the cluster (which is important for live migration) without the need for all of the involved nodes to use the same actual device names (which would impose a large administrative overhead). The writable disk images are empty, when the virtual machine is started.

The image daemon (imaged) of the XGE is responsible for downloading and caching base images (the read-only layers) and for managing the DRBD devices.

Pre-Migration Process

When the XGE node wants to initiate the live migration of a virtual machine from a source to a destination node, the following tasks are performed.

- The head node contacts the image daemons on both hosts and instructs them to prepare the migration. The source node responds with the port numbers used by the DRBD devices of the corresponding disk images. The destination node reserves DRBD devices, attaches LVM partitions or disk images, chooses free ports to use for the synchronization, and sends them back to the XGE.

- The head node communicates the configuration information to both nodes so that they can update their DRBD configuration accordingly and connect the corresponding DRBD endpoints. When the endpoints are connected, the synchronization starts in primary/secondary mode.

- Once the synchronization is finished, the DRBD devices on the destination node are put into primary mode, and the usual Xen live migration process is started.

- When the live migration has successfully been completed, the DRBD devices on the source node are disconnected so that the DRBD devices on the destination host run in standalone mode (with nearly native I/O speed). The corresponding resources (devices, ports, disk images) on the source node are freed.

5.2.5 Evaluation

In the following section, selected measurements of the developed components are presented in order to evaluate the overhead introduced. The machines used for the tests have a Intel Core 2 Duo CPU with 3.0 GHz, 4 GB RAM connected with switched Gigabit Ethernet network and run Debian/GNU Linux 5.0 and Xen Version 3.2.1.

Chapter 5. Network Security

There have been a number of performance studies of Xen and on the whole the author had made the same observations. The real overhead for most CPU intensive applications, including the turbulence simulation, is roughly 5%. For more detailed performance studies of Xen, consult the following papers: [20, 92, 8, 175, 17].

5.2.5.1 Execution Time

The following experiment quantifies the overhead introduced using operating system virtualization. The turbulence simulation (compare Section 1.1.1 on page 2) was executed both in a virtualized and native environment. Both the host and the virtual machine are assigned 1 GB of virtual memory.

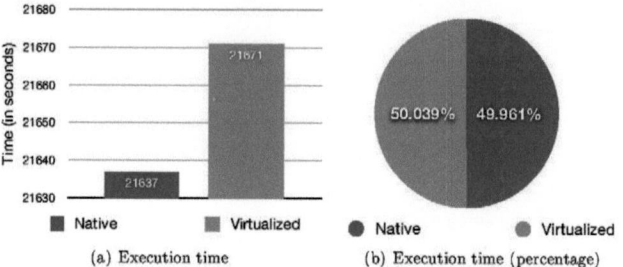

Figure 5.12: Comparing the turbulence simulation's execution times in a virtualized and a native environment

Figures 5.12(a) and 5.12(b) show the performance of the turbulence simulation in a virtual machine compared to the native performance. In total, 6 runs were performed to procure a robust mean. Execution in the virtual machine was 0.078% (or 34 seconds) slower compared to the native execution. Compared to the total execution time of over 6 hours, the performance penalty is negligible.

Figure 5.13 shows a comparison between the execution of a test application, which runs 10 seconds in total, on physical hardware and within a virtual machine. Here, Torque is used as scheduler and the job is submitted to either the virtual XGE queue and to the native queue. Looking at this figure, it is obvious that the prologue and epilogue of the XGE consume a significant amount of time. While this might be inappropriate when running short jobs, it is negligible when launching a long running computation like the turbulence simulation.

5.2. Virtualized Grid Computing

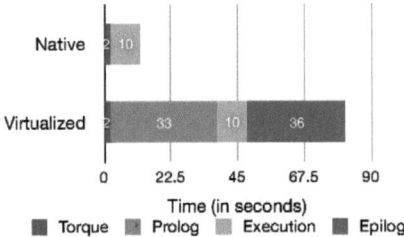

Figure 5.13: Submitting a test job over Torque in a virtualized and a native environment

5.2.5.2 XGE Internals

One of the most important measurements concerns the XGE's overhead. Therefore, a job is executed in a virtual machine with a 2 GB disk image. This process includes the time starting from the actual job submission, detecting and registering the job, deploying the disk images, stopping the placeholder virtual machines, starting the user's own machine, stopping this machine after the computation and finally, restarting the placeholder again. Figure 5.0(a) shows the percentage shares for every operation. To procure a robust mean, 500 trials were performed and the execution time was factored out of the measurement. Most time is consumed by the deployment and the placeholder restart process. Distributing the disk images takes 31.9 seconds on average; however, only for the first time. Since the disk image is unmodified during job execution, it is cached and there is no need to redistribute it. Although the detection process (in terms of code) is fast, it takes 1.3 seconds on average because the XGE only checks the shared job directory every 5 seconds.

Table 5.0(b) shows the detailed average time needed for every single step. The total job handling overhead is 34.4 seconds on average, which is small compared to the average runtime of grid or cloud jobs.

5.2.5.3 Scheduler Performance

The Linux operating system kernel offers several process- and I/O-schedulers. In order to improve the performance of an application, the preferably best possible scheduler should be used, based on runtime characteristics. For example, a CPU intensive application like the turbulence simulation has other I/O-throughput characteristics than massive parallel MPI application; there are other requirements

Chapter 5. Network Security

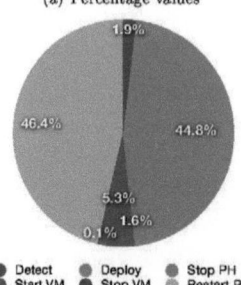

(a) Percentage values

(b) Detailed values of job submission times

Operation	Average
Detect	1.3323414 s
Deploy VM	31.934740 s
Stop PH	1.1271154 s
Start VM	3.7463749 s
Stop VM	0.0801703 s
Restart PH	33.120271 s

Table 5.1: Job processing within the XGE, split in single steps

related to the process response time either. Since the XGE uses tailored virtual machines, it could arrange the machines with an appropriate scheduling algorithm based on the application running inside. The following measurements try to clarify the question, if it is useful to set a tailored scheduling algorithm during virtual machine startup at all. A short introduction of the different schedulers follows; for more details the reader is referred to Maurer [90].

I/O Scheduler

The Linux kernel implements a number of I/O schedulers, which can be activated at run time through the sysfs file system module. Alternatively, there is a parameter to set the default I/O-scheduler at boot time.

Completely Fair Queuing Scheduling is the default since Linux Version 2.6.18 and shares the I/O-bandwidth in a fair manner between the different processes. CFQ replaced the anticipatory scheduler, the default scheduler since Version 2.5.

Anticipatory Scheduling anticipates process behavior as far as possible; it uses the locality principle between two or more disk read accesses to avoid unnecessary seek operations between one or more read- and a write-operation.

Deadline Scheduling implements a soft realtime scheduler, thus it attempts to reduce the number of disk seeks and that requests are served within a certain amount of time.

5.2. Virtualized Grid Computing

Noop is a simple first in, first out scheduler. It is only useful if the underlying hardware has a built-in logic for smart request reordering.

The first measurement uses the *kernbench*[2] benchmark, a CPU throughput benchmark. It compiles the Linux vanilla kernel using a different number of simultaneous jobs each run. The default value is four times the number of CPU cores. During the tests, *kernbench* compiles the kernel with n threads, where n ranges from one to 10.

The average benchmark results, running on the physical hardware and a virtual machine each with two CPU cores, are shown in Figures 5.14(a) and 5.14(b). While running the benchmark directly on the hardware takes less time (around 44 seconds), there is no real difference between the used I/O schedulers. The elapsed time is nearly the same both in the physical and the virtual environment. This effect is even more obvious when looking at the used CPU, since it was impossible to measure a real difference between the schedulers.

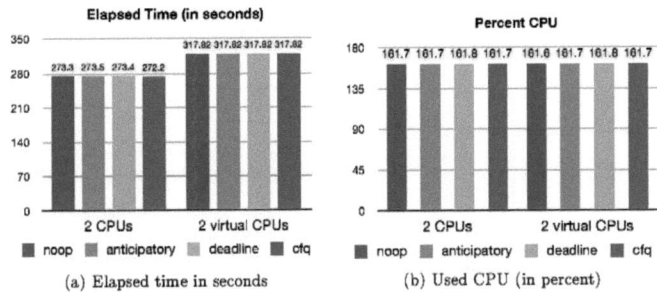

(a) Elapsed time in seconds

(b) Used CPU (in percent)

Figure 5.14: Results of the *kernbench* benchmark running on two physical and two virtual CPU cores

The second measurements were conducted using the bonnie++ [24] benchmark. In order to benchmark the file system and I/O, bonnie reads and writes a file (2 GB in all tests) using different operations. All figures show the the number of megabytes processed per elapsed second using the four different I/O schedulers. While Figure 5.15(a) shows the results while reading byte-by-byte, Figure 5.15(b) shows the results reading block-by-block. The throughput difference between both tests is as follows: *noop* 1.6 MB/s, *cfq* 2.7 MB/s, *anticipatory* 3.07 MB/s, *deadline* 3.1 MB/s.

---
[2]http://freshmeat.net/projects/kernbench/

Chapter 5. Network Security

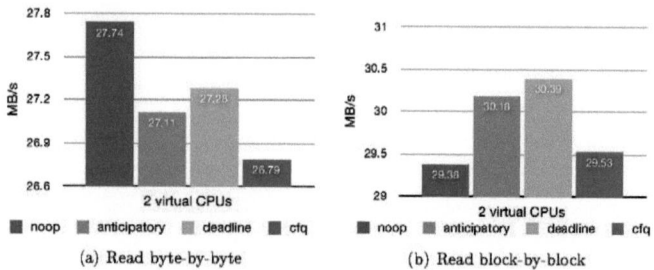

(a) Read byte-by-byte

(b) Read block-by-block

Figure 5.15: bonnie++ benchmark results: sequential input

Figures 5.16(a) and 5.16(b) show the result of the sequential output benchmark, the file is either written byte-by-byte or block-by-block. The throughput differences are as follows: *cfq* 0.1 MB/s, *anticipatory* 1.9 MB/s, *noop* 2.1 MB/s, *deadline* 4.6 MB/s.

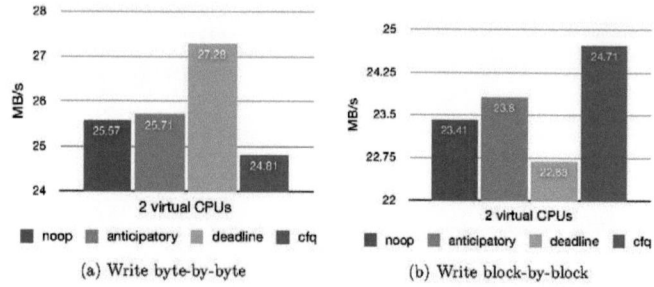

(a) Write byte-by-byte

(b) Write block-by-block

Figure 5.16: bonnie++ benchmark results: sequential output

Looking at these results, it is not obvious which I/O scheduler to use. While one scheduler achieves good writing results, it reaches worse reading results.

Process Scheduler

The process scheduler's main task is to distribute the available time slice fairly to the processes; thus, it has to take different priority levels for processes in account. On one hand, it has to reduce context switches in order to reduce the overhead of the scheduling algorithm itself; on the other hand, letting tasks run for too long increases the latency of a process response. The Linux kernel provides two

5.2. Virtualized Grid Computing

scheduling classes and five scheduling policies. Scheduling classes are used to decide which task runs next. The *completely fair scheduling class* provides a completely fair scheduling (NORMAL), with two variants (BATCH, IDLE) for less important tasks. The *real-time scheduling class* provides a round robin (RR) and a first in, first out mechanism (FIFO). In the following, the focus is on the completely fair scheduling class.

Two parameters in the *proc* file systems are used to control the behavior of the scheduler. *sched_latency_ns* controls the length of the interval during which a runnable process should run at least once (default is 20,000,000 nanoseconds) and *sched_nr_latency* controls the number of active tasks that are at most handled in one latency period (default is 4,000,000 nanoseconds). This parameter is controlled indirectly by *sched_min_granularity*.

The following measurements use the *hackbench*[3] test developed by Rusty Russell, a Linux kernel developer. Its aim is to measure the performance, overhead, and scalability of the Linux scheduler. It starts a number of client and server processes listening to network sockets and exchanging 100 messages. *Hackbench* measures the time taken to exchange the messages. This step is repeated multiple times with an increasing number of processes.

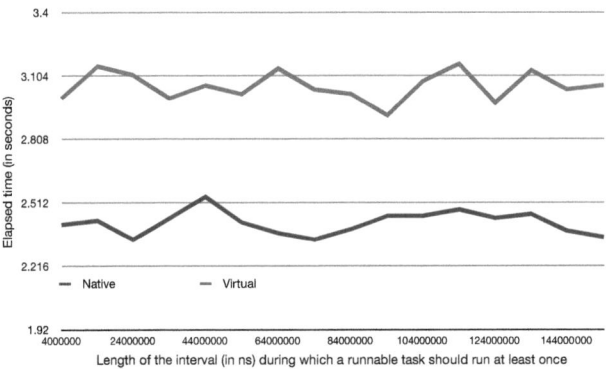

Figure 5.17: Results of *hackbech* runs varying the scheduler's granularity settings

Figures 5.17 and 5.18 show the results of the *hackbench* runs while varying both the scheduler's latency and granularity parameters. An obvious, but unimportant observation is that execution takes longer in the virtual machine. Since *hackbench*

---

[3] http://devresources.linuxfoundation.org/craiger/hackbench/

Chapter 5. Network Security

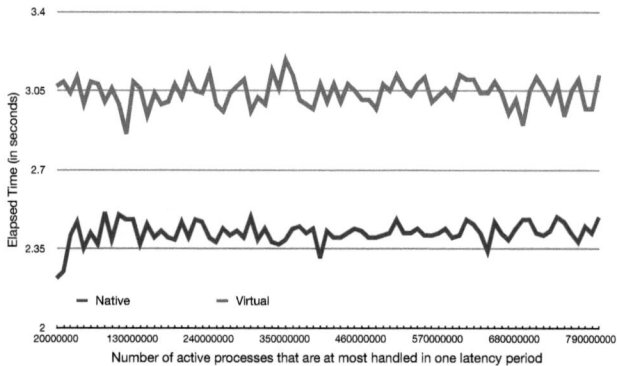

Figure 5.18: Results of *hackbech* runs varying the scheduler's latency settings

simulates a chat with interprocess communication, smaller execution times are better. Based on the results, it is obvious that varying both parameters does not reveal any performance gains.

Summary

In this section, several measurements related to I/O and process scheduling were presented. Unfortunately, the results revealed that it is unreasonable to chose a specific scheduler or its parameters for a virtual machine, depending on its workload.

5.2.6 Summary

A novel virtualized grid environment that offers advanced security mechanisms to enable users to safely install and use custom software on-demand was presented. Applications no longer run unprotected on shared resources; they are embedded into sandboxed environments. Existing components like the grid middleware and a scheduler were leveraged in order to provide a more efficient solution. Since the introduction of virtualization to traditional grids disclosed new issues, the designed software also presents a mechanism for efficient storage synchronization and integrated solutions for effective disk image distribution.

5.3 Grid Demilitarized Zone

5.3.1 Introduction

The grid computing paradigm aims to provide resources (such as compute clusters, data, access to special appliances and even people) as easily as electricity is provided through the electrical power grid. This necessitates that the grid must be easy and transparent to access and use. Unlike traditional cluster computing in which only a small number of users work in a closed system, grid computing exposes local clusters to a large number of users via the Internet using open grid middlewares such as Globus, gLite and Unicore. Like most complex IT systems, these middleware solutions exhibit a number security problems [148, 147, 53, 145], which open the entire system to attack. Unfortunately, these security holes not only expose grid users to attack, but also existing cluster users who up until now have worked in a local and secure environment. This changing nature of grid and cluster computing and the new threats arising thereof is discussed in Smith et al. [125, 124].

This leads us to two major requirements that a grid system must fulfill if widespread integration of existing cluster systems and an industrial adoption of grid technologies is desired. First, existing cluster environments need to be isolated from the weaknesses of the grid middleware, the numerous and possibly unknown, malicious grid users, while at the same time offering their computing power to the grid. Second, the grid user data must be protected from malicious users both during transport and during computation on the backend clusters.

The following section describes several approaches that try to enhance security within grid computing. Because the approaches presented in the related work are insufficient, a novel grid demilitarized zone is presented in this section. Finally, the performance of the presented solution and the security overhead is evaluated.

Parts of this section have been published in [118, 127, 126].

5.3.2 Related Work

Grid and Globus Security

This section presents related work dealing with grid and Globus security in general.

The Grid Security Infrastructure (GSI) (formerly known as Globus Security Infrastructure) was presented by Foster et al. [46] to guarantee security of the data in transit and utilizes Unix security to ensure the safety of data on the nodes in traditional grid/cluster setups, where the grid head node and the scheduler head node are within the same network. While GSI is absolutely sufficient in guaranteeing authentication, confidentiality, and integrity during the transport of grid user data, it does not prevent attackers from attacking the Globus Toolkit itself.

Humphrey et al. [59] group the grid activities that need to be secured into four categories: naming and authentication; secure communication; trust, policy, and authorization; and enforcement of access control. Authentication can be achieved using Public Key Infrastructures (PKI), which is standard in modern grids. The same applies to secure communication, where transport encryption protocols like TLS [31] are used by default. Grid level authorization rules are in the *gridmap* file, which maps a grid DN to a local user account. This scheme turned out not to scale to the case where remote administrators need to control access to local resources. CAS [100] and VOMS [104] solve this problem. Humphrey's paper presents a wide range of solutions for the stated grid security problems and serves as a good reference. However, it does not deal with grid middleware security, basic network security, and damage mitigation.

Two grid cases studies are described by Martin and Yau [88]. The first is an overview of the Grid Security Infrastructure, a de facto architecture that has been adopted by many grid implementations, which deals with the requirements of authentication and authorization. The second, *climateprediction.net*, reveals different security issues that relate to protecting hosts, and to the reliability of results. Based on the studies, they identify a number of security issues and mention, among others, the "fat" grid middleware:

> It is inevitable that it will contain numerous points of vulnerability. By its networked and distributed nature it offers a natural large surface to any would-be attacker: whether their motivation is the subversion of the resources of the Grid, the theft of the data and software being used, or an attack upon the integrity of calculations.

They also mention Trusted Computing (TC) [168] technologies, such as the Trusted Platform Module (TPM) [54]. Nevertheless, they have to admit that "proposals that use Trusted Computing for grid computing are rare, probably because the potential has not yet been fully realized". In conclusion, in order to enhance the security of the grid head node, including the middleware, additional security mechanisms are needed.

Johnston et al. [65] present an overview of security considerations for computational and data grids. In compliance with other authors' authentication, access

5.3. Grid Demilitarized Zone

control and confidentiality are mentioned as security considerations. Furthermore, they mention the following assets to be protected: grid resources, computing systems, data, and communication systems.

Grid and Firewalls

The papers in this section cover challenges, obstacles, and approaches in recent grid firewall research.

Because Globus offers a wide range of remote services, firewalls rules have to be chosen carefully in order to avoid disturbing legal users. Von Welch [169] analyzes Globus Versions 3 and 4 with respect to network ports and data streams. Based on these, a fine-grained firewall configuration can be created, so that authorized users can work without disruptions, while at the same time blocking most unwanted traffic. A similar study was done by Baker et al. [6]. In fact, the DGI of the German D-Grid project recommends a static firewall configuration [165] with about 25.000 open ports to guarantee communication from a grid client to the grid middleware without any problems.

Graupner and Reimann [51] present the most comprehensive study on the Globus Toolkit and firewalls. Regarding creating a demilitarized zone, the authors state: "Another solution is setting up the system under the corporation's control, but network-wise in front of the firewall. The main problem with this solution is that grid resources cannot easily be reached from inside the organization since, network-wise, resources are outside the firewall." Their approach is to use a SSH tunnel to connect grid resources from HP in Paolo Alto to the Technical University Dresden. Unfortunately, the authors do not provide any measurements regarding the overhead of their solution.

Tan et al. [146] present an architecture that facilitates inter-organization communication using existing grid middleware, without compromising the security policies in place at each of the participating sites. Therefore, they describe on a theoretical level how to detect and resolve port conflicts and block unwanted grid applications. They developed and tested a rerouting and multiplexing system called Remus and implemented it prototypically into Nimrod/G. While the paper presents a theoretical overview of grid and firewalling, it lacks a proper implementation based on standard grid middlewares like Globus.

Using a firewall as a grid site protection mechanism raises several problems. For example, the Globus Toolkit 4 uses a wide range of ports for communication with grid clients; thus, it is difficult to configure firewalls properly. Rowland et al. [111] illustrate that in their work. They use a grid installation in an environment working with sensitive medical data. A workflow service, which is installed on a

Chapter 5. Network Security

public location in the Internet, coordinates the execution of grid jobs. Hence, the service can only be reached through a firewall which does not allows connections from the Internet to the internal network. Since not every grid middleware can work with such restrictions, the approach is not feasible.

A dynamic firewall called *Dyna-Fire* has been introduced by Green et al. [52] for a Globus grid middleware environment. The authors state that "the most secure resource is one that does not permit any network connections from any external system. However, this is an impractical solution because it renders the resource useless in terms of grid computing" before they present their approach. *Dyna-Fire* is based on a multi-level authentication, which is based on port knocking. Furthermore, it supports VO-based security policies. *Dyna-Fire* is a solution for enforcing access control on the grid head node. Due it close relationship to the Globus gatekeeper, it enables fine-grained access control to grid sites. Nevertheless, it does not protect other nodes close to the grid head node (e.g., infrastructure nodes) or the compute nodes.

Vinay Bansal [7] presents an approach for granting different rights to grid users based on the WS-Security model. The presented component is a mix between firewall and proxy that analyzes the network traffic and checks the WS-Credentials to grant or deny firewall traversal. By using a parsing engine, the proxy can detect web service-based protocols. A whitelist-based approach (the list contains host names and protocols) is used to determine if the connection is valid or not. Due to its restriction on web service-based protocols, the approach is not suitable. The grid head node can be attacked by a number of other protocols as well. Furthermore, the enormous amount of data in a grid network could overflow the self-written Java parsing engine.

Volpato and Grimm [164] present an approach to partially overcome the limitations in grid computing introduced by firewalls. The first method, based on the extension of a firewall implementation enables dynamic behavior of the firewall itself to better adapt to the needs of the grid environment. The second approach creates a grid demilitarized zone that aims to minimize the interactions between grid middleware and the cluster network. However, since no virtualization of the nodes is present, the following Globus services need to be allowed access from the demilitarized zone into the private cluster network: GridFTP and a login service that transfers the GRAM calls to the cluster scheduler. It is also recommended that the grid middleware in the demilitarized zone and the internal head node share a common file system.

Grid Intrusion Detection Systems

As of today, there are not many mature grid intrusion detection systems. Existing approaches are presented in the following:

Schulter et al. [120] describe a grid IDS, which combines host- and network-IDS to analyze the users' behavior. A scheduler loads the users' profiles and starts one or more analysis processes to detect anomalies. All components interact closely with a database to update changed profiles regularly. The IDS utilizes stored user behavior to detect anomalous activities. Due to the fact that the grid head node can not see most of the users' grid activities in a demilitarized setup, this approach is not applicable to our scenario.

Fang-Yie Lue et al. [83, 82] also integrate an IDS into a grid. Their solution uses existing grid resources to detect high volume packets, especially distributed Denial of Service attacks. Instead of standard technologies, they use their own solution to overcome possible performance bottlenecks. Their approach deals mainly with the distribution of load for the IDS and requires several Globus nodes to be utilized, which raises the risks of being compromised though a middleware. Furthermore, it is not clear whether an implementation of the system is available.

Silva et al. [122] describe a system named *Distributed IDS on Grid* (DIDSoG), that aims to join heterogeneous Intrusion Detection System over a grid middleware. This should be achieved using a two-dimensional hierarchy of sensors, correlators/aggregators, analysers, monitoring services, and countermeasure services. The infrastructure should be used to combine the strengths and reduce the weaknesses of various existing IDS systems. However, no IDS or grid systems are used; rather, a GridSim simulation is presented covering the graph construction. Thus, it is difficult to judge the capabilities of the system.

Kenny and Coghlan [69] present SANTA-G (Grid-enabled System Area Networks Trace Analysis), which is a generic template for ad-hoc, non-invasive monitoring with external instruments. They use it and Snort [128] as the basis for grid-wide intrusion detection. A special sensor monitors the log files created by Snort and notifies an engine when new log files are detected. This engine saves the information into a database and processes incoming SQL queries that request this information. Communication is socket-based and XML is used as communication protocol. There is also a graphical user interface for the administrator. Due to its design, SANTA-G could be used as a distributed intrusion detection system to monitor multiple grid sites. Although the design of SANTA-G looks promising, it is unclear whether an implementation exits. Furthermore, the system does not deal with specific intrusion signatures for grids.

5.3.3 Design

Based on the related work presented in the last section, it is possible to derive the following requirements for security measurements of the grid head node:

- Since most grid head nodes are located inside the same network as the computing resources, a compromise of the former leads to access of the latter. Therefore, a separation of the grid/internal network into two isolated networks is needed. As this creates new problems, these problems need to be addressed as well.

- In a standard setup, GSI is responsible for the integrity of the data, but the assumption is that the grid head node has full access to the cluster. Data encrypted with the GSI is decrypted by the grid head node, which could be compromised. As a result, GSI-secured job data stored on the grid head node is no longer safe or private. To protect grid user data, GSI encryption must be extended to encompass both the grid and the internal network.

- Since a grid middleware requires a number of open network ports, a specialized solution is not feasible. Though a more generic solution could leave space for attacks, other solutions could interrupt the workflow or even the whole operation of grid users.

- Grid user data must never be stored in unencrypted form on the grid head node, and the grid middleware must not be able to decrypt the data, for it could potentially be compromised.

- Since it is impossible to create countermeasures against all known attacks, it would be beneficial if there were logs in the event of a successful compromise. Therefore, a Network Intrusion Detection (NIDS) could be used. Most intrusion detection systems are not able to detect attacks against grid environments due to grid-specific attacks; thus, new rules have to be developed.

An important design goal is simple integration into an existing infrastructure. This is, as prescribed by the German D-Grid, the Globus Toolkit as grid middleware and Torque as scheduler. Incoming jobs are submitted via the GRAM interface; therefore, it is important that this interface remains functional and no modifications on the Globus source should be necessary. Additional modifications to the source are inappropriate, as the mere amount of code could lead to new, unintended bugs.

A working group of the German D-Grid reviewed the cooperation between different grid middlewares, including Globus, and firewalls [165]. In order to guarantee

5.3. Grid Demilitarized Zone

Service	Port (TCP)
GRAM	2119, Range 20000 - 25000
WS-GRAM	8443, Range 20000 - 25000
WS-MDS	8443
GridFTP	2811, Range 20000 - 25000
RFT	8443
GSI-SSH	2222

Table 5.2: Globus Toolkit 4 network configuration. Source: [165]

a seamless workflow between users and grid services, a number of ports that must not be filtered were identified. The results are shown in Table 5.2. To achieve at least some protection, they recommended letting only certain IP addresses or IP ranges pass the firewall. To prevent overloading the Globus Toolkit, they further recommend restricting the number of users who can access it simultaneously to 20.

Due to the stated firewall restrictions, it is unreasonable to proceed with the traditional grid network architecture: a shared network with both the grid head node and the computing nodes. Derived from these requirements, a grid enabled demilitarized zone was designed, which will be presented in the following. To be able to analyze attack traces after a successful compromise, the nodes inside the demilitarized zone are monitored by a grid-capable Network Intrusion Detection System.

5.3.3.1 Architecture of the Demilitarized Zone

To prevent external intruders from accessing the computing resources by exploiting weaknesses in the grid middleware, the grid/internal subnet is divided into two separate subnetworks, the border network and the internal network.

The demilitarized zone guards both networks with a firewall configured to the specific needs of the network in question. The border firewall filters connections from the Internet and denies unwanted connections to all machines within the demilitarized zone. However, since grid middlewares require a large number of open ports to function correctly and efficiently, and a large number of fluctuating users need to access the grid, the border firewall has to be relatively open. The grid head node is located in the demilitarized zone. The inner firewall guards the internal network and prevents direct connections to the cluster subnetwork. To protect the internal network, the inner firewall is very strict and only allows one specially designed connector to pass through. Moreover, it does not allow any

Chapter 5. Network Security

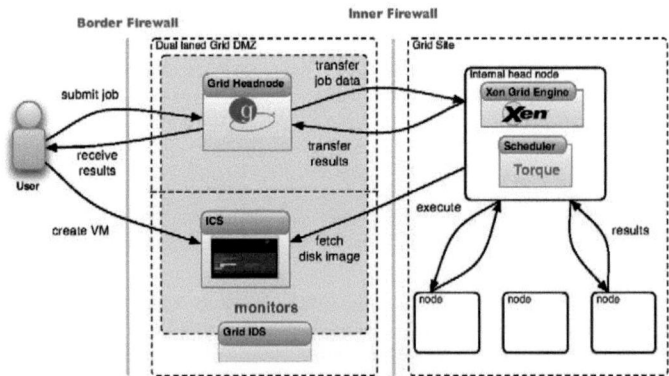

Figure 5.19: Architectural overview

interactive sessions to pass into the cluster network. The computing resources reside in the internal network and consist of a cluster head node and a set of nodes. An architectural overview is presented in Figure 5.19.

Grid Job Submission

The following section describes the steps involved in submitting a grid job through a firewall, ranging from the initial submission up to the termination.

In order to submit a grid job, the user has different choices. She could use a simple command line client, a portal (e.g., Gridsphere [150]) or a grid service. Depending on method used, different actions are triggered within Globus. All files needed for execution are created by the job manager, be it either a local or a portal job. If it used grid service invocation, the service also calls GRAM and, hence, the job manager.

In the third step, the job manager calls a local daemon that transfer the generated job files over to another daemon on the internal head node. This is done step by step for all files belonging to the job.

The daemon on the internal head node accepts the information in the fourth step. All received data is stored on the local hard disk. Another service located on the grid head node now transfers all grid job data to the daemon mentioned in the previous step.

Once the transfer is finished, the job manager is notified and sets the job state from pending to active in Step 6. In the seventh and final step, the job manager notifies the user. All of the described steps are shown in Figure 5.20.

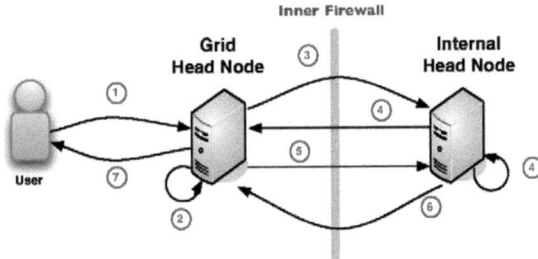

Figure 5.20: Step-by-step processing of a job through the inner firewall

In order to use the virtualized grid enhancements previously described in this chapter, the user has to create a virtual machine using the Image Creation Station (ICS). The ICS provides a software installation process based on virtualization technology. A user receives a private virtual environment that looks and behaves exactly like a node that belongs to the grid to be used. The user has root access and can install software in the same way that software is installed on a local machine.

Since the ICS must also allow users to log on from the Internet, it is located inside a part of the demilitarized zone. Based on the X.509 grid identity, the user can log onto an individually created disk image and install all required software. The user only gets to log on to his or her own disk image and thus can not compromise other disk images in the demilitarized zone. To prevent an attacker from compromising the grid head node, from there, the ICS, a dual-laned demilitarized zone approach is employed that restricts access to either the grid head node lane or the ICS lane. Thus, if one lane is compromised, the other lane remains unaffected.

5.3.3.2 End-to-End Encryption

Since jobs are no longer executed in the same realm of the network as the grid head node, a new encryption scheme is required. When a user submits a job, the client software (e.g. the Gridsphere portal) generates a 48-byte session key, which is encrypted with the public key of the XGE. This session key is used to encrypt both the job data and later also the results. Both the job and the encrypted session key can now be transferred through the insecure demilitarized zone. Due to its location in the demilitarized zone, the grid head node is considered unsafe, so the job data remains encrypted and the corresponding keys are not available outside of the secure network environment.

Job submission with full encryption is divided into several steps. The steps are shown in Figure 5.21 and explained in the following:

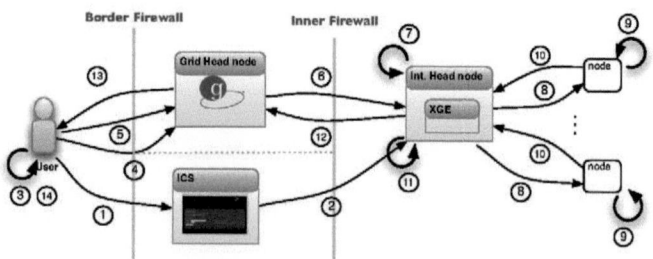

Figure 5.21: All steps required for a end-to-end encryption

1. The user creates a fully-customized virtual machine for execution at the ICS. This machine represents the basis for the upcoming computation.

2. The disk image is transferred to the internal head node. The connection is initialized from the internal network. This ensures maximum security because there is no need for an open incoming port towards the cluster network.

3. The client generates a session key and encrypts the session key with the XGE public key. It then archives and encrypts the job data with the session key and creates a customized RSL file. The RSL file contains the name of the archive and the encrypted session key.

4. The job data is copied to the grid head node via GridFTP.

5. A Globus GRAM call is launched according to the RSL file.

6. Globus hands over the job to a special software that will be described later, which transfers the new job to the internal head node.

7. The XGE parses the job description, decrypts the session key, and decrypts the data within the virtual machines. Furthermore, the scheduler is now invoked and schedules the job for execution.

5.3. Grid Demilitarized Zone

8. After the scheduler calls the XGE, it distributes and boots the images created in Step 1.

9. The job is executed within the virtual machines on behalf of the scheduler.

10. The results are encrypted with the session key, extracted from the machines and copied back to the internal head node.

11. The encrypted results handed over to Fence.

12. The encrypted results are copied back to the grid head node.

13. The user fetches the results with GridFTP.

14. The user decrypts the results.

Job Submission, Transfer and Execution

Since direct communication between the grid head node and the scheduler is no longer possible, a new mechanism is required to transfer and execute a grid job. A newly developed software called *Fence* (short for Fence Head Node Security Environment) deals with the task of transferring job data to the internal head node. Fence consists of the following components, which will be explained in greater detail later on.

- Job manager: Tightly integrated into the Globus Toolkit. One component is a *Scheduler Event Generator* (SEG). The other one hands over a new job to the scheduler.

- DMZ Head Node Client (*dhnc*): Provides the communication between the grid head node and the internal head node.

- Cluster Head Node Daemon (*chnd*): Represents the interface between the services on the grid head node and the scheduler on the cluster head node. Due to its location, the *chnd* is a critical security component and needs additional protection.

- DMZ Head Node Daemon (*dhnd*): The second service on the grid head node. It is a background task, serving requests from the *chnd*.

All connections between the aforementioned components are encrypted using the TLS protocol, which guarantees confidentiality and authenticity.

Chapter 5. Network Security

Job Manager

In the last stage of processing, Globus hands over the job to the novel job manager. To use it, a new job must use a specific factory type. In order to forward the job to the installed scheduler, a number of parameters must be included:

- The working directory of the job binary
- The absolute path pointing to the binary
- Command line arguments possible
- Command line variables required
- Additional files needed for execution
- Maximum amount of virtual memory

These parameters are written into two files that the XGE and the scheduler need to launch the grid job. The first one is a shell script containing calls to the actual binary, the second an XML description of the job.

Since the job manager is integrated into Globus, is has to implement an interface that consists of the following functions:

- Start a job
- Delete a job
- Request status information about a job

In general, all Globus job managers are written in the Perl programming language. Since Globus itself offers no interface for Perl, one has to chose another way instead. A log file, written by the job manager, is used as gateway between the two. After handing over a job to a scheduler (or Fence, respectively), the job manager writes a first entry to the log and sets the job's state to *pending*. Once the data transfer between Fence's components is finished, another entry is added that marks the job as *active*. As soon as the job terminates, the last entry is written, setting the job to *deleted*.

While the job manager writes entries to that log, a *Scheduler Event Generator* (SEG) reads from it. This SEG is a small daemon, written in the C programming language and bound to the C interface of Globus. Once it reads a legitimate entry, it triggers an action. All of the described steps are shown in Figure 5.22

5.3. Grid Demilitarized Zone

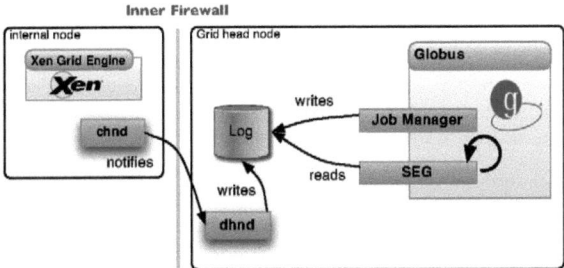

Figure 5.22: Interaction between Globus, the job manager and the XGE

DMZ Head Node Client

The DMZ Head Node Client, short *dhnc*, provides the interface between the job manager and the internal head node. Its primary task is to notify the software on the internal head node about a new grid job. In order to provide maximum security, no job data other than a small and simple info message is sent from the border network to internal network. Thus, only one port needs to be open. All further data transfers are initiated from within the internal network.

Cluster Head Node Daemon

The Cluster Head Node Daemon, short *chnd*, is the counterpart of the *dhnc* installed on the internal head node. Besides handling the communication between the two networks, it is also responsible for interacting with the XGE. As a consequence, the daemon must support a great variety of functions.

After the daemon receives an info message about a new job, it opens up a connection to the border network and exchanges data. Since the daemon is bound to the only open port of the internal firewall, additional protection is needed. First, it must be impossible to connect directly from the Internet to this port. Second, the runtime environment must be restricted as much as possible to mitigate the risks after a possible compromise.

In order to support all of the job manager's functions (start, delete, request status), the *chnd* acts as a gateway between the mentioned components and the XGE.

Chapter 5. Network Security

DMZ Head Node Daemon

The DMZ Head Node Daemon, short *dhnd* is running in the background of the grid head node. Its task is to bind to a network port, accept connections from its counterpart, the *chnd*, and transfer the requested data. Since the daemon only communicates with Fence components, it is independent from the grid middleware.

Like the *chnd*, the *dhnd* offers a possible attack surface since it is bound to a network port inside the border network. As a result, the process' runtime environment is restricted and the process runs as unprivileged user.

Summary

The last few sections illustrated the design of a grid demilitarized zone that includes Fence, a software that enables secure data transfers between the border and the internal network. Figure 5.23 shows an overview of all of the components within Fence, including the node on which they are installed.

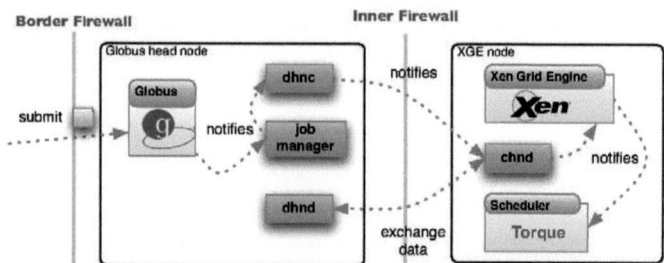

Figure 5.23: Fence embedded into the demilitarized zone. Furthermore, the relations between all components are shown.

5.3.3.3 Optimizing Security Configurations

All of the security mechanisms presented introduce a performance overhead in the overall grid operation. While some of the mechanisms, such as the border firewall, work on a per site basis and must be coped with by all applications, others can be configured on a per user or even per job/service call basis:

- Encryption of input data
- Encryption of working data
- Encryption of result data
- Secure ClassLoaders[1]
- Jailing[1]
- Virtualization[1]
- Inter-node firewalls

This opens up the opportunity to optimize application performance by selectively downgrading or switching off certain security measures that are not required by some applications. To better accommodate the different usage scenarios, a service-oriented description and configuration mechanism is required to allow manual as well as automated selection and configuration of security mechanisms. This allows applications to optimize performance by selectively turning off certain security mechanisms automatically in an otherwise high security grid environment.

WS-Agreement Security Description

This section proposes a ws-Agreement compatible approach to describing security requirements and capabilities in addition to the traditional ws-Negotiation attributes such as computational needs, quality-of-service (QoS), and pricing. Listing 5.18 shows a simplified version of a ws-Agreement scheme for the security mechanisms a grid site could offer. This allows the environment to optimize the security settings for different applications using standardized mechanisms like ws-Negotiation. When a client wants to submit a job or use a service, he or she can create an instance using this template to specify his or her fine-grained security and performance needs. This allows the user to specify in detail which security mechanisms are required at what strength, thus giving the grid middleware the possibility to optimize performance based on those requirements.

---

[1] If sandboxing is implemented for a site, the user has a choice of sandboxing technology. It is not advisable to let users run their software outside a sandbox if there are also users requiring the sandbox's protection. While it should be possible to prevent users from attacking other sandboxed software using standard operating system security, the risk to other users requiring sandbox protection is high; thus, sandboxing should be a per site decision. However, what type of sandbox is used can be left up to the users and depends on the type of software to be sandboxed and the amount of configuration the users and the administrator are willing to spend setting up the sandbox. See Smith et al. [125] for a discussion of the different sandboxing mechanisms and their performance and configuration constraints.

```xml
<xsd:complexType name="AgreementTermType">
<xsd:sequence>
  <xsd:element name="parties" type="tns:AgreementPartiesType"/>
  <xsd:element name="serviceInstanceHandle" type="xsd:anyURI"/>
  <xsd:element name="dependency" type="xsd:anyURI"
    minOccurs="0"
    maxOccurs="unbound"/>
  <xsd:element name="sandbox" type="tns:SandboxType"/>
  <xsd:element name="firewall" type="tns:FirewallType"/>
  <xsd:element name="input_encryption" type="tns:EncryptionType"/>
  <xsd:element name="result_encryption" type="tns:EncryptionType"/>
  <xsd:element name="working_encryption" type="tns:EncryptionType"/>
</xsd:sequence>
</xsd:complexType>

<xsd:complexType name="AgreementPartiesType">
<xsd:sequence>
  <xsd:element name="client" type="xsd:anyURI"/>
  <xsd:element name="provider" type="xsd:anyURI"/>
</xsd:sequence>
</xsd:complexType>

<xsd:simpleType name="SandboxType">
  <xsd:restriction base="xsd:string">
    <xsd:enumeration value="Java"/>
    <xsd:enumeration value="Jail"/>
    <xsd:enumeration value="Xen"/>
  </xsd:restriction>
</xsd:simpleType>

<xsd:complexType name="FirewallType">
<xsd:sequence>
  <xsd:element name="firewall" type="xsd:boolean"/>
  <xsd:element name="throughput" type="xsd:int"/>
  <xsd:element name="ports" type="tns:PortRange"
    minOccurs="0"
    maxOccurs="unbound"/>
</xsd:sequence>
</xsd:complexType>

<xsd:complexType name="PortRange">
<xsd:sequence>
  <xsd:element name="lower" type="xsd:int"/>
  <xsd:element name="upper" type="xsd:int"/>
</xsd:sequence>
</xsd:complexType>

<xsd:complexType name="EncryptionType">
<xsd:sequence>
  <xsd:element name="algorithm" type="tns:AlgorithmType"/>
  <xsd:element name="strength" type="xsd:int"/>
```

```
52  <xsd:element name="sign" type="xsd:boolean"/>
53  </xsd:sequence>
54  </xsd:complexType>
55
56  <xsd:simpleType name="AlgorithmType">
57    <xsd:restriction base="xsd:string">
58      <xsd:enumeration value="AES"/>
59    </xsd:restriction>
60  </xsd:simpleType>
```

Listing 5.18: Grid Security Schema

Processing of the Description

The user creates and submits a WS-Agreement file specifying his or his or her functional requirements (CPU, RAM, time to finish, etc.) as well as his or her security requirements (encryption, sandboxing, required ports, etc). The WS-Agreement document is processed by the AgreementFactory. Based on the evaluation whether the job can be executed to the user's satisfaction, a positive or negative reply is sent.

If both functional and security requirements are met, no changes are needed and the job can be optimized according to the required security settings. If, however, some requirements can not be met, such as number of CPUs, or required closed ports, but the site policy does not allow automatic those ports to be opened automatically, or the user requires native execution (this is particularly relevant for Infiniband grid applications), but the site policy only allows jobs to be executed in virtual environments, the user is informed about the restriction that apply to the given site.

The previous two steps can then be repeated a number of times using WS-Negotiation until either a mutually acceptable setting is found or the request is canceled. The WS-Agreement accepted by both parties is stored by the AgreementManager and can be accessed by Globus and XGE to facilitate user-centric system configuration.

5.3.3.4 Grid-enabled Intrusion Detection

While the introduction of the demilitarized zone protects the internal network from attacks and the new encryption scheme protects the confidentiality and integrity of grid job data, there is still the danger of Denial-of-Service or unknown attacks against insecure grid middleware within the demilitarized zone. To face this threat, a setup that detects possible attacks and takes appropriate countermeasures is needed. To accomplish this task, a standard Network Intrusion Detection Systems (NIDS) was extended by grid specific attack signatures.

To detect possible intruders in advance, a NIDS is installed between the border firewall and the border network. Most intrusion detection systems are not able to detect attacks against grid environments due to grid specific attacks; thus, new rules have to be developed. There are a number of relevant attacks against a grid:

- Simple Denial-of-Service Attacks: This type is very similar to common DoS attacks, except that they focus on grid components, such as the Globus Toolkit, gLite, Unicore, GridFTP, etc.

- Complex Denial-of-Service Attacks: Complex DoS attacks try to misuse certain components of the grid software. For example, an intruder could generate numerous false certificates to generate a high load on the grid AAI components.

- Use of exploits: No software component is really free of bugs, so the use of an exploit against a security vulnerability is always possible.

Grid specific rules and a proof-of-concept attack are described in Section 5.3.4.8 on page 163.

5.3.4 Implementation

This section describes the implementation of the demilitarized zone and the GSI extension. The design of a network has a certain impact on the security of a demilitarized zone. A poorly configured firewall or an ill-designed network could lead to a number of problems, e.g. unnecessary filtered ports reveal the existence of a transparent firewall.

5.3.4.1 Border Network

The border network is guarded by both firewalls and builds the demilitarized zone. All machines are directly connected to the outside network. Currently, this includes the head node running Globus and the Image Creation Station. Traffic between the Internet and the demilitarized zone is filtered by the border firewall. Invalid packets are dropped immediately. This includes:

- External connections that have a private IP address as source address. This

5.3. Grid Demilitarized Zone

prevents that external packets are masked as internal ones. Of course, this only applies if Network Address Translation is used.

- Unrouteable packets.

- Various types of network scans such as port or SSH scans. This rule prevents an attacker from gaining knowledge about the network's structure. While a good firewall can filter known scans, it is still possible for yet unknown or advanced scans to pass through the filter.

- Any traffic which is not explicitly permitted.

It is only possible to lock down the border firewall to a certain degree. Too restrictive rules can disturb the legal operations of complex software such as Globus.

5.3.4.2 Internal Network

The inner firewall guards the internal network that is a private network according to RFC 1918; thus, no direct connection from the Internet is possible. Internet connectivity for the XGE is provided via Network Address Translation (NAT).

Connections initiated by nodes in the internal network are only filtered for invalid or blocked ports as the internal network is trusted one. Connections initiated by nodes in the demilitarized zone are blocked. Only one exception is permitted: connections to the Cluster Head Node Daemon (see Section 5.3.3.2). Furthermore, these connections are only permitted if they originate from the demilitarized zone. Stateful inspection is enabled on both firewalls to minimize load.

5.3.4.3 End-to-End Encryption with Fence

The following steps are required for end-to-end encryption.

- Session key generation and job submission: First, the session key is generated. The software encrypts the job data with this key. Then, the session key is encrypted with the XGE public key and appended to the GRAM-RSL file. Finally, a GRAM call is sent to the Globus machine, and GridFTP is used to transfer the encrypted job data.

- New job arrives: After a new job arrives at the grid head node, Fence transfers this job to the cluster head node. All transferred data remains encrypted at all times.

- New job arrives at the internal head node: After the XGE recognizes a new job, it extracts the session key from the job description and decrypts the job data with the private key within the corresponding user image.

- Computation finished: After successful computation, the results are encrypted within the secure virtual environment and are then handed back to the grid head node.

The RSL extension field is used to integrate the session keys into Globus and two new tags were introduced: <inputArchive> and <ID>. On the client-side, the job data is stored inside a Zip-archive (named by the first tag), which is encrypted with the session key. The second tag holds the encrypted key. Encrypting the session key with a public key ensures the secure transfer of the key over insecure channels and storing the key on untrusted storage, e.g. the grid head node. The secret key is stored securely on the cluster head node and is not accessible to any users.

5.3.4.4 Connection to the Globus Toolkit

The connection between Fence and the Globus Toolkit is managed by a newly developed module. Usually, a Globus module called the job manager is responsible for processing new jobs. New jobs, submitted either directly from the command line or via GRAM call a job manager. There is one job manager for every scheduler of which Globus is aware, e.g. *Fork*, *PBS* or *Condor*. The new job manager module is an extension of the previous PBS module and the SGE module developed by London E-Science [35]. The final version was optimized for security.

A job manager consists of two parts, one written in C, the other one written in Perl. The C part is responsible for the integration into Globus and the Perl part is the interface to Fence. To use the new module, one has to specify PBS as job manager or factory type.

Every job manager is a subclass of *Globus::GRAM::JobManager* and has to implement three methods:

> submit() is called when a job is forwarded from the job manager to the scheduler. The method has access to the whole job description (e.g., the content of the RSL file). Its main purpose is to check if the parameters for the scheduler call are valid. Invalid parameters could lead to a direct abortion of the job. Finally, the method submits the job to the scheduler.
>
> poll() queries the state of the job. Among others, this could be *active* or *failed*.

cancel() stops the stop and removes it from the system. A message informs the user about the details.

The module generates two files: a XML file with the description of the job and a shell script containing the needed commands to launch the job. The syntax of the XML file is derived from the Globus GRAM RSL schema [28] and the job description is encoded as follows:

<user>: The user who submitted the job via Globus.

<script>: The name of the job script calling the job's executable.

<files>: This meta tag encodes a number of <file> entries describing the file needed for job execution.

<maxMemory>: Maximum amount of virtual memory (in megabytes).

<maxCpuTime>: Maximum amount of CPU time (in minutes).

<sessionKey>: This field contains the session key encrypted with the public key of the XGE.

A sample XML file is shown in Listing 5.19. The file job.sh is executed on behalf of the user *testuser* (line 3 and 4). Input and output streams are saved in two files in the users home directory (lines 9 through 11) and the job is bound to resource requirements (lines 6 and 7).

```
1  <?xml version='1.0'?>
2  <job>
3      <script>job.sh</script>
4      <user>matthias</user>
5
6      <maxCpuTime>100000</maxCpuTime>
7      <maxMemory>1024</maxMemory>
8
9      <files>
10         <file>$HOME/input</file>
11         <file>$HOME/output</file>
12     </files>
13 </job>
```

Listing 5.19: Auto-generated XML file describing a job

A shell script is needed to let the scheduler start the job. The script calls the actual binary and sets possible environment variables.

5.3.4.5 DMZ Head Node Client

The DMZ Head Node Client, *dhnc* for short, establishes the connection between the job manager and the cluster node. It can be called from either the command line client or directly from the job manager.

As mentioned in the previous section, several generated files are needed for job execution. Due to the demilitarized zone, the job manager cannot communicate directly with the XGE node, so another solution is needed. A naive solution would allow the *dhnc* to copy the files directly. Due to security considerations, this method is not acceptable. A direct copy of nodes in the demilitarized zone requires exact parsing on the internal node. This is necessary to avoid malicious data from triggering a buffer overflow on the receivers side, for example. To avoid that issue, a pull strategy is used. The *dhnc* opens up a connection to the corresponding service on the internal node and sends a simple INFO message. This message is easy to parse so that it cannot be misused. Listing 5.20 shows an INFO message being transferred, which informs the daemon running on the XGE node about a new job. A new network socket is opened (lines 2 through 5). Parameters, such as the IP address, the protocol, and the port, are set in lines 7 through 10. The *dhnc* either obtains the IP address from the command line client or it is set by the job manager. Using the socket and the parameters, the connect system call opens a connection that will be used to transfer the data (lines 12 through 16). Finally, the INFO message is constructed and written to the socket (lines 20 through 24). The INFO message length is limited to 1024 characters to prevent buffer overflows. Due to the design of an INFO message, the string will never hit that limit.

```
1  [...]
2  if ((fd = socket(AF_INET, SOCK_STREAM, 0)) < 0) {
3      if (flag_q == 0) printf("Cannot open socket\n");
4      return(-1);
5  }
6
7  memset(&addr, 0, sizeof(addr));
8  addr.sin_family = AF_INET;
9  addr.sin_port = htons(CHND_PORT);
10 inet_pton(AF_INET, ip, &addr.sin_addr);
11
12 if (connect(fd, (struct sockaddr *)&addr, sizeof(addr)) < 0) {
13     if (flag_q == 0) printf("Connect to %s failed\n", ip);
14     close(fd);
15     return(-1);
16 }
17
18 [...]
19
20 snprintf(snd, 1024, "INFO %s\r\n", (char*)string);
```

5.3. Grid Demilitarized Zone

```
21
22  [...]
23
24  len = write(fd, snd, strlen(snd));
```

Listing 5.20: Code snippet that shows the process of creating and transferring an INFO message

After the transfer ends successfully, the connection is closed.

5.3.4.6 Cluster Head Node Daemon

The Cluster Head Node Daemon, *chnd* for short, is the interface between the grid head node and the XGE on the internal head node. It runs in the background, is bound to the only port open in the internal firewall, and is written in the C programming language.

A frequent message arriving at the *chnd* is the aforementioned INFO message reporting that a new job is waiting on the grid head node. In order to avoid an attacker from exploiting a possible bug, the message is carefully parsed. Only well-known parts are accepted, all other information is discarded. This is possible since Globus used a well-defined format for its job IDs. The message is split to extract the job ID and the file name. The extracted file is requested by using the ID. Thus, a connection to the *dhnd* is opened. A GET message is constructed to request a file. This procedure is repeated for all files mentioned in the job description. If an error occurs, the connection is canceled and the user is informed.

Due to its prominent location, the runtime environment has to be restricted. A successful compromise of the *chnd* could lead to access of the internal head node. Further details about the restriction of the runtime environment are described in the next section.

5.3.4.7 DMZ Head Node Daemon

The second service running on the grid head node is the DMZ Head Node Daemon, or *dhnd*. Its a background daemon that answers requests from the *chnd* and transfers data to the internal network. It is written in the C programming language.

The *dhnd*'s primary task is to transfer job data. An incoming message from the internal network is split and then parsed for invalid characters. The *dhnd* searches for the given file is in the file system and sends it over the established connection. After a successful transfer, the file is removed from the file system to avoid the hard disk from filling up. Once all files belonging to a job are transmitted, the whole directory is removed. If an error occurs, the connection is aborted.

Runtime Environment Restrictions

Due to the fact that the *dhnd* is permanently bound to a network port, it represents a critical service. While the border firewall prevents connections from the Internet, it cannot prevent connections from the border network. To increase the difficulty a possible attacker faces when trying to compromise the system, the run time environment of *dhnd* is restricted. After start-up, the working directory is changed to a special directory with the help of the chroot system call. Now, the process can no longer access files outside of this directory. In the event of a compromise, no working environment (e.g., a shell and system utilities) is available. To prevent the attacker from escaping from the working directory, the process runs with reduced privileges, i.e. it is running as a special user. It is possible to procure the user ID with the initgroups system call (line 16). Then the user and group ID are set for this process (lines 18 - 21). It is possible to use the setuid system call because the process is started as root. Theoretically, it is even now still possible to escape from jailed environment. To avoid that, further modifications of the operating system kernel are needed (e.g., as with the Openwall [152] or grsecurity [137] kernel hardening patch). The aforementioned implementation is shown in Listing 5.21

```
int
drop_root(char *server_user, char *server_jail)
{
    struct passwd *pw;

    if (!(pw = getpwnam(server_user)))
        return -1;
    if (!pw->pw_uid)
        return -1;

    if (chroot(server_jail))
        return -1;
    if (chdir("/"))
        return -1;

    if (initgroups(server_user, pw->pw_gid))
        return -1;
    if (setgid(pw->pw_gid))
        return -1;
    if (setuid(pw->pw_uid))
        return -1;

    return 0;
}
```

Listing 5.21: Runtime Environment Restrictions

Under Linux, the proc file system shows the current working directory (cwd) as well as the root directory of a process ($root$). For an instance of $dhnd$ this looks as follows:

```
[...]
lrwxrwxrwx 1 root root 0 2011-01-13 08:10 cwd -> /usr/dhnd
lrwxrwxrwx 1 root root 0 2011-01-13 08:10 exe -> /usr/local/bin/dhnd
lrwxrwxrwx 1 root root 0 2011-01-13 08:10 root -> /usr/dhnd
[...]
```

The new working and root directory is /usr/dhnd.

5.3.4.8 Grid Enabled Intrusion Detection System

To protect the grid infrastructure, Snort [128] is placed between the border firewall and the border network as Network Intrusion Detection System. Snort analyzes all incoming traffic and compares it to its signature database. If a positive match occurs, an alarm is sounded. Usually, an alert is just an entry to a special alert log file. However, Snort has multiple ways to contact an administrator, such as e-mail or SMS. To reduce the scan time the signature database should be as small as possible. As a result, it is not important to search for SMTP attacks if no SMTP server is available.

A fraction of an attack log showing an example portscan of the grid head node running Globus is shown in Listing 5.22. In addition to the grid software, a *finger* daemon[4] was installed to test the functionality of the NIDS. *finger* is a simple service used to query information about other users and has an inglorious security history (legacy versions of the daemon contained some severe bugs). Both the scan and the attempt to execute code were detected by Snort and logged.

```
[**] [122:1:0] (portscan) TCP Portscan [**]
02/20-15:06:12.016821 172.16.1.2 -> 172.16.1.1
PROTO255 TTL:0 TOS:0x0 ID:0 IpLen:20 DgmLen:155 DF

[**] [1:327:8] FINGER remote command pipe execution attempt [**]
[Classification: Attempted User Privilege Gain] [Priority: 1]
02/20-15:06:31.281091 172.16.1.2:49312 -> 172.16.1.1:79
TCP TTL:64 TOS:0x0 ID:11583 IpLen:20 DgmLen:96 DF
***AP*** Seq: 0x9A4F576D  Ack: 0x95BF2F6D  Win: 0x8218  TcpLen: 32
```

---

[4] http://tools.ietf.org/html/rfc742

```
10 TCP Options (3) => NOP NOP TS: 641186081 607311459
```

Listing 5.22: Fraction of the snort alert log after a portscan and a break-in attempt

Grid IDS Signatures

To enhance the security of the installed grid head node, the signature database was extended with Globus-specific attack signatures. Since Globus offers a wide range of services (e.g., GridFTP, GSI-SSH, gatekeeper, service container, etc.), it is impossible to develop signatures for all of them. Furthermore, developing a new signature for a service requires a new, yet unknown attack. As a result, only two proof-of-concept attacks and the corresponding signatures were developed in the course of this thesis: one attack against WSRF, another against GridFTP.

The attack is a simple Denial-of-Service attack; hence, it attempts to overflow Globus with a enormous amount of connections until the service stalls. Listing 5.23 shows a shell script that uses the *netcat* tool to open up a connection and to send 500 bytes of random data. Since the number of parallel connections is the cause of the problem, the size of the payload is negligible. The script connects to the web service container port (8443), however it can also be used to attack GridFTP by simply changing the port number to 2811.

```
1  #!/bin/sh
2
3  # Network port (here, the WSRF service)
4  port=8443
5  # IP address of the grid head node
6  host=172.16.1.1
7  # Maximum number of packets
8  max=100000
9
10 for ((i=0; i<$max; i++)); do
11     nc $host $port < paket_content
12 done
```

Listing 5.23: Globus WSRF-Denial of Service

Based on the evaluation of these attacks, new Snort detection rules were created, which are shown in Listing 5.24.

```
1 alert tcp $EXTERNAL_NET any -> $HOME_NET 8443 (msg:"Globus WSRF DoS
2 attack"; flow:stateless; flags:S; threshold: type both, track by_src
   ,
3 count 1000,seconds 30; classtype:denial-of-service;)
4
```

5.3. Grid Demilitarized Zone

```
5 alert tcp $EXTERNAL_NET any -> $HOME_NET 2811(msg:"Globus GridFTP
    DoS
6 attack"; flow:stateless; flags:S; threshold: type both, track by_src
    ,
7 count 1000,seconds 30; classtype:denial-of-service;)
```

Listing 5.24: New signatures to detect a Globus Denial of Service attack

Since the difference between the two rules is the port number, only the WSRF signature is explained here:

- `alert tcp $EXTERNAL_NET any -> $HOME_NET 8443`: Snort triggers an alarm as soon as a TCP connection to port 8443 is opened from the Internet into the border network and once the following conditions are true:

- `msg:Globus GridFTP DoS attack`: This message is logged if the rules fires.

- `flow:stateless`: In general, a TCP connection that is part of DoS attack does not perform a correct 3-way handshake; thus, Snort has to treat all packets as isolated ones.

- `flags:S`: Since all packets want to open up a connection, the SYN flag has to be set.

- `threshold: type both, track by_src, count 1000, seconds 30`: The rule only fires, if more than a 1000 TCP packets arrive within 30 seconds. This high threshold ensures that the normal volume of legal grid connections observed at our site does not raise a false alarm. The threshold needs to be adjusted to each site's expected usage.

- `classtype:denial-of-service`: The classification tag for DoS attack rules.

Using these rules, Snort can now detect the proof-of-concept attacks (Listing 5.25). If an attack is registered, there are three responses: First, a log entry is written solely for documentation purposes. Second, the grid and cluster administrators receive an alert message. Third, the attack is displayed on the local WebMDS, which enables end users to view Globus monitoring information via a standard web browser interface. The icon for the registered resource changes from green to red to enable quick visual recognition of which sites are under attack.

```
1 [**] [1:9998:0] Globus GridFTP DoS attack [**]
2 [Classification: Detection of a Denial of Service Attack] [Priority:
    2]
```

Chapter 5. Network Security

```
3 03/16-09:40:24.037370 10.0.1.10:45941 -> 10.0.1.68:2811
4 TCP TTL:64 TOS:0x0 ID:44334 IpLen:20 DgmLen:60 DF
5 ******S* Seq: 0xE8A4D535  Ack: 0x0  Win: 0x16D0  TcpLen: 40
6 TCP Options (5) => MSS: 1460 SackOK TS: 679901211 0 NOP WS: 7
```

Listing 5.25: Snort detects the attack on the GridFTP service

5.3.5 Evaluation

While the presented features are required for effective security in grid environments, they create a certain amount of overhead. The transmission time is extended due to the extra hop via Fence, and encryption and decryption also consume some time compared to a completely unsecured grid operation.

The test environment consists of 6 machines connected with a switched 100 Mbit Ethernet network. The firewalls are Pentium III machines with 1 GHz, 512 MB RAM and FreeBSD installed. The grid head node is a Pentium IV with 3 GHz, 1 GB RAM and Debian Linux installed. The same configuration applies to the client machine. The Cluster head node is a Pentium IV with 1.8 GHz, 512 MB RAM and Solaris 10 installed. There are also 4 Pentium IV with 1.8 GHz, 512 MB RAM worker nodes running Debian Linux in a Xen environment. The NIDS is a passive component, which does not influence job execution time.

The most important measurement concerns end-to-end encryption. It introduces improved security, but it also consumes time. To show that the introduced overhead is negligible, two measurements were conducted. The first one measures the time for an encrypted job from the client to the XGE. The second measurement is the same, except that the data is unencrypted. The execution time is job dependent and thus factored out of the measurements.

Figure 5.24 shows the times required for the following steps:

1. Start a job on the client side and encrypt the job data with a 48-byte key
2. Transfer the job data via Fence to the XGE
3. The XGE detects the new job and decrypts the data

The test application is the casting simulation package CASTS (Computer Aided Solidification TechnologieS) [36], which is one of the engineering applications in the D-Grid. CASTS is a dedicated software tool developed for the full range of casting processes. CASTS calculates transient temperature distributions in mold, core and alloy, taking into account both latent heat release as a function of

5.3. Grid Demilitarized Zone

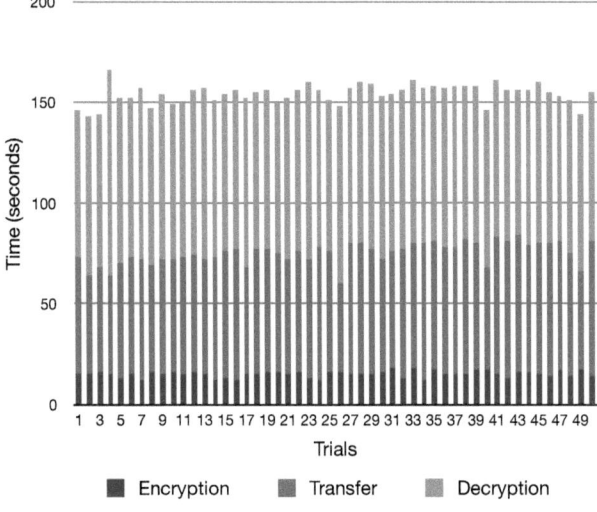

Figure 5.24: Time for fully-encrypted job submissions

fraction solid, and heat transfer resistance at material interfaces. The typical data volume for CASTS is about 290 MB.

50 trials were conducted to get a robust mean, which is about 154 seconds. The chart is divided into three parts. The bottom part displays the time needed to encrypt the data. The middle part displays the time needed to transfer the files via Fence from the grid head node to the internal head node. The upper part displays the time needed to decrypt the data. The difference between the two cryptographic processes results from diverse hardware (1.8 GHz CPU vs. 3 GHz CPU). The small variance in transfer time is due to the polling nature of the XGE.

The second measurement is exactly the same as the first, except no job data is encrypted or decrypted. Figure 5.25 shows the time in seconds on the ordinate and 50 trials on the abscissa. The mean is about 49 seconds. Due to the watchdog characteristic of the XGE, the same variance can be seen here as already described in the last case.

The difference between the means of the two trials is 105 seconds, so about twice the time for full end-to-end encryption is needed. Compared with the time this

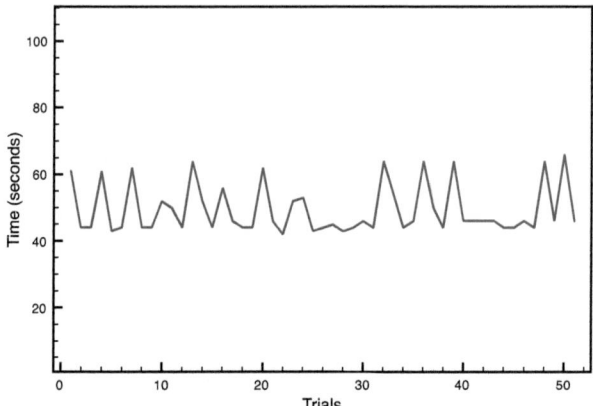

Figure 5.25: Time required for unencrypted job submissions

CASTS job needs to be completed (about one hour), the extra time (an additional 105 seconds) is worth the security gained.

To compare the filter overhead introduced by the firewalls, data was transferred with and without the firewalls. To gain a robust mean, the data was transferred 100 times. The volume of the data is the same as above. Figure 5.26 shows the results of the measurement. The upper curve displays the transfer time through the firewalls; the lower curve displays the transfer time without firewalls. The mean of the upper curve is about 26.7 seconds; the mean of the lower curve is about 25.7 seconds. The resulting difference is very small, so the measurements indicate that the use of firewalls for a demilitarized zone helps to improve the security at little cost.

A sample Denial-of-Service attack (described in Section 5.3.4.8 on page 164) was launched against the Globus Toolkit Version 4.2.1 on the grid head node to show how vulnerable Globus is to attacks. Hereby, Globus was installed on a Quad-Core Intel Xeon CPU with 2.27 GHz and 1 GB RAM. The interconnection between the source and the target machine was switched Gigabit Ethernet network. Overall, the attack lasted over 6 minutes, targeted the GridFTP service and 100,000,000 packets were sent. In order to keep the monitoring overhead as small as possible, the load value was measured every 2 seconds; thus, the small variance in the curve. Figure 5.27(a) shows the system load on the ordinate and

5.3. Grid Demilitarized Zone

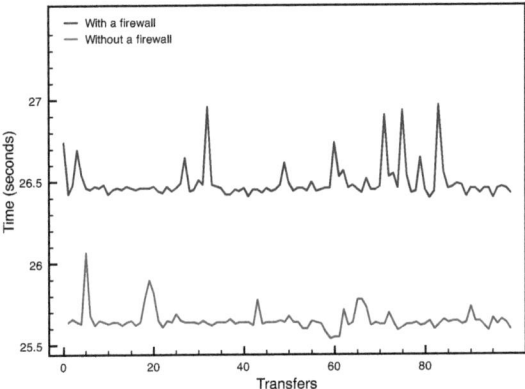

Figure 5.26: Transfer data chart with/without a firewall

the passed time in seconds on the abscissa. The system reacts faster if the load is lower. The load increased up to its maximum after the attack was started (after 382 seconds) and decreased immediately after the attack was stopped. As a comparison: the usual system load of a server ranges from 1 to 10, so the attacked system is heavily overloaded and barely usable anymore. Figure 5.27(b) shows the same attack on the system; however, the system is now installed within the demilitarized zone and guarded by a snort intrusion detection system with custom grid-specific rules. Snort detects the attack after about 145 seconds and a custom script is called that blocks the attackers IP address; thus, the load decreases and normal operation continues.

Due to the increasing load, it is no longer possible to actually work with the system. GridFTP's behavior is the root cause of the problem, as it creates a new child process for every incoming connection. Although there is no data exchange after the connection is established, the increasing number of processes is sufficient to bring down the system. GridFTP uses the *xinetd* superserver, which restricts the number of parallel connections. While this is indeed a proper security mechanism, it fails here for process creation, termination, and the context switches involved simply use too many resources.

For comparison purposes, the attack was also launched on the Apache web server,[5] which handled the number of parallel connections without any hassles.

---

[5] http://httpd.apache.org/

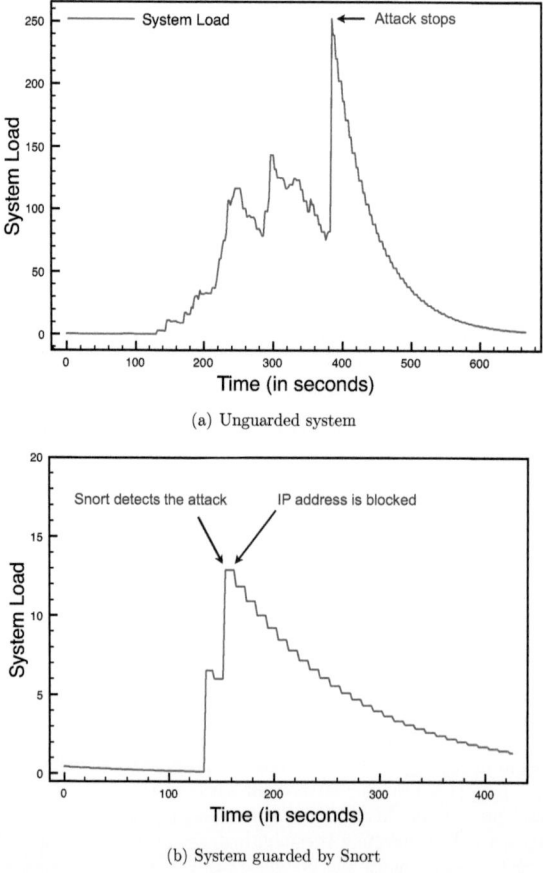

(a) Unguarded system

(b) System guarded by Snort

Figure 5.27: System load of the grid head node during an Denial-of-Service attack on GridFTP

Although the system load increased, it was irreducible compared to GridFTP because Apache creates a new thread, instead of a child process for every connection. Since thread creation is quite cheap and lightweight, the systems remains responsible.

The attacks carried out demonstrate the vulnerability of the grid head node to Denial-of-Service attacks. If an attacker has access to a variety of resources (e.g., a botnet), he or she could bring down the head node and thus the entry point of a grid site. Consequently, the head node needs additional protection mechanisms like the one presented in this thesis.

5.3.6 Summary

By using the novel dual-lane demilitarized zone, the grid environment was separated into several zones to protect local resources from grid middleware. The grid head node and the image creation station are both confined into separate compartments in the grid demilitarized zone. A new solution, called Fence, guarantees that job data is encrypted during all stages of transmission and storage in insecure networks. Extending a Network Intrusion Detection System according to several grid-specific rules further protects the network.

5.4 Dynamic Firewalls for Grid Computing

5.4.1 Introduction

The relationship between grid users and resource providers changed from highly trusted to mostly untrusted [124]. This change occurred because grid computing itself changed from a research topic with few users to a widely deployed product with commercial adoption. The traditional open research communities have very low security requirements, while, in contrast, business customers often operate on sensitive data representing intellectual property; thus, their security demands are very high. In traditional grid computing, most users share the same resources concurrently. Consequently, information about other users and their jobs can usually be accessed quite easily. This includes, for example, the fact that a user can see the another user's running processes. For business users, this is unacceptable since even the meta-data of their jobs is classified [125]. As a consequence, most commercial customers are not convinced that their intellectual property in the form of software and data is protected in the grid.

Using virtual machines to enhance security for job applications already fulfills the requirements posed by the industrial partners in the German D-Grid. All computation takes place inside a shielded environment in which there is no inter-user communication and no connection to the Internet. However, for service-oriented grid applications consisting of several grid services that are potentially executed from different users on multiple sites, using virtual machines without

Internet access or inter-node communication capabilities is not sufficient. Such an application was described in Section 3.3.5 on page 33.

The basic idea is to virtualize grid resources in order to offer the same freedom that network access cloud computing offers but in a multi-organizational and shared use environment, without endangering existing users or resources. This allows service-oriented applications direct, multi-site access to the computing nodes, without endangering the resources or other computations running on the nodes.

Parts of this section have been published in [126, 116, 121, 117].

5.4.2 Related Work

One method of granting access to network resources is to use firewall traversal techniques. A system that uses such techniques is CODO (Cooperative On-Demand Opening) [131]. CODO permits both inbound and outbound network traffic only for privileged applications. Apart from the fact that these decisions are made on the application level, the corresponding applications need to be linked with specific client libraries and require the use of firewall agents. A program's client library interacts with an agent to aquire permission to traverse the firewall itself. However, using client libraries is unacceptable since commercial software users are not able to link the application to the required libraries.

Another idea is to use a semantic firewall [144]. Applications present a profile describing their needs to the semantic firewall. The firewall itself also has access to the policies of the grid community to which the application instance belongs, and of the domain whose resources it protects. The firewall only allows traffic to pass through if the application requests (from both local and remote processes) are consistent with the policies, regardless of which ports and protocols are used. Unfortunately, the applications must present a profile describing their needs to the semantic firewall, such that an application has to be aware of the firewall's existence. Furthermore, it is not clear if there is a usable implementation available.

Rezmerita et al. [108] propose a new approach called *Instant Grid* (IG), which combines various Grid, P2P and VPN approaches, allowing simple deployment of applications over different administration domains. The paper proposed a P2P-based middleware which is able to establish encrypted connections between peers. Since the approach uses non-standard software and techniques, it is not possible to integrate it into an existing infrastructure. This includes existing grid or virtualization software. Unfortunately, is relationship to grid computing is not at all clear.

5.4. Dynamic Firewalls for Grid Computing

Matthews et al. [89] state that virtualization is an important enabling technology for many large private datacenters and cloud computing environments and propose Virtual Machine Contracts (VMCs). A VMC is a specification of the requirements and parameters that a virtual machine needs to operate. This includes network access control criteria or limits on the type and quantity of network traffic generated by the virtual machine. VMCs offer a flexible way to specify information about virtual machines. Therefore, it could be desirable to extending the approach that will be presented in this thesis using VMCs.

Wood et al. [172] argue that current cloud computing services need to further evolve to fully meet the needs of businesses. Therefore, cloud computing resources should be integrated into an enterprise's current infrastructure. The authors propose Virtual Private Clouds (VPCs), a framework used to integrate virtual private networks into the cloud. A new software called Cloud Manager creates virtual machines and embeds them into a MPLS network. So-called provider edge (PE) routers span the virtual network between the cloud site and the customer's own network. While the presented approach interconnects a cloud site and an enterprise's network, it relies on its own components to create the infrastructure, including virtual machines. As a result, it is not possible to use this approach in a grid context or in a default cloud environment.

Sundararaj and Dinda [142, 143] present VNET, a simple layer 2 virtual network tool. Using VNET, virtual machines have no network presence at all on a remote site. Instead, VNET provides a mechanism to project their virtual network cards onto another network. Therefore, they developed a VNET client, proxy and a server based on VMWare GSX Server. A virtual machine is connected to the VNET host which captures outbound and injects inbound Ethernet packets from the bridge to which the machine is connected. These packets are relayed (either locally or remotely) between the host and the VNET proxy on the client's side. Here, the proxy injects inbound and captures outbound Ethernet packets from the local network to which client is connected. While the proposed idea is a good one, due to the restrictions of the German D-Grid (which uses mostly open source components), it is not possible to use commercial software like GSX.

Tsugawa and Fortes [156] present a virtual network (ViNe) architecture for grid computing. ViNe is an IP-overlay network on top of the Internet. Routing between different sites is achieved by placing a dedicated virtual router in every site's virtual subnet. Hosts can join this subnet if they have a virtual IP address. ViNe is similar to the approach presented in the following and represents a step towards homogeneous multi-site network connections. While ViNe also takes care of routing packets between different sites, the upcoming approach delegates routing to the existing infrastructure.

There are several proposals for how to create a secure container in which (untrusted) software can be executed. For example, Batheja and Parashar [9] use JavaSpaces to create a homogenous computing environment in a heterogeneous hardware landscape. The author's approach is limited to Java applications. Since most of the cluster jobs are natively running Unix binaries, this approach is not suitable.

5.4.3 Design

Based on the related work presented in the last section, the following requirements for dynamic firewalling in virtualized grids and can be derived:

- One of the big advantages of grid computing is its ability to use multiple remote sites for computing. Thus, a virtualization solution should be able to support jobs running on different sites. This support takes the form of a virtual private network that encapsulates all virtual machines that belong to a job.

- Network security on a grid site is important as it might be possible for a job inside a virtual machine to sniff the traffic of another virtual machine's job. Besides sniffing, a malicious job could also launch Denial-of-Service attacks on other machines or even worse, against critical infrastructure components. Dynamic firewalls and static routes can mitigate these problems and should be a part of the proposed solution.

- Simply making the nodes of a computing site public is not a viable option since public nodes would clash with the requirements of the traditional batch-job oriented use case. The reason that batch-job and service-oriented computing paradigms clash is that submitting batch jobs only requires a publicly accessible head node, while the computing nodes can be operated in a private network, reducing the risk of an external attack. Service-oriented grid applications require a more complex and dynamic setup with accessible cluster nodes, which would also endanger all other users on those resources.

- The approach must address internal attacks on other users' virtual machines. A malicious user could try to remotely compromise other virtual machines to gain sensitive data or corrupt the work of other users. This can be achieved by exploiting software vulnerabilities. To cope with this threat, users must be carefully shielded from each other. By default, no user should be allowed to connect or reach virtual machines that are operated by another user. However, user-specified exceptions need to be supported. For example, users from the same virtual organization could request open access between their nodes.

5.4. Dynamic Firewalls for Grid Computing

- Internal attacks against the grid/cluster infrastructure are a serious threat that must be addressed. This includes attacks to corrupt parts of the infrastructure or attacks on particular machines (e.g. the head node). It must be kept in mind that since users have root access to their virtual machines, they can install privileged software such as DHCP or DNS servers legally. This could enable malicious users to subvert a site's normal operation and enable inter-user attacks. The security solution must be able to ensure that such infrastructure services do not propagate beyond the users' virtual images and network partitions.

- Giving all nodes publicly accessible IP addresses also means that the nodes can be accessed from everywhere in the world. This includes valid connection requests from trusted users and infrastructure services as well as malicious connection requests trying to compromise the node or gain sensitive data. The network security mechanism needs to ensure that users can access their services on a node, and that the node is guarded from both internal and external attacks.

- The network security configuration as well as its deployment must be easy, dynamic and scalable.

Based on the requirements, a dynamic firewalling architecture was designed. While the approach was tested and implemented with grid-specific tools, it is also adaptable to a public cloud.

Architecture

An overview over the proposed architecture is shown in Figure 5.28. A user submits a job to a meta-scheduler instead of to a site-specific head node. The meta-scheduler distributes the job to a number of chosen sites where an instance of the Globus Toolkit is installed. Every Globus handles the local scheduling in conjunction with the XGE. At this point, the XGEs on all sites are invoked and coordinate the distribution of the virtual machine disk images to the nodes. The firewall solution, as proposed in the following, as well as inter-virtual machine communication channels are set up. Once the virtual machines are ready on all sites, job execution continues. Now, the user is able to communicate with all of the assigned virtual machines.

5.4.3.1 Secure Infrastructure Communication

An important issue is to ensure secure communication between the virtual machines and the infrastructure services. This could include access to shared storage

Chapter 5. Network Security

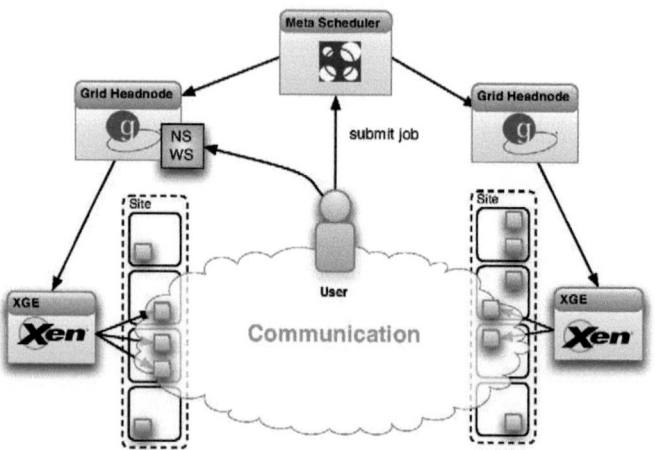

Figure 5.28: Inter-Site communication between the user and the virtual machines on two sites

(accessible via NFS or Samba), automatic IP address configuration (DHCP) or host name resolution (DNS), as described below.

Access to Shared Storage

If the shared storage is only accessible from local, private IP addresses, devices with external IP addresses cannot access it. If all virtual machine nodes have public IP addresses, there are two possible solutions:

- Only allow access from known IP addresses. This is the easiest solution and would be sufficient in most cases. However, this solution does not offer flexibility in case of address range changes, new nodes, etc. Furthermore, it creates additional complexity in multi-site setups.

- Allow access on an application/job basis. Every application run has one or more virtual machines assigned with dynamically assigned IP address(es). Based on these addresses, access is granted on the same dynamic basis. This approach is more complex than the previous solution, but increases flexibility and scalability.

5.4. Dynamic Firewalls for Grid Computing

- Place all virtual machines and the storage server (commonly a NFS server) inside a dynamic, virtual VLAN. A virtual VLAN is the same as a physical VLAN, except that so-called virtual switches are used instead of real ones. The VDE switches of the VirtualSquare Project [27], which try to interconnect different virtualized entities, can be used to achieve this goal. VirtualSquare even supports an encrypted virtual cable connection to interconnect the switches.

Due to the scalability benefits, the second solution was chosen. The solution guarantees that all virtual machines running on a particular cluster site only have access to their assigned storage. Multi-site shared storage is not possible due to known problems with exporting file systems over network borders. This drawback can be circumvented with a dynamic Virtual Private Network (VPN) assigned between all participating sites.

Grid Node IP Address Configuration

Every virtual machine has a dynamically assigned IP address that is fixed for the duration of a job. After the associated application finishes, the address is released. On each participating site, a DHCP server is set up to distribute the IP addresses. To prevent abuse of the service, DHCP requests are not allowed to pass through the routers guarding the network. Thus, all nodes with a known MAC address can request an IP address. Nodes with unknown MAC addresses will not receive IP addresses. Due to the fact that all users are superusers inside their virtual machine, they could set a new MAC address and try to get another IP address from the DHCP. In the presented solution this can be prevented by a fine-grained MAC address filter installed in the node's host domain. The filter knows the legal MAC addresses of the running virtual machines and thus only allows DHCP requests if the valid MAC address is used. A properly chosen lease time ensures that no connection between the DHCP server and the virtual machines is necessary once the application has started running. With this setup, automatic address configuration is guaranteed for nodes on all sites.

There is one official DHCP server on every site that assigns IP addresses to the virtual machines. These IP addresses are the official ones. If a number of virtual machines join a job's private network, a second network interface and DHCP server are needed. All virtual machines have two network interfaces, yet only one is used by default; the other one is only activated if the machines joins a private subnetwork. IP address are granted by either a second DHCP server or the VPN software itself. OpenVPN for example contains a DHCP server that is only able to grant IP addresses for hosts joining the network. IP addresses are taken from a private subnet.

One problem arises when using the presented setup: the management hassles associated with using multiple DHCP servers on several sites. To provide reliable IP addresses for the virtual machines, all DHCP servers need to be synchronized. This is accomplished using central resource management the DHCP configuration. This configuration is automatically distributed to all participating sites. Due to the fact that the number of virtual machines on one site is limited (the offered resources can only handle a certain number of virtual machines effectively), the distribution interval is not critical. It could run on a daily basis.

If virtual machines can be suspended or resumed while running, they could lose their DHCP lease and leave their personal firewall rules behind on the nodes. Currently, suspending virtual machines is not supported by the XGE, so this is not possible. But this is a point that must be addressed in the future. One could think about a controlled suspend/resume initiated by the XGE. Thus, it could take care of removing all firewall rules and bringing the computing nodes back to a coherent state. Once the virtual machines resume, they automatically apply for a new DHCP lease.

Host Name Resolution

Assigning host names to virtual machines is a necessary step to ensure identification for users and services (e.g. the resource manager or monitoring software). Host name resolution is done by a DNS resolver installed on each site. After a virtual machine is started, only connections to the well-known DNS resolvers on the local site are allowed; connections to the DNS port on other machines are forbidden.

5.4.3.2 Dynamic Network Security

The following presents the novel design for guarding the virtual machines and satisfying the stated challenges.

Rule Set Generation

Network security and protection of the virtual machines is enforced on the node by dynamic firewall rules. A default XML template is used to create firewall rules for a particular user's application. It represents a secure default setting for the average user, i.e. an uninterrupted workflow is possible without endangering other components. Based on this template, the user can apply his or her own rules. The basic template allows access to the LDAP, NFS and HTTP services by default

5.4. Dynamic Firewalls for Grid Computing

and limits the network speed (this could be a default value or a value given by a SLA.)

```
1  <fw name="script.sh">
2      <policy name="common" value="DENY" />
3      <policy name="INPUT" value="DENY" />
4      <policy name="OUTPUT" value="DENY" />
5      <policy name="FORWARD" value="DENY" />
6
7      <src>VMs</src>
8
9      <dst>common</dst>
10
11     <set name="common">
12         <host ip="10.0.0.1" proto="tcp" port="22, 2119, 8443" />
13         <host ip="10.0.0.2" proto="tcp" port="22" />
14     </set>
15
16     <set name="VMs">
17         <host ip="10.0.0.100" />
18         <host ip="10.0.0.101" />
19         <host ip="10.0.0.102" />
20         <host ip="10.0.0.103" />
21     </set>
22 </fw>
```

Listing 5.26: Common firewall rule set template

An example template is shown in Listing 5.26. All users can access several of the head node's ports (10.0.0.1) from all participating nodes (10.0.0.100/30). Access involves normal container operations as well as Secure Shell (SSH) Login. Additionally, SSH access to 10.0.0.2 is granted. Connections to the user's participating virtual machines are permitted, but connections to other nodes or resources are denied.

Every template starts with an `<fw name="" >` entry. A template's attribute name is initially empty and is replaced with a unique name when the actual firewall rule set is generated. This step is important because a given rule set must be explicitly identified. If is is not possible to identify the rule set, it would be impossible to remove the firewall rules after the computation is finished. Furthermore, it would generate a mess of firewall rules on all computing nodes.

Every template supports default rules for iptables-chains with the `<policy name="" value="" />` tag. Normally, the default policy for all standard chains (INPUT, OUTPUT, FORWARD) is deny all packets. Default policies for user-defined chains are also supported.

Chapter 5. Network Security

To ease the parsing and the complexity of the template, support for sets is provided. A set starts with a `<set>` tag and contains one or more `<host>` entries. The host tag supports various attributes. It contains at least an IP address, a complete IP range or a specific host name. Several protocols (TCP, TCP) and ports are also supported. A port is either a single port, an enumeration of ports or a complete port range.

Two tags are special. The `<src>` tag points to a set representing all virtual machines in which the current job is executed. In contrast, the `<dst>` tag points to a set representing all hosts which can be accessed.

Firewall Actions

To actually protect the network with the generated rules, the XGE has to deploy the script to the node on which the virtual machine is running. Figure 5.29 shows how the firewalls deployed on the host will protect the infrastructure and shield the users and their virtual machines from each other.

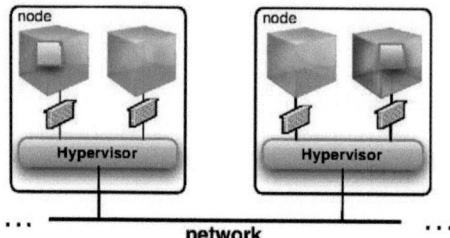

Figure 5.29: Multiple dynamic firewalls installed on the node

The XGE contains a list of virtual machines on which the application is executed. The list is obtained from the local scheduler, which decides on which hosts (virtual machines and corresponding nodes) the jobs will be executed. The firewall rules generated are now copied to all of these machines. Afterwards, the rules are deployed and become active. After the computation is finished, the XGE is also responsible for the removal of the deployed firewall rules. The XGE removes only the rules that belong to a certain application and user by managing a unique mapping between application, user and firewall rules.

It is indispensable to install the firewall rules on the host machine, rather than on the virtual machine itself. All users are superusers inside their own virtual

5.4. Dynamic Firewalls for Grid Computing

machine, so they could easily remove the rules and thus bypass the protection. To enforce the protection offered by the installed rules, every connection that is not explicitly allowed is denied. In a starting state, a virtual machine is not permitted to open outgoing connections. When the template rules are first applied, connections to local services are allowed. Furthermore, due to the use of the Network Security Web Service, users and administrators can define more targets to which to connect.

Traffic Limitations

To ensure that network connection bandwidth is not misused, the traffic of virtual machines can be limited. A default rate for all traffic is defined by the basic template. Furthermore, it is possible to define limits for all types of connections based on a single port or port ranges, protocols or sets of hosts (e.g. the virtual machine interconnection rate is higher than the connection to hosts outside of this set). A user can limit his or her own rate with the web service (see Section 5.4.3.4). Administrators can limit or raise users' bandwidth based on the experience over time.

Protection against Denial-of-Service attacks

Besides preventing bandwidth abuse from internal users, Denial-of-Service (DoS) protection is another threat the solution has to address. However, a complete and bullet-proof protection against this type of attack is not available. If the attackers' bandwidth and the number of attack nodes is high enough, it could spam nearly every infrastructure with unwanted traffic. To mitigate the Denial-of-Service risk, some on-by-default countermeasures are put in place:

- Dynamic traffic limitation of ICMP messages to broadcast and multicast destinations from outside connections to prevent the so-called *smurf* attack [16].

- A limitation of 100 incoming TCP SYN-packets per seconds ensures a good SYN flood protection. The protection is bucked-based, so it does not affect performance if the number of SYN-packets is under the given threshold.

- Incoming connections to ports that are likely to get scanned or abused (e.g. OpenSSH) are limited.

Chapter 5. Network Security

5.4.3.3 Inter-Virtual Machine Communication

An encrypted connection is set up between all virtual machines. This can be accomplished with a small overhead, as all virtual machines are equipped with a SSH public/private key pair by default. This key pair is generated when the machine is generated and is unique for every virtual machine. After the virtual machines are deployed to the worker nodes, every virtual machine contains the same key pair; thus, password-less access between all virtual machines is possible. OpenSSH is used to setup an encrypted tunnel. Since Version 4.3, OpenSSH can be used to set up virtual private networks. With the built-in scripting support, a tunnel is set up automatically during start-up or afterwards by issuing certain commands.

Nevertheless, it is up to an administrator to decide that the communication between the virtual machines should not be encrypted. This is mainly due to overhead concerns. Encrypting the communication using a common cryptographic protocol produces CPU load, and the transfer rate is decreased.

Information Exchange

To handle multi-site applications, a permanent communication channel between all running XGEs is needed. The purpose of the channel is to exchange information that needs to be present on all of the involved XGEs. Strong cryptography and authentication ensures that this information stays private and cannot be intercepted by malicious entities.

5.4.3.4 Network Security Web Service

A special web service was designed that allows users to decide which external resources they want to reach through specified ports. This is necessary when a user's application needs to connect to a remote location to receive data needed for the appropriate execution of a computing job. After the job starts, the user's application may connect, for example, to a license server to receive positive acknowledgement and start running.

The service affects the firewall of all virtual machines for incoming and outgoing connections. The newly opened ports can be a security risk, depending on the software attached to those ports; however, only the user's own virtual machine can be reached from the outside network, so other users are not endangered. If a user decides to open a port, he or she also opens him or herself up to an attack.

These additions do not decrease the level of network security. All outgoing ports that can be opened by users and their corresponding protocols are marked. This ensures that only marked ports can be opened. For example, all users can open a secure shell connection to an external machine. But users cannot open an unencrypted remote login session. Only selected users are allowed to open ports considered potentially dangerous (e.g. common virus or file sharing ports). All additions to the firewall are assigned to the user's virtual machine IP addresses. Thus, if a user requests an open port to reach an outside resource, only he or she can connect to it. Connections from other users' virtual machines are denied.

To add, change or remove firewall rules in a service-oriented manner, a service running on the head node is provided. Common mechanisms like TLS and a PKI are used to apply authentication and authorization on this security critical service, so users can only set and unset rules for their own virtual machines. All valid rule set will be transferred into the database by the backend running on the head node.

5.4.4 Implementation

This section describes the enhancements made to the XGE to support dynamic firewalls for grid and cloud nodes.

5.4.4.1 Rule Set Generation

The firewall rule sets are based upon an XML template defining a number of default rules for this computing site. Such a template is shown in Listing 5.26 on page 179. A specially written firewall rule set generator, which is connected to the XGE, parses the template and outputs a ready-to-start shell script. Therefore, the Expat XML parser is used. All of the XML file's entries are converted to an internal object representation. The representation consists of one ore more trees representing the firewall rules. Figure 5.30 shows the tree-based representation of a firewall template.

To generate the shell script, the trees are traversed in a special order:

1. The first entry represents the *default policy tree*.
2. The second entry represents the network source and destination hosts.
3. The third entry represents all of the connections allowed to one or more hosts (including protocol and ports)

During the traversal, every object has a special method that outputs the corre-

Chapter 5. Network Security

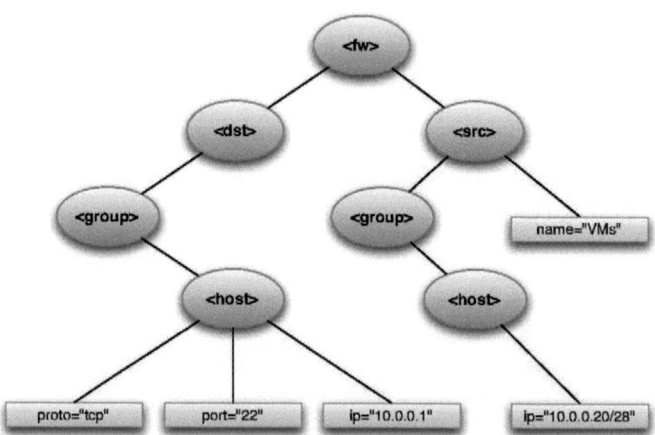

Figure 5.30: Tree-based representation of a firewall template

sponding rule (see Listing 5.27). The rules are all connected to an iptables chain uniquely named after the username and the job ID. This step is necessary because it is important to match a set of rules to a specific job. The default policy of all templates is deny, so everything which is not explicitly permitted is forbidden. All connections originating from one of the hosts in the <src> tag are allowed. All rules are inserted into a temporary shell script. Finally, a static, pre-defined number of rules is also added. These rules are standard techniques to prevent spoofing and a number of other well known attacks.

```
def genSrcRateRule(action, ipt, ip, dev, proto, port, rate):
    iptable = ipt + " -t mangle -" + action + " POSTROUTING"
    iptable += " -m physdev --physdev-out " + dev
    if ip != "":
        iptable += " --src " + ip
    if proto != "":
        iptable += " -p " + proto + " -m " + proto
    if port != "":
        iptable += " --dport " + port
    iptable += " -j CLASSIFY --set-class " + rate
    return iptable
```

Listing 5.27: Iptables rule generation

Traffic shaping is accomplished using the Traffic Control (tc) [55] tool for Linux.

5.4. Dynamic Firewalls for Grid Computing

`tc` is part of the `iproute2` tool suite and thus part of nearly all Linux distributions. Listing 5.28 shows a code fragment responsible for creating traffic shaping rules. Line 2 shows the creation of a *qdisk* rule with a hierarchical token bucket filter. A *qdisc* is a scheduler providing a set of rules to order packets entering a scheduler's queue. The default is a simple FIFO scheduler. The default rate from the XML template is assigned to the device in lines 3 through 5. Any further rates given by the template or configured by the user are assigned at the end (lines 8 through 13).

```
for dev in [ "peth1" ] + hostdevices:
    rules.append(tc+" qdisc add dev "+dev+" root handle 1: htb")
    rules.append(tc+" class add dev "+dev+" parent 1:1"
        + " classid 1:" + str(job.tid) + "1"
        + " htb rate " + str(fwrs.defaultrate))
    classid = 2

    for rate in fwrs.rates:
        rules.append(tc + " class add dev "
            + dev + " parent 1:1"
            + " classid 1:" + str(job.tid) + str(classid)
            + " htb rate " + str(rate.rate))
        classid += 1
```

Listing 5.28: Fragment of the XGE traffic shaping code

5.4.4.2 Deployment, Execution and Removal

Before the final rule set is deployed, it needs to be distributed to all participating XGEs that themselves distribute the rule set to the associated nodes. All XGEs are connected with each other with a TLS-secured communication channel. The final set of rules is copied to all nodes hosting virtual machines. The list containing the nodes on all sites is available to the XGE. All rules are executed; thus, the virtual machine and the network are protected before the computation starts. After the computation is finished, all rules that belong to this job are flushed.

5.4.4.3 Packet Filtering

The *iptables*[6] packet filter is used because the Linux operating system is the most commonly used operating system in such environments today. To match all packets that originate from one virtual machine, the *physdev*-module of the Linux kernel is used. This module allows the traffic to be filtered on the data link layer, which is needed due to the fact that Xen uses a bridge to connect the virtual machine to the network.

---
[6] http://www.netfilter.org/

185

Chapter 5. Network Security

5.4.5 Evaluation

A number of measurements were conducted to investigate the properties of the presented proposal. The participating nodes are all AMD Dual-Core machines with 16 GB RAM running Debian GNU/Linux. The head node also runs the Globus Toolkit 4.0.5 and the Xen Grid Engine. The native cluster nodes are interconnected with switched Gigabit Ethernet network. All virtual machines have 2 GB RAM, one assigned CPU core and a local-loopback mounted hard disk image. The cross-site connection to other grid sites is a one Gigabit link.

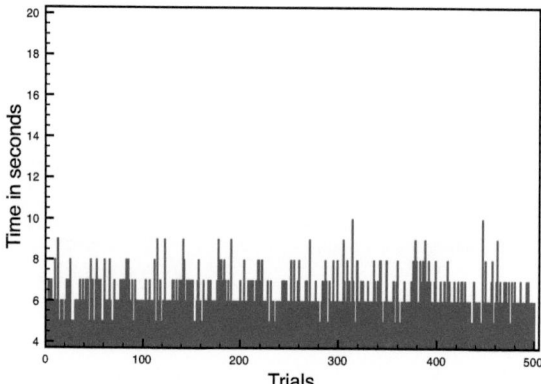

Figure 5.31: Dynamic firewall deployment time

One of the important measurements is the time needed for rule propagation and final set up. The entire process includes rule generation for a particular application, determining all nodes that belong to that application, propagating the rules, and setting them up to protect the virtual machine. The face detection application runs on 20 different virtual machines and 30 different rules protect the virtual machines. 500 trials were conducted to calculate a robust mean. The results are shown in Figure 5.31. The mean of the results is 6 seconds and the deployment time is nearly constant over all trials. The small variance is due to changing load on the XGE node. The deployment time can increase if a larger number or a more complex set of firewall rules is applied. This performance degradation is based on the performance of iptables.

In Figure 5.32, the time needed to deploy a continuously increasing number of firewall rules with iptables is measured. Applying a small number of rules, i.e.

5.4. Dynamic Firewalls for Grid Computing

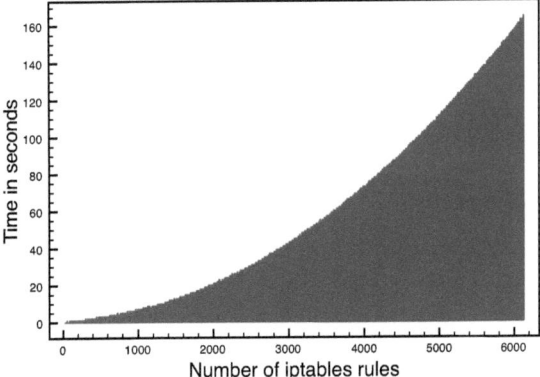

Figure 5.32: iptables rule deployment time

between one and 100 (which is the average case for most applications in the local installation), takes one second on average. Overall, the time needed for the installation increases exponentially with the number of rules. Since the rule setup is executed on all nodes in parallel, the additional cost is only counted once. Flushing the rules does not affect the performance at all. Even with a high number of rules, it was not possible to measure a real impact.

Besides the time needed to install and deploy the firewall rules, using firewalls also has an impact. Measurements were taken between virtual machines on different physical nodes on two different academic locations interconnected via the German Research Network (DFN). As shown in Figure 5.33, there is no drawback to use firewalls to shield the virtual machines from each other, even when the machines are located on different sites. In total, 3600 samples were recorded during a one-hour-analysis of the network performance using *iperf*[7] as measurement tool. The ordinate shows the network throughput in MBits per second, while the abscissa shows the time in seconds. When firewalls were used, an average network performance of 938.67 MBit/s was reached; when no firewalls were used, an average performance of 939 MBit/s was reached. A comparison measurement of the network performance between two physical machines using no firewalls shows a mean of 940.45 KBit/s. The slight decrease in network performance between virtual machines is due to the use of virtualization and the virtualized network

---
[7] http://dast.nlanr.net/Projects/Iperf/

Chapter 5. Network Security

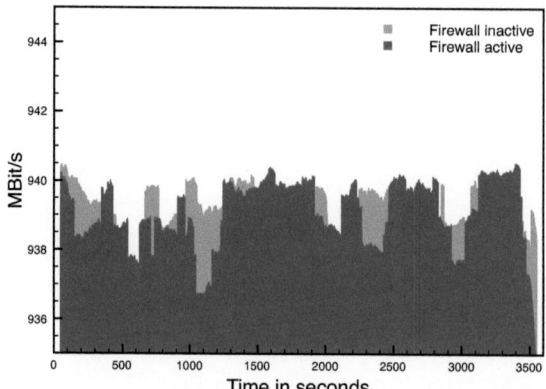

Figure 5.33: Cross-site measurements with and without firewalls

stack. This measurement shows that applying an average number of rules does not affect the network's performance.

For the sake of completeness, a number of measurements were conducted with significantly more rules than are commonly needed for service-oriented applications. The set of measurements was conducted with a linear growing number of rules. The results are shown in Figure 5.34. As the number of rules increases, the maximum throughput decreases. Overall, the throughput is decreased by about 80 MBits/s when using over 2000 rules.

In the next experiment, measurements were performed with the face detection application developed by Ewerth et al. [37]. The service's execution time is not relevant to the firewall overhead and thus is factored out of the measurement; only the time needed to transfer the application data (enclosed in SOAP messages) is measured. Figure 5.35 shows the result. The mean transfer time without a firewall (left bar) is 79.9 s; the mean transfer time with a firewall (right bar) is 88.0 s. The resulting difference is about 8 s.

Thus, the measurement indicates that the use of firewalls helps to improve the security for a negligibly small cost.

5.4. Dynamic Firewalls for Grid Computing

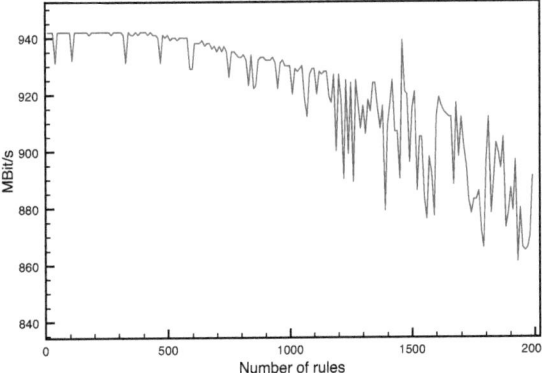

Figure 5.34: Maximum throughput with an increasing number of firewall rules

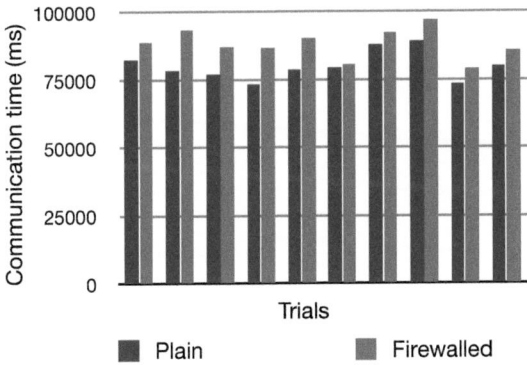

Figure 5.35: Inter-application communication time (milliseconds) with and without dynamic firewalls

5.5 Summary

In this chapter, several solutions for providing network security were presented. The first includes a software that provides transparent virtualization for grids and thus protects the users' applications and data. A novel grid demilitarized zone breaks up the traditional grid network structures and separates the grid head node from the backend. Fence, a new software that connects the head node and the internal node, guarantees that job data is encrypted at all times. Even if it is stored in possibly compromised storage or transferred over insecure networks. Dynamic firewalls guard the virtual machines running on the nodes. While this adds additional network security, it is sometimes beneficial for both users and administrators to allow users to modify their own rule set in both directions and in a controlled manner. This can be achieved using a special web service.

"Reason, observation, and experience - the Holy Trinity of Science"
Robert G. Ingersoll (1833–1899)

6 Experimental Results

6.1 Introduction

In the following chapter, selected measurements of the developed components are presented to evaluate the overhead introduced by the various measures introduced in this work. Contrary to the measurements presented in the previous chapters, the measurements are not directly related to a specific component.

6.2 Efficient Transfer of Virtual Machines

To evaluate the performance of the presented distribution methods, several measurements have been performed. The test environment consists of Intel Xeon 2.5 GHz machines with a total of 80 cores connected with a switched Gigabit Ethernet network. All machines have 16 GB RAM and Debian Linux stable with Xen 3.0.2 installed. The local hard disks have a capacity of 250 GB.

6.2.1 Distribution Methods

All distribution mechanisms have advantages and disadvantages. While multicast and BitTorrent are promising candidates to distribute large amounts of data to

Chapter 6. Experimental Results

hundreds or thousands of clients, they are not suitable for every scenario. As already mentioned, routing multicast packets between networks is not possible without additional protocols, and BitTorrent needs a torrent file for every transfer of a different disk image. This generates an overhead if only small pieces of data are transferred. On the contrary, the tree-based distribution method only scales to a certain degree, but it is ready to go and needs no preliminary work like generating and distributing torrent files. Thus, choosing the right method depends on the amount of data to distribute and the number of receiving nodes.

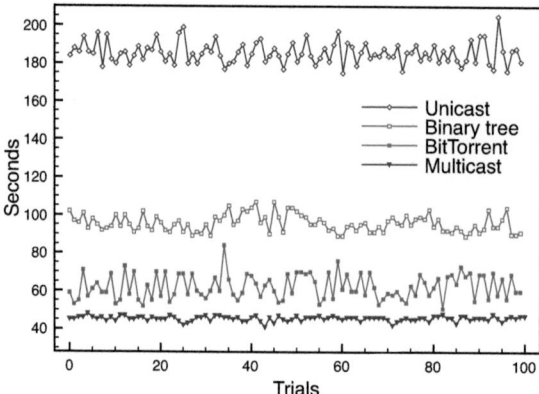

Figure 6.1: Deployment times for a 1024 MB virtual disk image

In Figures 6.1, 6.2, 6.3 and 6.4 all measurements with unencrypted transfer are shown. As already stated, the unicast distribution method is the slowest method to distribute the disk images and is thus not really suitable for practical use, it only serves as a reference value. The binary tree distribution method is significantly faster than unicast distribution, but slower than the P2P distribution method based on BitTorrent and the multicast method. Even though BitTorrent was designed with desktop file sharing in mind, it performed very well in the structured cluster environment. Multicast is significantly faster than all other algorithms. In figure 6.4 the results of unicast and the binary tree are skipped, because they are about three times slower and thus unusable to transfer larger data sizes. The mean values (of 100 measurements) of all transfers are shown in Table 6.1. The transfer times with different virtual machine image disk sizes was measured, where 512 MB refers to a basic image or layer with few modifications and 8192 MB to a highly customized disk image or layer. Based on experiments

6.2. Efficient Transfer of Virtual Machines

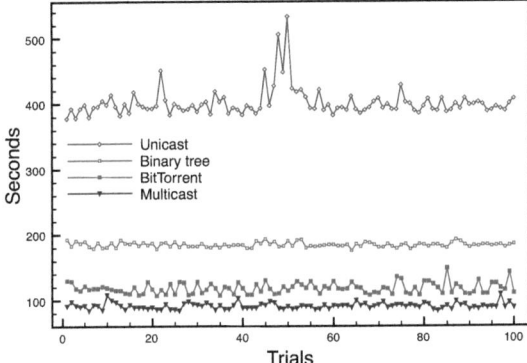

Figure 6.2: Deployment times for a 2048 MB virtual disk image

with several users, the average disk image size is about 4 GB and the average user layer size is about 1 GB.

Image Size	Unicast	Binary tree	BitTorrent	Multicast
512 MB	89.4 s	50.0 s	29.0 s	27.9 s
1024 MB	191.1 s	95.7 s	62.3 s	45.5 s
2048 MB	401.0 s	183.8 s	120.9 s	90.6 s
4096 MB	815.2 s	367.4 s	214.3 s	121.8 s
8192 MB	1634.1 s	727.6 s	465.0 s	383.5 s

Table 6.1: Measured mean values of all deployment methods

In the P2P distribution method, a torrent file needs to be generated for every distribution process, thus the time needed for the generation of the torrent file must be added to the actual transfer time. The generation time grows with the size of the file – generating a torrent file for a 512 MB disk image takes less time than for a 8192 MB disk image. As a compromise, the generation time needed for a 4096 MB disk image was measured. 100 trials were conducted to calculate a mean of about 27 seconds. Thus, the complete time needed to transfer a 4096 MB disk image is about 241 seconds (instead of 214 seconds without considering the generation of the torrent file) on the average. Obviously, this is still better than the transfer time for a 4096 MB disk image (367 seconds) using the binary tree distribution method.

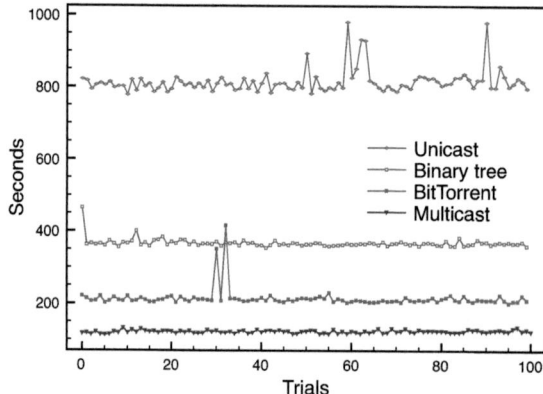

Figure 6.3: Deployment times for a 4096 MB virtual disk image

The jitter that can be seen in the figures is caused by network activity produced by other users in the test environment. The effect of others users' activities is, however, small compared to the jitter effect of the BitTorrent protocol. Thus, the jitter that can be seen is mainly caused by the BitTorrent protocol itself.

6.2.2 Virtual Disk Encryption

When encrypted transfer over the binary tree is used, encryption, transfer and decryption are performed in parallel. The encryption methods offered by BitTorrent clients mainly aim to prevent filtering of BitTorrent traffic by ISPs. Thus, both the algorithm (RC4) and the bit lengths (60-80) used are not sufficient for confidential data. Thus, for the BitTorrent and multicast cases the entire virtual machine is encrypted before transfer, and can only be decrypted once the entire file has been received, which significantly slows down the approach.

Figures 6.5 and 6.6 show the times needed to encrypt and decrypt different sized images, respectively. The size ranges from 512 MB to 8 GB and the AES algorithm with 256 bit is used. Encrypting and decrypting a 2048 MB disk images takes 62 and 65 seconds on average, respectively. To summarize, these additional times have to be taken into account when sending an encrypted disk image over the network and the encryption is not built in the transport protocol (e.g., as in TLS or SSH).

6.2. Efficient Transfer of Virtual Machines

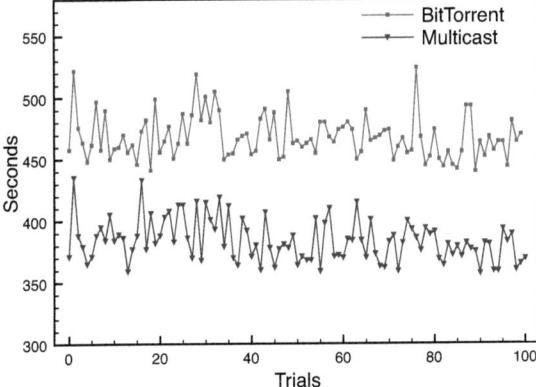

Figure 6.4: Deployment times for a 8192 MB virtual disk image

The complete time needed to encrypt a disk image with AES 256, transfer it with BitTorrent and decrypt it again is depicted in Figure 6.7.

6.2.3 Multi-Layered Virtual Machines

Adding COW layers to virtual machines using UnionFS produces additional costs when intensive file related tasks are performed. Measurements were conducted using the bonnie++ [24] benchmark as a well-known testing suite for file systems to investigate this overhead. The used virtual machines have 1024 MB RAM and a single assigned CPU core. A total of 100 tests was performed. The average of the results is shown in Figure 6.8. When writing the file block by block, the non-layered virtual machine outperformed the layered virtual machine (206277 KB/s vs. 198015 KB/s), thus the COW layer introduces a slight performance reduction. The character test does not reveal any notable difference (48775 KB/s vs. 48319 KB/s), whereas in the rewrite test the layered virtual machine had a significantly higher throughput than the non-layered virtual machine (67951 KB/s vs.' 33472 KB/s). This is due to the COW cache of the UnionFS file system. As a conclusion, it can be stated that the introduction of the additional layers consumes some performance if files are written in large blocks. Once this step has been performed, the performance benefits from the effective caching of the layered file system are evident. Due to the fact that most files of a regular job

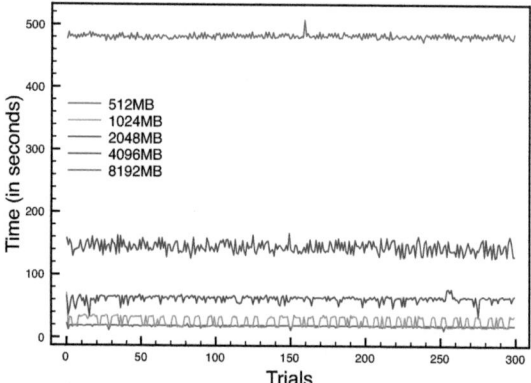

Figure 6.5: Encryption times for different sized images

are written in the user's home directory that is natively accessible, the overhead only comes into play in certain, special circumstances.

Without the multi-layered file system, every time the user updates his or her virtual machine and submits a job, the complete disk image of this machine has to be copied to the particular nodes (because a virtual machine that was cached earlier is marked as invalid after a software update). When the multi-layered file system is used, only the user layer needs to be copied, which is significantly smaller. The base layer needs to be copied only once, because it is cached locally at the compute nodes. In case of an update, only the changes are copied and merged into the corresponding layer. A measurement of the transfer time in both cases was conducted, comparing a virtual machine with and without a multi-layered file system.

The base installation consists of 162 packages using about 468 MB, and the user installs 14 additional packages using about 58 MB. The update includes 3 updated and 1 added package, using about 12 MB plus about 40 MB Debian Package Manager metadata (package lists, etc). Both virtual machines use a 4 GB sparse disk image containing an ext3 file system. The difference between the used space within the images and the sizes is caused by file system structures and the space allocated for files that have been deleted afterwards. Since sparse files are used for the disk images, only the used parts of the image need to be transferred.

Table 6.2 shows the measured time needed to transfer different images from one

6.2. Efficient Transfer of Virtual Machines

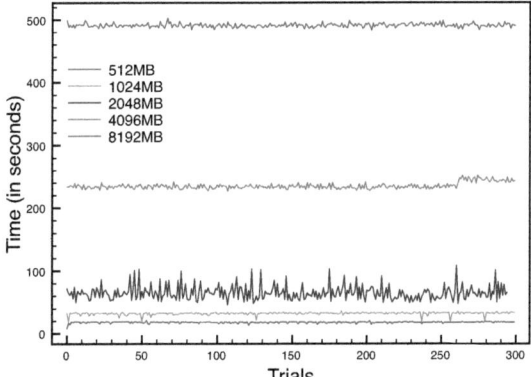

Figure 6.6: Decryption times for different sized images

			Transfer times	
Size (MB)		single site	multi site	
			uncompressed	compressed
Single disk image	691	40.59 secs	660.83 secs	460.12 secs
Base layer (BL)	666	39.12 secs	636.92 secs	443.47 secs
BL update	72	15.06 secs	106.23 secs	100.11 secs
User layer	67	14.45 secs	101.51 secs	91.58 secs

Table 6.2: Transfer times of virtual machine images and file system layers

compute node to another without compressing the data during the copy process. The difference between the size of the single disk image and the sum of the sizes of base and user layer (691 MB vs. 733 MB) is due to the fact that the base layer as well as the user layer each contain a package database. Furthermore, the updated packages are cached within the respective layers, which also adds some space to the layers. 60 transfer operations were conducted to calculate a robust mean value. When virtual machine images must be copied between remote sites, the time needed for the copy operations increases dramatically. The table also shows the measurements of uncompressed and gzip-compressed data transfer between compute nodes on two different academic locations connected by the German Research Network (DFN).

Summing up, without the multi-layered file system the amount of data to be transferred for the virtual machine including the update is about 1380 MB, taking

197

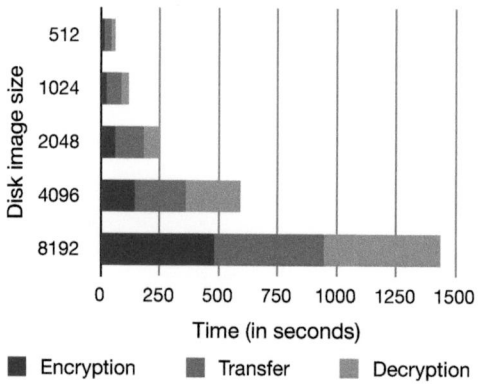

Figure 6.7: Disk image distribution with BitTorrent and data en-/decryption

about 81, 1330 or 925 seconds (LAN, WAN, WAN compressed). Using the presented solution, the amount of data reduces to 140 MB, taking about 34, 212 or 196 seconds when the base image is already cached or 805 MB and 73, 850 or 640 seconds otherwise, although the latter case should be rare. This means that the use of the multi-layered file system saves up to 90% traffic and 60% – 85% of the time in the scenario.

6.3 Storage Synchronization

This section evaluates the impact of disk synchronization on the total migration time and on the performance of the virtual machine. All participating physical nodes are AMD Dual-Core machines with 2.2 GHz, 16 GB RAM running Debian GNU/Linux. All nodes are interconnected with Gigabit Ethernet.

Figures 6.3 and 6.3 show the synchronization time of an idle disk image for several disk image sizes via the DRBD driver. The left bars represent the tests with *full disk images* (randomly filled from /dev/urandom), and the right bars show the corresponding tests with *sparse images* (which are observed as zero-filled images by the synchronization partner). It is evident (especially from Figure 6.3, which draws the results over a logarithmic scale) that the synchronization time increases linearly with the disk size. The results also show that the synchronization time can be reduced by up to 13% when working with sparse images, where only a small fraction of the image size is actually in use.

6.3. Storage Synchronization

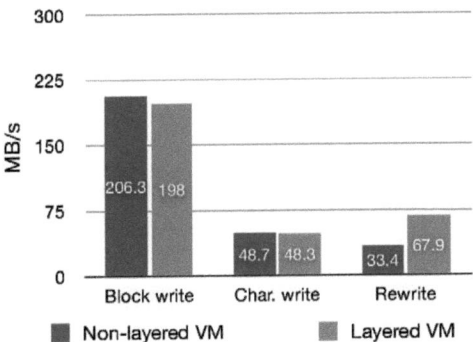

Figure 6.8: Results of the bonnie++ benchmark with layered and unlayered virtual machines

As a core test, the kernel compile benchmark, was used. This test measures the total time required to build a recent Linux kernel with the default configuration. The test was chosen because it represents a balanced workload with respect to stressing the virtual memory system, doing moderate disk I/O as well as being relatively CPU-intensive. The kernel compilation was done inside a virtual machine while being live migrated to another host. Six tests with slightly different setups were performed:

1. 256 MB RAM in the virtual machine with a 2 GB disk image attached to a DRBD driver and 1 G RAM in the node

2. 256 MB RAM in the virtual machine with a 2 GB disk image attached to a DRBD driver and 13 G RAM in the node

3. 3 GB RAM in the virtual machine with a 2 GB disk image attached to a DRBD driver and 1 GB RAM in the node

4. 3 GB RAM in the virtual machine with a 2 GB disk image attached to a DRBD driver and 13 GB RAM in the node

5. 3 GB RAM in the virtual machine with a tmpfs writable layer and 1 GB RAM in the node

6. 3 GB RAM in the virtual machine with a tmpfs writable layer and 13 GB RAM in the node

Chapter 6. Experimental Results

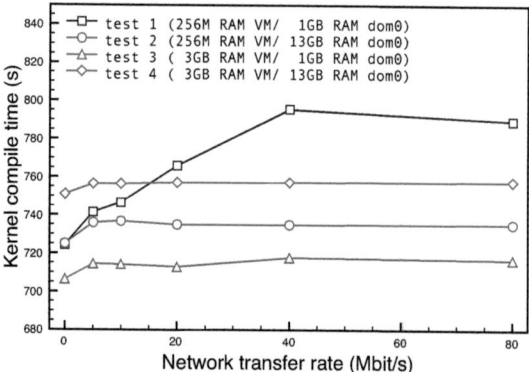

Figure 6.9: Impact of background synchronization limits on virtual machine performance

In tests 1-4, the compile output was written to the disk image being synchronized via the DRBD module, in tests 5 and 6 the output went to tmpfs. The duration of the kernel compilation, the synchronization, and the Xen migration were measured, and all tests were repeated at least 50 times to procure a robust mean. The kernel compilation tests were also done without migration as a reference. The tests involving disk synchronization were performed with transfer rates of 5, 10, 20, 40 and 80 MByte/s for the background synchronization (a transfer rate configuration of more than 80 MByte/s did not result in a further increase of synchronization speed). The third proposed possibility for layering the read-only and the writable layer using a large swap space on disk was not tested separately because from the synchronization viewpoint, there is no difference between synchronizing a disk image or a disk containing a swap partition.

The results of Tests 1-4 are shown in Tables 6.3 and 6.4 and Figure 6.9; Table 6.5 shows the results of Tests 5 and 6, and in Table 6.6, the reference values for all tests without migration are summarized.

Several observations can be made:

- The total performance degradation in the tests involving disk synchronization compared to the reference values ranges from 0.7% (in Test 4) to 9% (in Test 1 with maximum bandwidth utilization for background synchronization). These values are relative to one migration process per kernel

6.3. Storage Synchronization

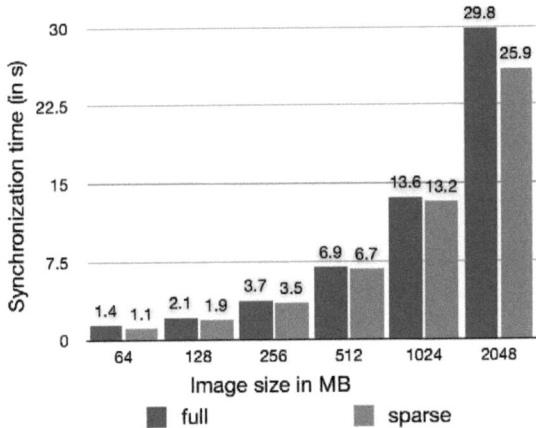

Figure 6.10: Disk synchronization

compilation. If the values are extrapolated to one migration per hour, the performance degradation ranges from 0.2% to 1.9%, which are acceptable values.

- The Xen live migration process itself has little impact on the performance of the migrating virtual machine, as indicated when comparing the test results of Tests 5 and 6 (see Table 6.5) to their reference values. Thus, most of the overhead observed in the other tests can be assumed to be caused by disk synchronization.

- The migration time does not increase when using a tmpfs as a writable layer. Hence, the total migration time is reduced by about 90% compared to using a local disk image (when using a medium value of 20 Mbit/s for background synchronization). Thus, the tmpfs solution is suitable for workloads that do not produce large amounts of data.

- The amount of RAM allocated to the node dictates an upper bound to the transfer rate for background synchronization. In the tests with only 1 GB of RAM (see Table 6.3, column one and two), the synchronization time does not decrease between 20 and 80 Mbit/s, which means that the network bandwidth is higher than the rate at which the incoming data can be processed at the destination host. In general, the synchronization time is inversely proportional to the transfer rate in a linear fashion.

Chapter 6. Experimental Results

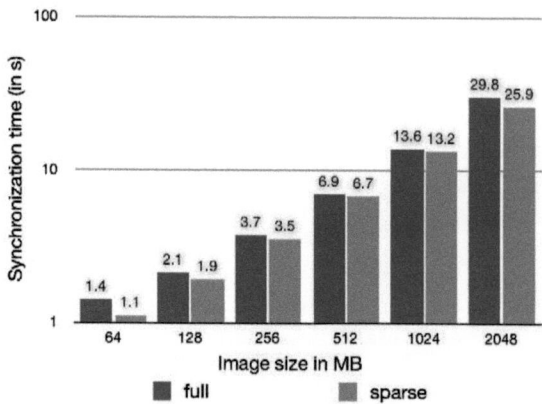

Figure 6.11: Disk synchronization (logarithmic scale)

- Increasing the transfer rate for background synchronization only has an observable impact in Test 1, where both the node and the virtual machine have a small amount of RAM. This test case represents the most write-intensive workload in the sense that the kernel can cache fewer writes in main memory (both in the node and the virtual machine). In all other cases, the overhead compared to the non-migrating reference values is mostly caused by the the synchronous disk writes. Thus, especially for write-intensive workloads, choosing the transfer rate will always be a trade-off between the total migration time and the performance impact on the virtual machine.

- Strangely enough, in all tests with 3 GB of RAM in the virtual machine, the duration of the kernel compilation increases considerably when allocating more memory to the node (e.g from 714 s to 757 s between Tests 3 and 4). At the time of writing, no reasonable explanation for this phenomenon could be found; however, since these observations do not affect the area under test (disk synchronization), they are simply stated as observed. This topic has to be investigated in more detail in the future.

In normal operation, all of the virtual machine's disk I/O goes through the DRBD driver running in standalone mode. The bonnie benchmark was used to measure the driver's overhead. The bonnie test was performed on a disk image file mounted through a loopback device and on a LVM partition.

6.3. Storage Synchronization

	Test 1			Test 2		
speed	sync	migration	compile	sync	migration	compile
5 Mbit/s	400.2 s	8.2 s	741.5 s	398.2 s	7.0 s	736.0 s
10 Mbit/s	203.0 s	8.7 s	746.5 s	201.7 s	7.2 s	736.7 s
20 Mbit/s	119.7 s	8.2 s	766.0 s	103.0 s	6.7 s	735.0 s
40 Mbit/s	104.7 s	8.0 s	795.5 s	52.7 s	6.5 s	735.0 s
80 Mbit/s	108.5 s	7.5 s	789.5 s	27.0 s	5.7 s	735.2 s

Table 6.3: Results for live migration with storage synchronization (Tests 1 and 2).

	Test 3			Test 4		
speed	sync	migration	compile	sync	migration	compile
5 Mbit/s	397.5 s	34.3 s	714.4 s	401.7 s	32.7 s	756.5 s
10 Mbit/s	202.0 s	34.4 s	714.2 s	202.6 s	33.0 s	756.4 s
20 Mbit/s	119.3 s	34.1 s	712.9 s	102.7 s	32.7 s	757.1 s
40 Mbit/s	102.4 s	34.0 s	717.8 s	52.7 s	32.8 s	757.2 s
80 Mbit/s	100.3 s	34.3 s	716.8 s	27.3 s	32.7 s	757.5 s

Table 6.4: Results for live migration with storage synchronization (Tests 3 and 4).

Table 6.7 shows the results. The highest impact on performance can be observed on the write throughput on the disk image file (decreased by 6.7%) followed by the read throughput on the LVM volume (decreased by 2.4%). The other two values only differ by around 1% in both directions. Designed for disk performance tests, the bonnie benchmark represents an unusual workload that stresses the I/O facilities to a maximum. Hence, average applications running in a virtual machine will usually have more moderate disk I/O throughput, which, in turn would mean that the observable overhead due to the DRBD driver is expected to be much lower. Especially when comparing these values to shared storage solutions[1] (which are commonly required for enabling live migration), the results indicate that the proposed solution is suitable for virtualized grid environments like the XGE. In addition, the performance of shared storage access is expected to decrease with a number of clients using it simultaneously and with higher network utilization. The DRBD approach presented here allows the virtual machines to do their I/O locally and thus only introduces performance penalties during a live migration process.

---

[1] write throughput on an NFS file system is decreased by approximately 48% in synchronous mode and 9% in asynchronous mode according to Softpanorama [129].

Chapter 6. Experimental Results

node RAM	migration time	compile time
1 GB	32.40 s	721.00 s
13 GB	32.90 s	765.10 s

Table 6.5: Results for live migration with tmpfs as a writable layer (Tests 5 and 6)

Test no.	node RAM	VM RAM	compile time
1	1 GB	256 MB	724.38 s
2	13 GB	256 MB	725.00 s
3	1 GB	3 GB	706.38 s
4	13 GB	3 GB	751.00 s
5	1 GB	3 GB	722.00 s
6	13 GB	3 GB	762.88 s

Table 6.6: Reference values for the kernel compile benchmark without migration

6.4 Summary

This chapter presented an evaluation that showed that multicast offers the best performance for disk image distribution. Nevertheless, when transferring disk images between remote sites, BitTorrent is the method to choose. The evaluation of the layered file system showed that it saves a considerable amount of traffic, up to 90%. Finally, the evaluation of the storage synchronization has shown satisfactory performance for this approach.

Setup	writes in KB/s	reads in KB/s
File image	44003	59081
File image standalone	41070	59717
LVM	43781	57027
LVM standalone	43239	55634

Table 6.7: Overhead of the DRBD driver in standalone mode

"It is not for man to rest in absolute contentment."
Robert Southey (1774–1843)

7 Conclusions

7.1 Summary

In this thesis, a new security infrastructure for virtualized grid computing was presented. An analysis of the job submission procedure was conducted and resulted in the identification of four different areas in need of additional protection: the environment containing the head node, the actual execution of applications on shared resources, specific issues concerning host security, and problems that occur in multi-site computing.

Two solutions were presented to enhance the security of a host machine, i.e. dedicated infrastructure nodes as well as a ordinary computing nodes. An effective and lightweight mechanism prevents an attacker from loading kernel rootkits after a successful compromise. Since the module loading function of the operating system kernel was modified, only authorized modules can be loaded. Since a kernel rootkit is never authorized, it can no longer be loaded.

Furthermore, a malware scanner for virtualized grids using virtual machine introspection was presented. It is located within a protected area of the virtual machine's kernel; hence, it cannot be disabled by an attacker. The scanner sends the entire executable to one or more classical anti-virus engines running on dedicated grid nodes along with the continuous stream of system calls generated by this executable. This enables the detection of yet unknown malware, making

Chapter 7. Conclusions

it possible to look for malware-typical traces in the stream, which are not yet available as a signature.

A novel virtualized grid concept was introduced that allows execution of grid jobs within virtual environments. This environment protects the data as well as the application. A malicious process can no longer gather information about other processes running on the same resource. Within this context, several of the problems that arose were addressed as well. Different methods were implemented that speed up the distribution of virtual machine disk images and hence lead to less network congestion. Further, a new method was implemented to synchronize data between physical hosts during live migrations. While the virtualized environment leads to more security for the user as well as for the provider, it integrates seamlessly into existing infrastructures. This means that it works together with middlewares already installed on the system and uses the decisions of that system's scheduler.

A novel dual-lane grid demilitarized zone was introduced, securing existing setups from attacks that stem from the open grid world. The dual-lane nature of the demilitarized zone further subdivides the demilitarized zone into sub-compartments, allowing for secure network-based image creation and job submission, respectively. The Grid Security Infrastructure was extended to cope with the new demilitarized zone and the new grid virtualization. Job data is encrypted during all stages of transmission and storage in insecure networks. The extension of a Network Intrusion Detection System (NIDS) using several grid specific rules further protects the grid network.

An approach to secure multi-site virtual grid computing was presented. Dynamic and user adjustable firewalls protect the infrastructure and shield users from each other. The firewalls are dynamically applied to the host operating systems to filter the traffic between the users' virtual machines and the connected network. The decision to let users modify their own rule set in both directions and in a controlled manner is beneficial for both users and administrators. Running complex grid applications requiring multi-site interaction is possible without bothering the grid authorities to open ports on demand.

Overall, this thesis presented selected solutions for host and network security of grids. While the presented solutions are grid specific, some enhance the security of cloud computing. All solutions benefit from making use of the advantages found in virtualization technologies.

7.2 Future Work

There are several areas of future research to be conducted in the area of infrastructure security for virtualized grids. This includes extending the techniques presented in this thesis, which will briefly be discussed here.

7.2.1 Virtual Machine Lifecycle Management

Currently, the mechanisms introduced in this thesis deal only with host and network security of running virtual machines. Since virtual machines rest on a disk while they are not running, a future area to explore is the security during the whole life cycle. This includes scanning the suspended virtual disk image for malware or known vulnerabilities and patching them accordingly. One could also perform live vulnerability scans in a sandboxed environment to find further bugs.

7.2.2 Robustness and Scalability

Although all components presented in this thesis are well-tested and already used by research institutes and commercial partners, further improvement in terms of robustness and scalability is always desired. This includes tests on large scale testbeds with hundreds or even thousand of nodes.

7.2.3 Energy-efficient Virtual Machine Management

The virtualization management software is aimed to achieve a trade-off between security and performance. While these are important goals, energy-conscious high performance computing is a leading research direction for the future. In order to save energy, new management algorithms have to be developed that take advantage of the existing mechanisms such as live migration. A simple, but effective solution would be to consolidate virtual machines on a small number of nodes and shut down the remaining, idle nodes.

7.2.4 Intrusion Detection

To be able to detect even more attacks on grids in the future, there is a need for more precise signatures describing novel attacks. While this thesis focused on a grid intrusion detection system, there is also potential for special cloud-tailored signatures. New computing paradigms like Google's MapReduce or cloud data flow systems generate unique traffic signatures that are not covered by current network intrusion detection systems.

7.2.5 Malware and Rootkit Prevention

The lightweight kernel rootkit prevention and the malware scanner are currently only implemented for BSD derived operating systems. In order to make the approach available to a wider audience, it is desirable to port the approach to Xen and/or KVM on Linux and leverage existing technologies, such as XenAccess [99].

7.2.6 Complex Event Processing

In the future, real-time monitoring of grid and cloud resources will be a crucial field of research, as the vertical integration of monitoring solutions (i.e., being able to correlate cross-layer information) leads to more accurate decisions and actions. Of course, this also applies to the area of cloud-ready malware scanners. Using Complex Event Processing (CEP) technologies, it will be possible to perform complex operations on input data in real-time and thus react on time.

List of Figures

1.1 Typical turbulent state on the chaotic saddle. 3

2.1 Globus Toolkit 4: Components. Source: [149] 12
2.2 Grid Security Infrastructure overview. Source: [149] 14
2.3 Ring usage in native and paravirtualized systems. Source: [18] . . 18
2.4 Layered cloud computing architecture 20

3.1 Job submission and executions initiated by a user. A meta-scheduler distributes the job to one of the two sites and it is executed on the site's nodes. 25
3.2 Detailed view of a job submission process. An appropriate site is chosen by the meta-scheduler and the middleware acts as the first point of contact. 27
3.3 Multiple job applications executed on shared resources without any shielding. 30
3.4 XGE connected to backend resources on shared storage 35
3.5 Grid DMZ shielding the head node as well as the internal network with all resources 36
3.6 Multiple virtual machines introspected by a kernel agent that reports continuously over a middleware to various anti-virus/-maleware backends 37
3.7 Multi-site virtual private network, including the users own computer and the computing nodes of his or her actual job 38

List of Figures

3.8 Every virtual machine is guarded by a dynamic firewall installed on the administrative domain 39

4.1 Runtime kernel memory patching 47

4.2 Hooking a system call 48

4.3 Authorized module loading state transition diagram 52

4.4 Module loading activity 57

4.5 Time needed to load up to 2000 kernel modules 59

4.6 Time needed to unload up to 2000 kernel modules 60

4.7 Time needed to mark up to 2000 kernel modules as authorized . . 61

4.8 Malware scanner architecture 65

4.9 Comparing host, virtual machine and modified virtual machine speed 72

4.10 Transfer times for various binaries from the KernelAgent to the antivirus backend 73

4.11 Benchmark comparing speed of a modified kernel without running TCP receiver for binaries, single-threaded and multi-threaded transmission 74

4.12 Time needed to pass data in the kernel using static and dynamically allocated memory 75

5.1 Image Creation Station 85

5.2 The architecture of the XGE. The figure shows all modules and their relationship to each other. 86

5.3 Stacked architecture for virtual machine handling 90

5.4 Multilayer Disk Images 94

5.5 DRBD module overview. Source: [86] 95

5.6 Database tables 98

5.7 Binary tree distribution 101

5.8 Distributed file sharing between multiple peers including a tracker 102

List of Figures

5.9 Distribution of two disk images via BitTorrent 103

5.10 Usage scenarios for a layered virtual machine 105

5.11 Possible torrent states in the TorrentClient 128

5.12 Comparing the turbulence simulation's execution times in a virtualized and a native environment 132

5.13 Submitting a test job over Torque in a virtualized and a native environment 133

5.14 Results of the *kernbench* benchmark running on two physical and two virtual CPU cores 135

5.15 bonnie++ benchmark results: sequential input 136

5.16 bonnie++ benchmark results: sequential output 136

5.17 Results of *hackbech* runs varying the scheduler's granularity settings 137

5.18 Results of *hackbech* runs varying the scheduler's latency settings . 138

5.19 Architectural overview 146

5.20 Step-by-step processing of a job through the inner firewall 147

5.21 All steps required for a end-to-end encryption 148

5.22 Interaction between Globus, the job manager and the XGE 151

5.23 Fence embedded into the demilitarized zone. Furthermore, the relations between all components are shown. 152

5.24 Time for fully-encrypted job submissions 167

5.25 Time required for unencrypted job submissions 168

5.26 Transfer data chart with/without a firewall 169

5.27 System load of the grid head node during an Denial-of-Service attack on GridFTP 170

5.28 Inter-Site communication between the user and the virtual machines on two sites 176

5.29 Multiple dynamic firewalls installed on the node 180

5.30 Tree-based representation of a firewall template 184

List of Figures

5.31	Dynamic firewall deployment time	186
5.32	iptables rule deployment time	187
5.33	Cross-site measurements with and without firewalls	188
5.34	Maximum throughput with an increasing number of firewall rules	189
5.35	Inter-application communication time (milliseconds) with and without dynamic firewalls	189
6.1	Deployment times for a 1024 MB virtual disk image	192
6.2	Deployment times for a 2048 MB virtual disk image	193
6.3	Deployment times for a 4096 MB virtual disk image	194
6.4	Deployment times for a 8192 MB virtual disk image	195
6.5	Encryption times for different sized images	196
6.6	Decryption times for different sized images	197
6.7	Disk image distribution with BitTorrent and data en-/decryption	198
6.8	Results of the bonnie++ benchmark with layered and unlayered virtual machines	199
6.9	Impact of background synchronization limits on virtual machine performance	200
6.10	Disk synchronization	201
6.11	Disk synchronization (logarithmic scale)	202

List of Tables

4.1	Securelevel restrictions	50
5.1	Job processing within the XGE, split in single steps	134
5.2	Globus Toolkit 4 network configuration. Source: [165]	145
6.1	Measured mean values of all deployment methods	193
6.2	Transfer times of virtual machine images and file system layers	197
6.3	Results for live migration with storage synchronization (Tests 1 and 2)	203
6.4	Results for live migration with storage synchronization (Tests 3 and 4)	203
6.5	Results for live migration with tmpfs as a writable layer (Tests 5 and 6)	204
6.6	Reference values for the kernel compile benchmark without migration	204
6.7	Overhead of the DRBD driver in standalone mode	205

Listings

2.1	Sample job submission via Globus command line utilities	13
2.2	RSL description of a sample job	13
2.3	Libvirt example: show all running virtual machines	19
4.1	Fraction of kernel rootkit code that hooks the system call table and is able to provide root permissions to the calling process	48
4.2	Parts of the function that manages the trusted module list	53
4.3	An excerpt of the function that reads the module through the VFS layer from the disk and calculates the hash	54
4.4	Structure of the internal list	56
4.5	Marking a kernel module as loaded	57
4.6	Kernel function that traces system calls	68
4.7	vsyscall data structure	70
4.8	ktrace dump of a malware binary stealing the password file	71
5.1	Job description file as provided by a scheduler	88
5.2	Part of the ConnectionHandler that starts a virtual machine, catches and forwards possible exceptions back to the requester	108
5.3	Database worker class, which handles concurrent access to the SQLite database	109
5.4	Method in the LxGEd used to copy virtual machine hard disk images between client and daemon node	110

Listings

5.5 Abstract of the JobInformation class describing vital details about a XGE job 111

5.6 Method to register a job in the XGE 112

5.7 Initialization of the backend connection in the VNodesManager . 113

5.8 Method used to start a virtual machine in the VNodesManager . 114

5.9 Method used to stop a virtual machine in the VNodesManager . . 115

5.10 Method used to migrate a virtual machine in the VNodesManager 117

5.11 One TCP connection is opened to the libvirt daemon running on every node 118

5.12 XML document describing a virtual machine 120

5.13 Backend method used to start a virtual machine 121

5.14 Fragment of the sequential virtual machine hard disk image distribution code 122

5.15 First part of the method used to distribute a disk image via BitTorrent 125

5.16 Second part of the method used to distribute a disk image via BitTorrent 126

5.17 BitTorrent client within the imaged 127

5.18 Grid Security Schema 154

5.19 Auto-generated XML file describing a job 159

5.20 Code snippet that shows the process of creating and transferring an INFO message 160

5.21 Runtime Environment Restrictions 162

5.22 Fraction of the snort alert log after a portscan and a break-in attempt 163

5.23 Globus WSRF-Denial of Service 164

5.24 New signatures to detect a Globus Denial of Service attack 164

5.25 Snort detects the attack on the GridFTP service 165

5.26 Common firewall rule set template 179

5.27 Iptables rule generation 184
5.28 Fragment of the XGE traffic shaping code 185

Bibliography

[1] W. Allcock, J. Bester, J. Bresnahan, S. Meder, P. Plaszczak, and S. Tuecke. GridFTP: Protocol Extensions to FTP for the Grid. April 2003.

[2] Amazon Web Services LLC. Amazon Elastic Compute Cloud. http://aws.amazon.com/ec2/, 2010.

[3] AMD. AMD Virtualization (AMD V) Technology. http://www.amd.com/virtualization, 2010.

[4] Axelle Apvrille, David Gordon, Serge Hallyn, Makan Pourzandi, and Vincent Roy. Digsig: Run-time Authentication of Binaries at Kernel Level. *Proceedings of the 18th USENIX Conference on System Administration: LISA*, pages 59–66, Jan 2004.

[5] Michael Armbrust, Armando Fox, Rean Griffith, and Aanthony Joseph. Above the Clouds: A Berkeley View of Cloud Computing. *EECS Department University of California Berkeley Tech Rep UCBEECS200928*, 53(UCB/EECS-2009-28), Jan 2009.

[6] Mark Baker, Hong Ong, and Garry Smith. A Report on Experiences Operating the Globus Toolkit through a Firewall. Technical report, Distributed Systems Group, University of Portsmouth, September 2001.

[7] Vinay Bansal. Policy Based Firewall for GRID Security. Technical report, Dept. of Computer Science, Duke University, 2004.

[8] Paul Barham, Boris Dragovic, Keir Fraser, Steven Hand, Tim Harris, Alex Ho, Rolf Neugebauer, Ian Pratt, and Andrew Warfield. Xen and the Art of Virtualization. In *SOSP '03: Proceedings of the 19th ACM Symposium on Operating Systems Principles*, pages 164–177. ACM Press, 2003.

[9] Jyoti Batheja and Manish Parashar. Adaptive Cluster Computing using JavaSpaces. In *Proceedings of the 3rd IEEE International Conference on Cluster Computing*, pages 323–331, Washington, DC, USA, 2001. IEEE Computer Society.

[10] BitTorrent Development Team. BitTorrent Website. http://www.bittorrent.com/, 2011.

[11] BMBF. Bundesministerium für Bildung und Forschung. http://www.bmbf.de/, 2010.

[12] Robert Bradford, Evangelos Kotsovinos, Anja Feldmann, and Harald Schöberg. Live Wide-area Migration of Virtual Machines Including Local Persistent State. In *VEE '07: Proceedings of the 3rd International Conference on Virtual Execution Environments*, pages 169–179, New York, NY, USA, 2007. ACM.

[13] Jon Brodkin. Gartner: Seven Cloud-Computing Security Risks. http://bit.ly/eyjAtB, July 2008.

[14] B. Callaghan, B. Pawlowski, and P. Staubach. NFS Version 3 Protocol Specification. *Request for Comments (RFC) 1813*, 1995.

[15] Luigi Catuogno and Ivan Visconti. An Architecture for Kernel-Level Verification of Executables at Run Time. *Computer Journal*, 47(5):511–526, 2004.

[16] CERT Advisory CA-1998-01. Smurf IP Denial-of-Service Attacks. http://www.cert.org/advisories/CA-1998-01.html, 2008.

[17] Ludmila Cherkasova and Rob Gardner. Measuring CPU Overhead for I/O Processing in the Xen Virtual Machine Monitor. In *USENIX Annual Technical Conference*, pages 387–390. USENIX Association, 2005.

[18] David Chisnall. *The definitive Guide to the Xen Hypervisor*. Prentice Hall Press, Upper Saddle River, NJ, USA, 2007.

[19] Clam AntiVirus Team. Clam AntiVirus. http://www.clamav.net, 2010.

[20] Bryan Clark, Todd Deshane, Eli Dow, Stephen Evanchik, Matthew Finlayson, Jason Herne, and Jeanna Neefe Matthews. Xen and the Art of Repeated Research. In *USENIX Annual Technical Conference, FREENIX Track*, pages 135–144, 2004.

[21] Christopher Clark, Keir Fraser, Steven Hand, Jacob Gorm Hansen, Eric Jul, Christian Limpach, Ian Pratt, and Andrew Warfield. Live Migration of Virtual Machines. In *NSDI'05: Proceedings of the 2nd Symposium on Networked Systems Design & Implementation*, pages 273–286, Berkeley, CA, USA, 2005. USENIX Association.

[22] Cluster Resources, Inc. TORQUE Resource Manager. http://www.clusterresources.com/pages/products/torque-resource-manager.php, September 2010.

[23] Bram Cohen. The BitTorrent Protocol Specification. http://www.bittorrent.org/beps/bep_0003.html, 2008.

[24] Russel Coker. bonnie++ Benchmark. http://www.coker.com.au/bonnie++/, 2010.

[25] Symantec Cooperation. Symantec Client Security and Symantec AntiVirus Elevation of Privilege. www.symantec.com/avcenter/security/Content/2006.05.25.html, May 2006.

[26] D-Grid. D-Grid Website, 2010. http://www.d-grid.de/.

[27] Renzo Davoli and Michael Goldweber. Virtual Square (V2) in Computer Science Education. In *Proceedings of the 10th Annual SIGCSE Conference on Innovation and Technology in Computer Science Education*, pages 301–305, 2005.

[28] Globus Developers. GT 4.0 WS GRAM: Job Description Schema Doc. http://www.globus.org/toolkit/docs/4.0/execution/wsgram/schemas/, 2010.

[29] Libvirt Developers. Libvirt - The Virtualization API. http://libvirt.org/, 2010.

[30] The OpenSSH developers. OpenSSH - Secure Shell Login. http://www.openssh.org, 2011.

[31] T. Dierks and E. Rescorla. The Transport Layer Security (TLS) Protocol - Version 1.2. *Proposed Standard of the IETF*, August 2008.

[32] Artem Dinaburg, Paul Royal, Monirul Sharif, and Wenke Lee. Ether: Malware Analysis via Hardware Virtualization Extensions. *Analysis*, pages 51–62, 2008.

[33] Kay Dörnemann, Tim Dörnemann, Bernd Freisleben, Tobias M. Schneider, and Bruno Eckhardt. A Hybrid Peer-to-Peer and Grid Job Scheduling System for Teaming Up Desktop Resources with Computer Clusters to Perform Turbulence Simulations. In *Proceedings of 4th IEEE International Conference on e-Science*, pages 418–419. IEEE Press, 2008.

[34] Christian Engelmann, Stephen L Scott, Hong Ong, Geoffroy Vallée, and Thomas Naughton. Configurable Virtualized System Environments for High Performance Computing. In *Proceedings of the 1st Workshop on System-level Virtualization for High Performance Computing (HPCVirt) 2007, in conjunction with the 2nd ACM SIGOPS European Conference on Computer Systems (EuroSys)*, 2007.

[35] The London eScience Centre. Sun Grid Engine Integration with Globus Toolkit 4. http://www.lesc.ic.ac.uk/projects/SGE-GT4.html, February 2007.

[36] Access e.V. Materials, Processes, Casts. http://www.access.rwth-aachen.de/, 2010.

[37] Ralf Ewerth, Markus Mühling, and Bernd Freisleben. Self-Supervised Learning of Face Appearances in TV Casts and Movies. In *International Journal on Semantic Computing (IJSC), Special Issue on ISM 2006*, pages 185–204. World Scientific, 2007.

[38] Niels Fallenbeck, Hans-Joachim Picht, Matthew Smith, and Bernd Freisleben. Xen and the Art of Cluster Scheduling. In *Proceedings of the 2006 ACM/IEEE Conference on Supercomputing, Virtualization Workshop*, pages 237–244. ACM Press, 2006.

[39] Niels Fallenbeck, Matthias Schmidt, Roland Schwarzkopf, and Bernd Freisleben. Inter-Site Virtual Machine Image Transfer in Grids and Clouds. In *Proceedings of the 2nd International ICST Conference on Cloud Computing (CloudComp 2010)*. Springer LNICST, 2010.

[40] Renato Figueiredo, Peter Dinda, and Jose Fortes. A Case for Grid Computing on Virtual Machines. *23rd International Conference on Distributed Computing Systems*, 0:550, Jan 2003.

[41] FinGrid Project. FinGrid Website. http://www.fingrid.de, 2010.

[42] Unicore Forum. Unicore/GS Website. http://www.unicore.eu, 2010.

[43] Ian Foster. The Anatomy of the Grid: Enabling Scalable Virtual Organizations. *First IEEE/ACM International Symposium on Cluster Computing and the Grid, 2001*, Jan 2001.

[44] Ian Foster. What is the Grid? A Three Point Checklist. *GRID Today*, 1(6):32–36, July 2002.

[45] Ian Foster, Carl Kesselman, C. Lee, R. Lindell, K. Nahrstedt, and A. Roy. A Distributed Resource Management Architecture that Supports Advance Reservations and Co-Allocation. In *Proceedings of the International Workshop on Quality of Service*, 1999.

[46] Ian Foster, Carl Kesselman, Gene Tsudik, and Steven Tueckee. A Security Architecture for Computational Grids. In *Proceedings of the 5th ACM Conference on Computer and Communications Security CCS 98*, pages 83–92. ACM Press, 1998.

[47] Python Software Foundation. Python Programming Language – Official Website. http://www.python.org, 2011.

[48] Timothy Freeman and Katarzyna Keahey. Flying Low: Simple Leases with Workspace Pilot. In *Euro-Par 2008 – Parallel Processing*, volume 5168 of *Lecture Notes in Computer Science*, pages 499–509. Springer Berlin / Heidelberg, 2008.

[49] Tal Garfinkel, Ben Pfaff, Jim Chow, Mendel Rosenblum, and Dan Boneh. Terra: A Virtual Machine-based Platform for Trusted Computing. *ACM SIGOPS Operating Systems Review*, 37(5):193–206, 2003.

[50] Tal Garfinkel and Mendel Rosenblum. A Virtual Machine Introspection Based Architecture for Intrusion Detection. In *In Proceedings of the Network and Distributed Systems Security Symposium*, pages 191–206, 2003.

[51] Sven Graupner and Carsten Reimann. Globus Grid and Firewalls: Issues and Solutions in a Utility Data Center Environment. http://www.hpl.hp.com/techreports/2002/HPL-2002-278.pdf, October 2002.

[52] Mark Green, Steven Gallo, and Russ Miller. Grid-enabled Virtual Organization Based Dynamic Firewall. *Fifth IEEEACM International Workshop on Grid Computing*, pages 208–216, 2004.

[53] The Grid Security Vulnerability Group. Critical Vulnerability: OpenPBS/Torque. http://security.fnal.gov/CriticalVuln/openpbs-10-23-2006.html, October 2006.

[54] Trusted Computing Group. TPM Main Part 1 Design Principles Specification. Technical Report Version 1.2, March 2006.

[55] Stephen Hemminger. Linux Iproute2 Utilities. http://www.linuxfoundation.org/collaborate/workgroups/networking/iproute2, 2011.

[56] Michael R. Hines, Umesh Deshpande, and Kartik Gopalan. Post-copy Live Migration of Virtual Machines. *SIGOPS Operating Systems Review*, 43(3):14–26, 2009.

[57] Björn Hof, Jerry Westerweel, Tobias M Schneider, and Bruno Eckhardt. Finite Lifetime of Turbulence in Shear Flows. *Nature*, 443:60–64, 2006.

[58] Eduardo Huedo, Rubén Santiago Montero, and Ignacio Martín Llorente. A Modular Meta-Scheduling Architecture for Interfacing with Pre-WS and WS Grid Resource Management Services. *Future Generation Computing Systems*, 23(3):252–261, 2007.

[59] M Humphrey, M R Thompson, and K R Jackson. Security for Grids. *Proceedings of the IEEE*, 93(3):644–652, 2005.

[60] InGrid Project. InGrid Website. http://www.ingrid-info.de, 2010.

[61] International Standard Organization (ISO/OSI). ISO/IEC 27000:2009 Information technology – Security techniques – Information security management systems - Fundamentals and vocabulary. http://www.iso27001security.com/, May 2009.

[62] International Standard Organization (ISO/OSI). ISO/IEC 27004:2009 Information technology — Security techniques Information security management — Measurement. http://www.iso27001security.com/, May 2009.

[63] International Standard Organization (ISO/OSI). ISO/IEC 27005:2008 Information technology – Security techniques – Information security risk management. http://www.iso27001security.com/, May 2009.

[64] Joanna Rutkowska. Introducing Blue Pill. http://theinvisiblethings.blogspot.com/2006/06/introducing-blue-pill.html, June 2006.

[65] W E Johnston, K R Jackson, and S Talwar. Overview of Security Considerations for Computational and Data Grids. *Proceedings 10th IEEE International Symposium on High Performance Distributed Computing*, pages 439–440, 2001.

[66] Katarzyna Keahey. Virtual Workspaces: Achieving Quality of Service and Quality of Life in the Grid. *Scientific Programming*, Jan 2005.

[67] Katarzyna Keahey, Karl Doering, and Ian Foster. From Sandbox to Playground: Dynamic Virtual Environments in the Grid. *GRID '04: Proceedings of the Fifth IEEE/ACM International Workshop on Grid Computing (GRID'04)*, pages 34–42, 2004.

[68] Katarzyna Keahey, Ian Foster, Timothy Freeman, X Zhang, and D Galron. Virtual Workspaces in the Grid. *Lecture Notes in Computer Science*, Jan 2005.

[69] Stuart Kenny and Brian Coghlan. Towards a Grid-wide Intrusion Detection System. In Peter M. A. Sloot, Alfons G. Hoekstra, Thierry Priol, Alexander Reinefeld, and Marian Bubak, editors, *Advances in Grid Computing - EGC 2005*, volume 3470 of *Lecture Notes in Computer Science*, pages 275–284. Springer Berlin / Heidelberg, 2005.

[70] S Kent and R Atkinson. RFC 2401: Security Architecture for the Internet Protocol. http://tools.ietf.org/html/rfc2401, 1998.

[71] Samuel T. King, Peter M. Chen, Yi min Wang, Chad Verbowski, Helen J. Wang, and Jacob R. Lorch. Subvirt: Implementing Malware with Virtual Machines. In *In IEEE Symposium on Security and Privacy*, pages 314–327, 2006.

[72] Nadir Kiyanclar, Gregory A. Koenig, and William Yurcik. Maestro-VC: A Paravirtualized Execution Environment for Secure On-Demand Cluster Computing. In *CCGRID '06: Proceedings of the Sixth IEEE International Symposium on Cluster Computing and the Grid (CCGRID'06)*, page 28. IEEE Computer Society, 2006.

[73] Joseph Kong. *Designing BSD Rootkits. An Introduction to Kernel Hacking*. No Starch Press, first edition, 2007.

[74] Björn Könning, Christian Engelmann, Stephen L Scott, and G Al Geist. Virtualized Environments for the Harness High Performance Computing Workbench. *Proceedings of the 16th Euromicro Conference on Parallel, Distributed and Network-Based Processing (PDP '08)*, pages 133–140, 2008.

[75] Michael Kozuch and M. Satyanarayanan. Internet Suspend/Resume. In *Proceedings Fourth IEEE Workshop on Mobile Computing Systems and Applications*, pages 40–46, Jan 2002.

[76] Greg Kroah-Hartman. Signed Kernel Modules. *Linux Journal*, pages 301–308, Jan 2004.

[77] Ivan Krsul, Arijit Ganguly, Jian Zhang, Jose A. B. Fortes, and Renato J. Figueiredo. VMPlants: Providing and Managing Virtual Machine Execution Environments for Grid Computing. In *Proceedings of the 2004 ACM/IEEE Conference on Supercomputing*, page 7. IEEE Computer Society, 2004.

[78] Christopher Kruegel, William Robertson, and Giovanni Vigna. Detecting Kernel-Level Rootkits Through Binary Analysis. *Computer Security Applications Conference*, (6-10):91–100, Jan 2004.

[79] Abhishek Kumar, Vern Paxson, and Nicholas Weaver. *Exploiting Underlying Structure for Detailed Reconstruction of an Internet-scale Event*, page 1. ACM Press, 2005.

[80] Marcos Laureano, Carlos Maziero, and Edgard Jamhour. Intrusion Detection In Virtual Machine Environments. *Proceedings 30th Euromicro Conference 2004*, pages 520–525, 2004.

[81] P. Leach, M. Mealling, and R. Salz. A Universally Unique IDentifier (UUID) URN Namespace. *Request for Comments (RFC) 4122*, 2005.

Bibliography

[82] Fang-Yie Leu, Jia-Chun Lin, Ming-Chang Li, and Chao-Tung Yang. A Performance-Based Grid Intrusion Detection System. In *Proceedings of the 29th Annual International Computer Software and Applications Conference - Volume 01*, COMPSAC '05, pages 525–530, Washington, DC, USA, 2005. IEEE Computer Society.

[83] Fang-Yie Leu, Jia-Chun Lin, Ming-Chang Li, Chao-Tung Yang, and Po-Chi Shih. Integrating Grid with Intrusion Detection. In *Proceedings of the 19th International Conference on Advanced Information Networking and Applications*, pages 304–309, 2005.

[84] Terrence V. Lillard, Clint P. Garrison, Craig A. Schiller, and James Steele. The Future of Cloud Computing. In *Digital Forensics for Network, Internet, and Cloud Computing*, pages 319 – 339. Syngress, Boston, 2010.

[85] Bin Lin and Peter A. Dinda. VSched: Mixing Batch And Interactive Virtual Machines Using Periodic Real-time Scheduling. In *Proceedings of the 2005 ACM/IEEE Conference on Supercomputing*, page 8. IEEE Computer Society, 2005.

[86] LINBIT HA-Solutions GmbH. DRBD - Software Development for High Availability Clusters. http://www.drbd.org/, 2011.

[87] Yingwei Luo, Binbin Zhang, Xiaolin Wang, Zhenlin Wang, Yifeng Sun, and Haogang Chen. Live and Incremental Whole-system Migration of Virtual Machines Using Block-Bitmap. In *2008 IEEE International Conference on Cluster Computing*, pages 99–106, 2008.

[88] Andrew Martin and Po-Wah Yau. Grid security: Next steps. *Information Security Technical Report*, 12(3):113–122, 2007.

[89] Jeanna Matthews, Tal Garfinkel, Christofer Hoff, and Jeff Wheeler. Virtual Machine Contracts for Datacenter and Cloud Computing Environments. In *Proceedings of the 1st Workshop on Automated Control for Datacenters and Clouds*, ACDC '09, pages 25–30, New York, NY, USA, 2009. ACM.

[90] Wolfgang Maurer. *Professional Linux Kernel Architecture*. Wiley Publishing, Inc., Indianapolis, Indiana, 2008.

[91] Marshall McKusick and Geroge Neville-Neil. *The Design and Implementation of the FreeBSD Operating System*. Addison-Wesley Publishing Company, Reading, MA, April 2005.

[92] Aravind Menon, Jose Renato Santos, Yoshio Turner, G. (John) Janakiraman, and Willy Zwaenepoel. Diagnosing Performance Overheads in the Xen Virtual Machine Environment. In *VEE '05: Proceedings of the 1st*

ACM/USENIX International Conference on Virtual Execution Environments, pages 13–23, New York, NY, USA, 2005. ACM Press.

[93] Michael Nelson, Beng-Hong Lim, and Greg Hutchins. Fast Transparent Migration for Virtual Machines. *Proceedings of the USENIX Annual Technical Conference 2005*, pages 391–394, Jan 2005.

[94] Nimbus Developers. Nimbus Open Source Toolkit. http://www.nimbusproject.org/, 2010.

[95] Jon Oberheide, Evan Cooke, and Farnam Jahanian. Rethinking Antivirus: Executable Analysis in the Network Cloud. *Proceedings of the 2nd USENIX Workshop on Hot topics in Security*, Jan 2007.

[96] Jon Oberheide, Evan Cooke, and Farnam Jahanian. *CloudAV: N-Version Antivirus In The Network Cloud*, pages 91–106. USENIX Association, 2008.

[97] OpenSSL Project. OpenSSL: The Open Source Toolkit for SSL/TLS. http://www.openssl.org/, 2011.

[98] Oracle. MySQL: The World's most popular Open Source Database. http://www.mysql.com/, 2011.

[99] Bryan D Payne, Martim D P De A Carbone, and Wenke Lee. Secure and Flexible Monitoring of Virtual Machines. In *23rd Annual Computer Security Applications Conference ACSAC*, pages 385–397. IEEE Press, 2007.

[100] Laura Pearlman, Von Welch, Ian Foster, Carl Kesselman, and Steven Tuecke. A Community Authorization Service for Group Collaboration. In *Proceedings of the Third International Workshop on Policies for Distributed Systems and Networks*, pages 50–59. Published by the IEEE Computer Society, 2002.

[101] Nick L. Petroni, Timothy Fraser, Jesus Molina, and William A. Arbaugh. Copilot - A Coprocessor-based Kernel Runtime Integrity Monitor. In *Proceedings of the 13th Conference on USENIX Security Symposium*, volume 13 of *SSYM'04*, pages 13–13, Berkeley, CA, USA, 2004. USENIX Association.

[102] PostgreSQL Global Development Group. PostgresSQL: The World's most advanced Open Source Database. http://www.postgresql.org/, 2011.

[103] EGEE Project. gLite – Lightweight Middleware for Grid Computing. http://glite.cern.ch/, 2010.

Bibliography

[104] European DataGrid Project. Virtual Organization Membership Service (VOMS). http://edg-wp2.web.cern.ch/edg-wp2/security/voms/voms.html, 2003.

[105] PT-Grid Project. PT-Grid Website. http://www.pt-grid.de, 2010.

[106] Nguyen Anh Quynh and Yoshiyasu Takefuji. Towards a Tamper-resistant Kernel Rootkit Detector. *Symposium on Applied Computing*, pages 276–283, 2007.

[107] Rafal Wojtczuk and Joanna Rutkowska. Attacking SMM Memory via Intel CPU Cache Poisoning. http://invisiblethingslab.com/resources/misc09/smm_cache_fun.pdf, March 2009.

[108] Ala Rezmerita, Tangui Morlier, Vincent Neri, and Franck Cappello. Private Virtual Cluster: Infrastructure and Protocol for Instant Grids. In *Euro-Par 2006 Parallel Processing*, volume 4128 of *Lecture Notes in Computer Science*, pages 393–404. Springer Berlin / Heidelberg, 2006.

[109] Ryan Riley, Xuxian Jiang, and Dongyan Xu. Guest-transparent Prevention of Kernel Rootkits with VMM-based Memory Shadowing. *Lecture Notes in Computer Science including subseries Lecture Notes in Artificial Intelligence and Lecture Notes in Bioinformatics*, 5230 LNCS:1–20, 2008.

[110] John Scott Robin and Cynthia Irvine. Analysis of the Intel Pentium's Ability to Support a Secure Virtual Machine Monitor. *Proceedings of the 9th Conference on USENIX Security Symposium*, 9:10–10, Jan 2000.

[111] AL Rowland, M Burns, JV Hajnal, and D.L.G. Hill. Using Grid Services From Behind A Firewall. *Imperial College London*, 2005.

[112] Constantine P Sapuntzakis, Ramesh Chandra, Ben Pfaff, Jim Chow, Monica S Lam, and Mendel Rosenblum. Optimizing the Migration of Virtual Computers. In *Proceedings of the 5th Symposium on Operating Systems Design and Implementation*, pages 377–390, 2002.

[113] Matthias Schmidt, Lars Baumgärtner, Pablo Graubner, David Böck, and Bernd Freisleben. Malware Detection and Kernel Rootkit Prevention in Cloud Computing Environments. In *Proceedings of the 19th Euromicro Conference on Parallel, Distributed and Network-based Processing (PDP)*, pages 603–610. IEEE press, 2011.

[114] Matthias Schmidt, Sascha Fahl, Roland Schwarzkopf, and Bernd Freisleben. TrustBox: A Security Architecture for Preventing Data Breaches. In *Proceedings of the 19th Euromicro Conference on Parallel, Distributed and Network-based Processing (PDP)*, pages 635–639. IEEE press, 2011.

[115] Matthias Schmidt, Niels Fallenbeck, Kay Dörnemann, Roland Schwarzkopf, Tobias Pontz, Manfred Grauer, and Bernd Freisleben. *Aufbau einer virtualisierten Cluster-Umgebung*, pages 119–131. Books on Demand, 2009.

[116] Matthias Schmidt, Niels Fallenbeck, Matthew Smith, and Bernd Freisleben. Secure Service-Oriented Grid Computing with Public Virtual Worker Nodes. In *Proceedings of 35th Euromicro Conference on Internet Technologies, Quality of Service and Applications (ITQSA)*, pages 555–562. IEEE press, 2009.

[117] Matthias Schmidt, Niels Fallenbeck, Matthew Smith, and Bernd Freisleben. Efficient Distribution of Virtual Machines for Cloud Computing. In *Proceedings of the 18th Euromicro Conference on Parallel, Distributed and Network-based Processing (PDP)*, pages 567–574. IEEE Press, 2010.

[118] Matthias Schmidt, Matthew Smith, Niels Fallenbeck, Hans-Joachim Picht, and Bernd Freisleben. Building a Demilitarized Zone with Data Encryption for Grid Environments. In *Proceedings of First International Conference on Networks for Grid Applications*, pages 8–16. ACM Press, 2007.

[119] Tobias M. Schneider, Filippo De Lillo, Jürgen Bührle, Bruno Eckhardt, Tim Dörnemann, Kay Dörnemann, and Bernd Freisleben. Transient Turbulence in Plane Couette Flow. *Physical Review E*, pages 15301–15305, 2010.

[120] Alexandre Schulter, Fabio Navarro, Fernando Koch, and Carlos Becker Westphall. Towards Grid-based Intrusion Detection. In *10th IEEE/IFIP Network Operations and Management Symposium*, pages 1–4, 2006.

[121] Roland Schwarzkopf, Matthias Schmidt, Niels Fallenbeck, and Bernd Freisleben. Multi-Layered Virtual Machines for Security Updates in Grid Environments. In *Proceedings of 35th Euromicro Conference on Internet Technologies, Quality of Service and Applications (ITQSA)*, pages 563–570. IEEE Press, 2009.

[122] Paulo F. Silva, Carlos B. Westphall, Carla M. Westphall, and Marcos D. Assunção. Composition of a DIDS by Integrating Heterogeneous IDSs on Grids. In *Proceedings of the 4th International Workshop on Middleware for Grid Computing*, MCG '06, pages 12–18, New York, NY, USA, 2006. ACM.

[123] Matthew Smith. *Security for Service-Oriented On-Demand Grid Computing*. PhD thesis, Philipps University of Marburg, 2008.

[124] Matthew Smith, Thomas Friese, Michael Engel, and Bernd Freisleben. Countering Security Threats in Service-Oriented On-Demand Grid Computing Using Sandboxing and Trusted Computing Techniques. *Journal of Parallel and Distributed Computing*, 66(9):1189–1204, 2006.

[125] Matthew Smith, Thomas Friese, Michael Engel, Bernd Freisleben, G. Koenig, and W. Yurcik. Security Issues in On-Demand Grid and Cluster Computing. In *Sixth IEEE International Symposium on Cluster Computing and the Grid Workshops (CCGRIDW'06)*, page 24. IEEE Press, 2006.

[126] Matthew Smith, Matthias Schmidt, Niels Fallenbeck, Tim Dörnemann, Christian Schridde, and Bernd Freisleben. Secure On-Demand Grid Computing. *Journal of Future Generation Computer Systems*, pages 315–325, 2008.

[127] Matthew Smith, Matthias Schmidt, Niels Fallenbeck, Christian Schridde, and Bernd Freisleben. Optimising Security Configurations with Service Level Agreements. In *Proceedings of the 7th International Conference on Optimization: Techniques and Applications (ICOTA7)*, pages 367–368. ICOTA, 2007.

[128] Snort Development Team. Snort Network Intrusion Detection. http://www.snort.org, August 2010.

[129] Softpanorama - Open Source Software Educational Society. NFS Performance Tuning. http://softpanorama.org/Net/Application_layer/NFS/nfs_performance_tuning.shtml, August 2009.

[130] Rasterbar Software. Libtorrent. http://www.rasterbar.com/products/libtorrent/, 2011.

[131] Sechang Son, Bill Allcock, and Miron Livny. CODO: Firewall Traversal by Cooperative On-Demand Opening. In *Proceedings of the Fourteenth IEEE Symposium on High Performance Distributed Computing*, pages 233–242, Jul 2005.

[132] Borja Sotomayor, Katarzyna Keahey, and Ian Foster. Combining Batch Execution and Leasing Using Virtual Machines. In *Proceedings of the 17th International Symposium on High Performance Distributed Computing*, HPDC '08, pages 87–96. ACM, 2008.

[133] Borja Sotomayor, Kate Keahey, Ian Foster, and Tim Freeman. Enabling Cost-Effective Resource Leases with Virtual Machines. *Hot Topics session in ACM/IEEE International Symposium on High Performance Distributed Computing*, pages 16–18, 2007.

[134] Borja Sotomayor, Rubén S Montero, Ignacio M Llorente, and Ian Foster. Virtual Infrastructure Management in Private and Hybrid Clouds. *IEEE Internet Computing*, 13(5):14–22, 2009.

[135] Borja Sotomayor, Rubén Santiago Montero, Ignacio Martin Llorente, and I Foster. Resource Leasing and the Art of Suspending Virtual Machines. *2009 11th IEEE International Conference on High Performance Computing and Communications*, pages 59–68, 2009.

[136] Borja Sotomayor, Rubén Santiago Montero, Ignacio Martín Llorente, and Ian Foster. Capacity Leasing in Cloud Systems using the OpenNebula Engine. *Workshop on Cloud Computing and its Applications (CCA08)*, 2008.

[137] Brad Spengler. GRsecurity. http://www.grsecurity.org, 2010.

[138] Diomidis Spinellis. Reflection as a Mechanism for Software Integrity Verification. *ACM Transactions on Information and System Security*, 3(1):51–62, 2000.

[139] SQLite developers. SQLite Database Engine. http://www.sqlite.org/, 2011.

[140] Stealth. Adore Next Generation Rootkit. http://stealth.openwall.net/rootkits/, 2007.

[141] Stealth. Kernel Rootkit Experiences. *Phrack Magazine*, 0x0b(0x03d), August 2008.

[142] Ananth I Sundararaj and Peter A Dinda. *Towards Virtual Networks for Virtual Machine Grid Computing*, page 14. USENIX Association, 2004.

[143] Ananth I Sundararaj, Ashish Gupta, and Peter A Dinda. Dynamic Topology Adaptation of Virtual Networks of Virtual Machines. *Proceedings of the 7th Workshop on Languages, Compilers and Runtime Support for Scalable Systems LCR 04*, pages 1–8, 2004.

[144] Mike Surridge and Colin Upstill. Grid Security: Lessons for Peer-to-Peer Systems. In *P2P '03: Proceedings of the 3rd International Conference on Peer-to-Peer Computing*, pages 2–6, Washington, DC, USA, 2003. IEEE Computer Society.

[145] Internet Security Systems. Unicore client keystore information disclosure. http://xforce.iss.net/xforce/xfdb/30157, November 2006.

[146] J Tan, D Abramson, and C Enticott. Bridging Organizational Network Boundaries on the Grid. *Proceedings of the 6th IEEE/ACM International Workshop on Grid Computing*, pages 327–332, 2005.

[147] Globus Security Team. Globus security advisory 2007-02: Gsi-openssh vulnerability. http://www-unix.globus.org/mail_archive/security-announce/2007/04/msg00000.html, March 2007.

[148] Globus Security Team. Globus security advisory 2007-03: Nexus vulnerability. http://www.globus.org/mail_archive/security-announce/2007/05/msg00000.html, May 2007.

[149] The Globus Project. The Globus Toolkit 4, 2010. http://www.globus.org/toolkit/.

[150] The GridSphere Project. The GridSphere Portal Framework. http://www.gridsphere.org, August 2010.

[151] The NetBSD Guide. NetBSD Veriexec Subsystem. http://www.netbsd.org/docs/guide/en/chap-veriexec.html, 2010.

[152] The Openwall Project. Linux Kernel Patch From The Openwall Project. http://www.openwall.com/linux/, August 2010.

[153] TIMaCS Project. TIMaCS Website. http://www.timacs.de, 2010.

[154] TIS Committee. Tool Interface Standard (TIS) Executable and Linking Format (ELF) Specification, May 1995. Version 1.2.

[155] Andrew Tridgell and Paul Mackerras. The rsync Algorithm. *Imagine*, (TR-CS-96-05), 1996.

[156] Mauricio Tsugawa and Jose A. B. Fortes. A Virtual Network (ViNe) Architecture for Grid Computing. *Proceedings 20th IEEE International Parallel Distributed Processing Symposium*, pages 1–10, 2006.

[157] Rich Uhlig, Gil Neiger, Dion Rodgers, Amy Santoni, Fernando Martins, Andrew Anderson, Steven Bennett, Alain Kagi, Felix Leung, and Larry Smith. Intel Virtualization Technology. *Computer*, 38(5):48–56, 2005.

[158] Unionfs Developers. Unionfs: A Stackable Unification File System. http://www.filesystems.org/project-unionfs.html, June 2008.

[159] Geoffroy Vallée, Thomas Naughton, Christian Engelmann, Hong Ong, and Stephen L Scott. System-Level Virtualization for High Performance Computing. *Proceedings of the 16th Euromicro Conference on Parallel, Distributed and Network-Based Processing (PDP '08)*, pages 636–643, 2008.

[160] Leendert van Doorn, Van Doorn, Gerco Ballintijn, and William A. Arbaugh. Signed Executables for Linux. Technical report, Technical Report CS-TR-4259, University of Maryland, 2001.

[161] Dimiter Velev and Plamena Zlateva. Cloud Infrastructure Security. In *Open Research Problems in Network Security*, volume 6555 of *Lecture Notes in Computer Science*, pages 140–148. Springer LNICST, 2011.

[162] VMWare Inc. VMWare GSX Server. http://www.vmware.com/products/server/, 2008.

[163] Eugen Volk, Jochen Buchholz, Stefan Wesner, Daniela Koudela, Matthias Schmidt, Niels Fallenbeck, Roland Schwarzkopf, Bernd Freisleben, Götz Isenmann, Jürgen Schwitalla, Marc Lohrer, Erich Focht, and Andreas Jeutter. Towards Intelligent Management of Very Large Computing Systems. In *Proceedings of Competence in High Performance Computing CiHPC*. Springer, 2010.

[164] Gian Luca Volpato and Christian Grimm. Dynamic Firewalls and Service Deployment Models for Grid Environments. In *In Proceedings of the Cracow Grid Workshop*, 2006.

[165] Gian Luca Volpato and Christian Grimm. Recommendations for Static Firewall Configuration in D-Grid. Technical Report Version 1.4, D-Grid Integrationsprojekt (DGI), Januar 2007.

[166] William von Hagen. *Professional Xen Virtualization*. Wrox Press Ltd., Birmingham, UK, UK, 2008.

[167] Gerard Wagener, Radu State, and Alexandre Dulaunoy. Malware Behaviour Analysis. *Journal in Computer Virology*, 4:279–287, 2008.

[168] Aaron Weiss. Trusted Computing. *netWorker*, 10:18–25, September 2006.

[169] Von Welch. Globus Toolkit Firewall Requirements. http://www.globus.org/toolkit/security/firewalls/Globus-Firewall-Requirements-9.pdf, October 2006.

[170] Jeffrey Wilhelm and Tzi-Cker Chiueh. A Forced Sampled Execution Approach to Kernel Rootkit Identification. *Lecture Notes in Computer Science*, 4637:219–235, 2007.

[171] David Wolinsky, Abhishek Agrawal, P Boykin, and Justin Davis. On the Design of Virtual Machine Sandboxes for Distributed Computing in Wide-area Overlays of Virtual Workstations. *Proceedings of the 2nd International Workshop on Virtualization Technology in Distributed Computing (VTDC)*, page 8, Jan 2006.

[172] Timothy Wood, Alexandre Gerber, Alexandre Gerber, Prashant Shenoy, and Jacobus Van Der Merwe. The Case for Enterprise-Ready Virtual Private Clouds. In *Proceedings of the 2009 Conference on Hot Topics in Cloud Computing*. USENIX, 2009.

[173] Glenn Wurster and P.C. van Oorschot. Self-signed Executables: Restricting Replacement of Program Binaries by Malware. *HOTSEC'07: Proceedings of the 2nd USENIX Workshop on Hot Topics in Security*, pages 1–5, Jul 2007.

[174] Wei Yan and Erik Wu. *Toward Automatic Discovery of Malware Signature for Anti-Virus Cloud Computing*, volume 4, pages 724–728. Springer Berlin Heidelberg, 2009.

[175] Lamia Youseff, Richard Wolski, Brent Gorda, and Chandra Krintz. Paravirtualization for HPC Systems. *ISPA Workshops*, pages 474–486, 2006.

[176] Xiaolan Zhang, Leendert van Doorn, Trent Jaeger, Ronald Perez, and Reiner Sailer. Secure Coprocessor-based Intrusion Detection. In *Proceedings of the 10th Workshop on ACM SIGOPS European Workshop*, EW 10, pages 239–242, New York, NY, USA, 2002. ACM.

[177] Xuehai Zhang, Katarzyna Keahey, Ian Foster, and Timothy Freeman. Virtual Cluster Workspaces for Grid Applications. *ANL Tech Report ANL/MCS-P1246-0405*, 2005.

Die VDM Verlagsservicegesellschaft sucht für wissenschaftliche Verlage abgeschlossene und herausragende

Dissertationen, Habilitationen, Diplomarbeiten, Master Theses, Magisterarbeiten usw.

für die kostenlose Publikation als Fachbuch.

Sie verfügen über eine Arbeit, die hohen inhaltlichen und formalen Ansprüchen genügt, und haben Interesse an einer honorarvergüteten Publikation?

Dann senden Sie bitte erste Informationen über sich und Ihre Arbeit per Email an *info@vdm-vsg.de*.

Sie erhalten kurzfristig unser Feedback!

VDM Verlagsservicegesellschaft mbH
Dudweiler Landstr. 99   Telefon +49 681 3720 174
D - 66123 Saarbrücken   Fax   +49 681 3720 1749
www.vdm-vsg.de

Die VDM Verlagsservicegesellschaft mbH vertritt

Printed by Books on Demand GmbH, Norderstedt / Germany